SPORE

PRIMA Official Game Guide

written by:

David S.J. Hodgson

Bryan Stratton

Michael Knight

Prima Games

An Imprint of Random House, Inc.

3000 Lava Ridge Court, Suite 100
Roseville, CA 95661
www.primagames.com

Product Manager: Jason Wigle
Associate Product Manager: Rebecca Chastain
Copyeditor: Asha Johnson
Design & Layout: Calibre Grafix
Manufacturing: Stephanie Sanchez

ISBN: 978-0-7615-5780-7
Library of Congress Catalog Card Number: 2007941172
Printed in the United States of America

08 09 10 11 GG 10 9 8 7 6 5 4 3 2 1

contents

acknowledgments

Prima would like to thank the following people at EA and Maxis for provided invaluable knowledge, help, cross-checking, and advice throughout this project: Cody Murry (extra-special thanks), Brodie Andersen, Darren Montgomery, Guillaume Pierre, Lucy Bradshaw, Steve Eng, Soren Johnson, Serena Lam, Kip Katsarelis, Stone Librande, John Khoo, Matt Powers, Morgan Roarty, Thomas Vu, Anthony Tunac, Renaud Ternynck, and Will Wright.

Prima would also like to thank Rick Wong for his invaluable and timely assistance.

cell stage creator

Let there be life!

In the **Cell Stage** of *Spore*, you create the most basic form of life: microscopic, mind-bogglingly small proto-creatures that exist in a primeval ocean with other simple creatures. Before you head into this primordial soup to swim for your very existence, you get to choose the type of cell with which you begin the game. You can select from an herbivore cell, which eats green plant cells, or a carnivore cell, which eats red meat cells. Once you collect DNA points and unlock Body Parts, then you can use the Cell Creator to create a variety of cell creatures. The Creator also shows off all the Body Parts available, so you can decide which ones you want to try out. After that, a quick swim-through of the Cell Stage itself is in order.

Initial Cell
Lumpy
(Vegrandis offa unda creatura)

The Birth of Lumpy: Look at this terror of the deep! Well, it's actually about the size of a sea monkey, and about as ferocious! When your meteorite first crashes into a distant planet, and your amoeba-like glob of life emerges from the cracked rock, you have a very simple cell. It consists of two beady eyes, a flagella, and one of two mouths: either a filter mouth for eating plants or a jaw for eating meat.

Mouth: Filter Mouth
These tendrils flap around and suck plant materials. They are essentially the beginnings of a Herbivorous Mouth part.

Statistics

Herbivore

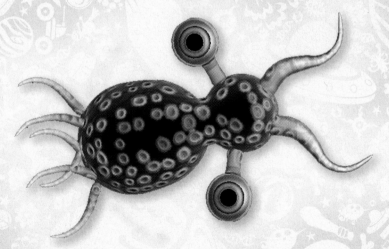

Propulsion: Flagella
Although two Filter Mouths and Flagella are shown, they still give you the same value when purchased as a set. Flagella propel Lumpy forward.

Eyes: Stalk Eyes
Try swimming without eyes and your field of vision becomes very limited. Try it and see, or rather, don't!

Body Manipulation

Creating Lumpy was an easy, but multi-stage process:

1. We removed all the different Body Parts so only the body was left, giving us a pool of DNA Points to play with!

2. Using the mouse wheel, we expanded the front and rear of the "blob," creating a dumbell-like effect.

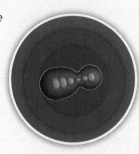

3. We added a Filter Mouth, allowing only plant life to be consumed. Delicious algae is Lumpy's dinner of choice!

4. A Flagellum was placed at the rear of Lumpy, to allow forward propulsion; two Flagella are shown, but they function as one.

5. We chose Stalk Eyes, but placed them to the rear of Lumpy, for a slightly different look!

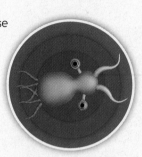

6. Then we entered Paint mode, and chose a rather pleasing red color combination with luminous blue spots...

7. ...which wasn't "Lumpy" enough, so we changed Lumpy's skin texture and coloration, and began to explore the deep!

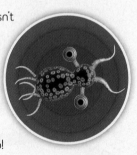

NOTE Place a Body Part in the middle of the creature for a single part. Place it to the side, and two parts are available (as shown during Lumpy's creation). Although statistically, this does not "double" any values, strategically it doubles the utility of the Body Part.

CAUTION Remember to give your creature a Mouth, Propulsion part, and Eyes, or you'll have difficulty surviving! Also try placing the Mouth part in the middle of the front of the creature, so it can easily access food.

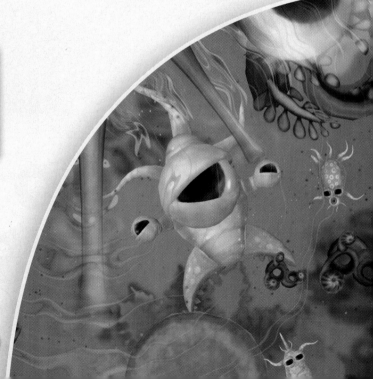

the cell creator

As you progress through the Cell Stage, you collect DNA points by eating plants and meat from other cells. In addition, part of your evolution involves locating "Shields" that allow you new Body Parts. These can be found when another cell organism is killed by you or another cell or by breaking open meteorites. In order to enter the Cell Creator and evolve your cell, you must collect 14 DNA points or collect a Body Part. Click on the "Call Mate" button at the bottom of the screen and then swim toward another cell of your species by following the little heart icons. This will open up the Cell Creator where you can spend the DNA points on adding Body Parts to your cell. By the time you reach Level 5 (of the five in this stage), you're likely to have unlocked all the Cell Body Parts, and can drastically change the way your cell looks. In this section, we show you the exact improvements each Body Part gives your cell, and give advice on maximizing your cell's different attributes.

Mouths

Your creature can consume plant matter, chunky pieces of meat, or cells and plants, depending on the chosen Mouth part.

Filter Mouth

 15 Availability: From the start
Attaching this enables the cell to eat Green Plants and Eggs.

Proboscis

25 Availability: During Cell Stage
Attaching this enables you to "slurp" Green Plants, Eggs, and other cells. You cannot eat Meat Chunks or dead cells, however.

Jaw

15 Availability: From the start
Attaching this enables your cell to eat other cells and Eggs. The Jaw can also repel an enemy Jaw mouth attack.

Design Hints: Choose the Filter Mouth if you're only interested in eating Green Plants. Choose the Jaw if you want to defeat foes, and then eat the Meat Chunks afterward. Choose the Proboscis if you want to suck a Prey-sized foe in and digest it. Of course, you can choose all three (as shown) so you can eat anything! Remember to position mouths around the front of your cell to easily guide food in. Multiple mouths are great (especially Jaws) as these can catch morsels of food your central mouth might miss.

Abilities

The parts you choose give you special advantages specific to the Body Part selected. One is "stackable."

Sight

Your creature needs eyes to see clearly in the world.

Beady Eye

5 Availability: From the start
Attaching these expands your cell's field of vision.

Stalk Eye

5 Availability: From the start
Attaching these expands your cell's field of vision.

Button Eye

5 Availability: From the start
Attaching these expands your cell's field of vision.

Design Hints: If your cell has no eyes attached, then your field of vision is reduced to a small circle around you. Your vision is the same whichever eye type you choose, and whether you have one eye or a dozen (as shown). Naturally, the more eyes you have, the fewer DNA Points you have left to distribute among more important aspects of your cell. Therefore, add more than two eyes to a cell only if you want a cool-looking creature. One final plan: place the Beady or Button Eye in the middle of your cell. It's the only part you can do this with, and this frees up the edges for Spikes or other parts.

 # Movement

Add Cilia, Flagella, and Jets parts to move faster and maneuver through the primordial soup. Every additional Movement part adds to the creature's speed. All are "stackable," so the more you add, the faster your cell will go—at least until you reach level 5.

Speed

Your creature moves faster.

Flagella

 15

Availability: From the start

Design Hints: Although Flagella are a cheap option compared to Jets, the burst of acceleration a Jet provides outweighs the usefulness of multiple Flagella on a single cell. However, Flagella produce a smooth, easy to control speed. Add multiple Flagella to further increase your speed, but be aware that Jets are twice as effective.

Burst Speed

Your creature Bursts forward quickly.

Jet

25

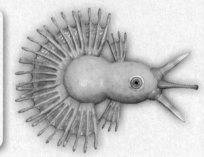

Availability: During Cell Stage

Design Hints: A Jet provides twice as much of a speed boost as Flagella or Cilia. Boost this effect by adding multiple Jets. This is the pinnacle of cell development when it comes to propulsion, so ignore the 10 extra DNA Points it costs, and always have at least one of these affixed to the back of your specimen.

Fast Turns

Your creature turns quickly.

Cilia

 15

Availability: During Cell Stage

Design Hints: These fin-like protrusions are the key to making very sharp turns, which is incredibly handy during the Cell Stage. You're wise to equip at least one of these. Stack them to be able to make quicker 180-degree turns, allowing you to dodge Epic cells and other dangers. They cost the same as Flagella and provide just as much Speed, so replace your Flagella with Cilia as soon as the part is unlocked.

Attack

Add Spikes, Poison, and Electric parts to attack other creatures. Two are "stackable."

Attack & Break

Charge into creatures to attack them. Some objects will break if you poke them.

Spike

 10

Availability: During Cell Stage

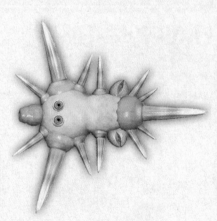

Design Hints: The Spike is a cheap, all-purpose weapon that provides exceptional advantages. First, you can ram or strike an enemy cell with one to damage them (exact damage ratings are shown later in the Cell Stage section). Secondly, they repel attacks from foes. With this in mind, attach at least two to the front of your cell (for ramming), and more around your cell so you're immune to attacks from the sides or rear.

Spit Poison

Your creature is poisonous and will spit out clouds of poison.

Poison

🦠 15

Availability: During Cell Stage

Design Hints: When a Poison sac is equipped, your cell automatically produces a trailing cloud of poison, which damages any other cell that contacts it. You can then turn around and attack the damaged cell, defeating it more easily. The more Poison sacs you equip (up to a maximum of five, if you spend any DNA points on a mouth and eyes), the longer the trail becomes.

TIP Always have one of these on your cell, because it makes you immune to all other poison attacks. This applies to poisonous rival cells, too.

Electrocute

Your creature is electric and will shock nearby creatures.

Electric

🦠 25

Availability: During Cell Stage

Design Hints: Attach this, and your cell emits an electric jolt to one nearby cell, stunning it. Afterward, there's a 5-10 second recharge. The more Electric sacs you add, the shorter the recharge. Simply ram and destroy a stunned cell.

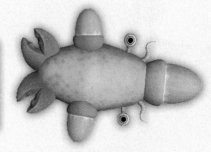

TIP Having an Electric sac makes you immune to all other enemies with Electric sacs! Conversely, don't try using this attack on an enemy with this Body Part because it doesn't affect them either!

✚ Health

The Health Bar shows you how much damage your cell can take. Each standard attack removes one-third of the bar.

NOTE The Health Bar is visible once you exit the Cell Creator.

Design Hints: As it doesn't matter what Body Parts you equip, because cells always have the same Health Bar no matter what you choose. It comes down to figuring out the best ways to prevent Health from being lost. With this in mind, try creating a cell that's thin and can easily maneuver around obstacles. Make sure it is covered in Spikes and therefore impervious to enemy bites or ramming. Finally, give it Poison and Electric sacs so it is immune to these attacks. You can gain back health by eating.

cell examples (various styles)

Finally, here are a few of the billions of different cells you could create, showing even more stylish critters you can take into the primordial ocean with you. Cells are divided into two different types; those created with style in mind, and others created to take advantage of "stackable" Body Parts that were detailed in the Ultimate Cell Creator.

NOTE Some of the cells shown are in a fully evolved form, just prior to exiting the ocean. If you want to construct similar-looking cells during the Cell Stage, you need to remove a number of Body Parts until you have the prerequisite DNA Points. The pictures of the different cells created are for illustrative purposes only.

Style 1. Personality-Driven

Xoidburg

Key Characteristics: Filter Mouth
Other Characteristics: Cilia

Despite a wide girth and a giant pair of unprotected eyes.. The two tiny Cilia flap effectively, but the evolved Filter Mouths keep a steady diet of plant matter flowing into his wide body.

Glossammer

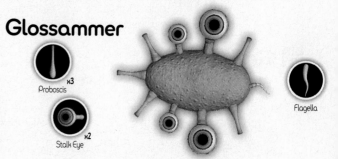

Key Characteristics: Proboscis, Stalk Eye
Other Characteristics: Flagella

Giving off an eerie glow in the darker reaches of the ooze it was birthed from, the Glossammer stalks its prey and suctions onto it at almost any angle, slurping the very life from it, before zipping back into cover. Its long-range eyes make up for a lack of defense.

Snooter Scooter

Key Characteristics: Poison
Other Characteristics: Proboscis, Beady Eyes

Traversing the water in a series of zigzag scoots, this specimen's bright purple color is usually warning enough of the trail it leaves behind. Plentiful Poison sacs on the beast's sides damage its prey. However, the Proboscis cannot be used to eat dead cells.

Zappy

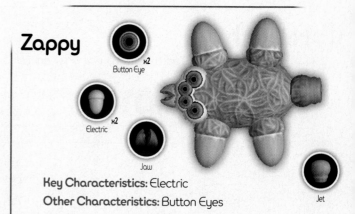

Key Characteristics: Electric
Other Characteristics: Button Eyes

Even the most fearsome predator tends to keep its distance from Zappy because of the massive charge of electricity it generates to paralyze its prey. Afterward, its tiny Jaw consumes the remains. Sneaking up and attacking from behind is the only way to defeat Zappy.

Maw the Mauler

Jaw · Spike · Flagella ×4 · Beady Eye

Key Characteristics: Jaw, Flagella
Other Characteristics: Spikes

One of the oddest and most vicious cells ever to exist, Maw lets its Jaw do the talking, or in this case, the wild thrashing into food, followed by the chopping into digestible morsels. A single, massive Beady Eye keeps watch for predators, while two tiny Spikes help defend it while feeding.

Thruster

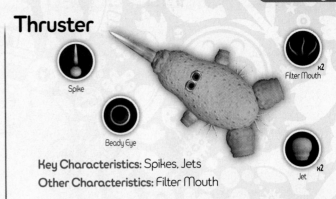

Spike · Beady Eye · Filter Mouth ×2 · Jet ×2

Key Characteristics: Spikes, Jets
Other Characteristics: Filter Mouth

The Thruster has a novel way of feeding; it positions its rear and sides near a large plant and begins to pick at the nutrients. If it spots an attacker, the Thruster brings the fight to the enemy, using Jets for a precise thrust, and skewering the enemy with its gigantic Spike.

Eyeful

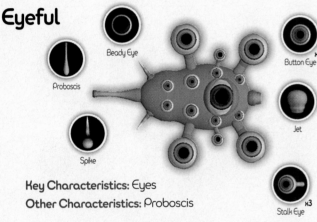

Proboscis · Beady Eye · Spike · Button Eye ×4 · Jet · Stalk Eye ×3

Key Characteristics: Eyes
Other Characteristics: Proboscis

An incredibly timid cell, the Eyeful can spot an enemy (or prey) from great distances thanks to the copious eyes and eye-like growths dotted around its body. A small Jet makes light thrusts until the Proboscis can clamp onto a foe and suck it dry.

Sea Spawn

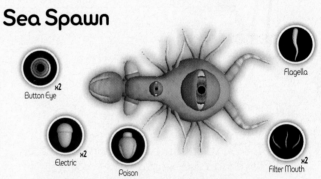

Button Eye ×2 · Electric ×2 · Poison · Flagella · Filter Mouth ×2

Key Characteristics: Filter Mouth, Flagella
Other Characteristics: Electric

With a mass of writhing tentacles and an eye that (legend has it) can see vast worlds beyond imagination, this odd little critter stares blankly into the void for days before drifting to a Large Green Plant to feed. It spits both poison and electricity at any would-be assailants.

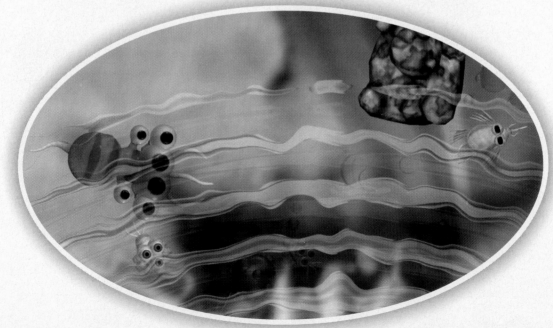

Style 2. Function-Based

Poppa

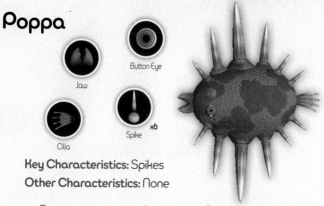

Jaw
Button Eye
Cilia
Spike x6

Key Characteristics: Spikes
Other Characteristics: None

Poppas are among the most proficient hunters in the vastly populated prehistoric oceans. Propelled by a single Cilium, it can spin around quickly, stabbing cells in almost any direction, after which its tiny Jaw grabs and digests the meat. It's a killer predator.

Frogling

Button Eye
Poison
Cilia x2
Electric
Filter Mouth

Key Characteristics: Cilia
Other Characteristics: Poison, Electric

The first ancestor of what would develop into the Tartywoad, this cell shows how a herbivore can defend against predators without resorting to Spikes. Electric and Poison sacs nullify attackers and make the cell immune to these attacks, while Cilia allow expert turning maneuvers.

Mass of Thun

Key Characteristics: Jaw, Spikes, Eyes
Other Characteristics: Jet

This ferocious little blighter is armed with a front-end filled with snapping Jaws, which allows it to attack and gulp down food in moments. At the rear is a single Jet, allowing speedy getaways from bigger cells, and two rows of nasty Spikes to stop would-be attackers.

Beady Eye x2
Spike x2
Jaw x3
Jet

cell stage advice

A Violent Birth

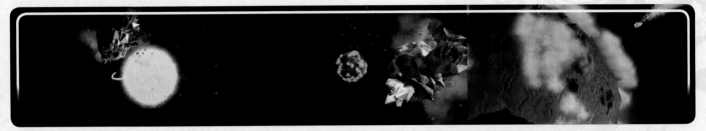

In the inky blackness of space, a tumbling meteorite twists and spins past a fiery star, skirting a solar flare, and heading for a small planet orbiting nearby. A tremendous explosion fills the planet's atmosphere, and chunks of the meteor detonate skyward, before falling into a large ocean. Smaller rocks slowly sink to the sea floor. A tiny rock splits in two. Out of the rock comes life....

Introduction

Lumpy

Level 1. Just after escaping from a crystalline rock meteor.

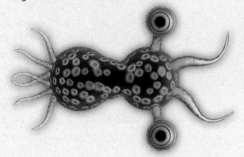

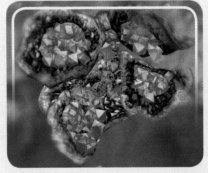

Welcome to the Cell Stage. This is a top-down, side-scrolling exploration of the primordial ooze, with a set of clearly defined levels. Your objectives are relatively straightforward: you need to eat to survive and thrive! As you eat, you grow in stature and can fend off other aggressive creatures, or attack living organisms. As your cell continues to expand, you can unlock additional Body Parts and augment your cell with them, changing the way you interact with other cells and the environment. Finally, after completing Level 5, you can evolve and crawl onto the surface of the world your rock crashed into!

TIP Refer to the previous Cell Creator for additional information on the different Body Parts and their specific advantages in this stage.

General Information

Dietary Needs

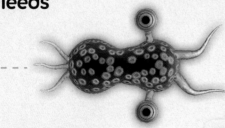

Your other option is to be a carnivore, utilizing the Jaw mouth, and attack other cells with it, feasting on their exploded remains!

Your first option is to begin this stage as a herbivore, using a Filter Mouth to suck plant remnants into your sac-like body.

NOTE The Cell Creator will not let you exit without a mouth. Fortunately, you start the Cell Stage with an herbivorous or carnivorous cell, complete with all of the bits you need to eat and survive!

DNA Accumulation

The key to creating a more complex cell is to expend DNA Points. These are collected by eating plant and meat cells. Once you have enough to buy a new part (as shown), enter the Cell Creator (detailed previously). Here, we show how DNA is specifically added.

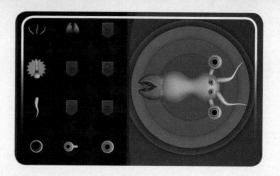

Level Progression

The base of your screen has a series of bars, which gradually fill up with a green color as you progress through the levels. To fill the bars, simply eat food. Your cell grows twice per level: once halfway through a level, and again at the start of the next level.

Transparency

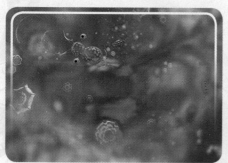

As you begin your first level, your cell's skin is transparent, allowing you to see the background and other debris floating behind it.

As you progress through the five Cell Stage levels, the skin becomes less see-through, until it reaches a completely solid state.

Field of Vision

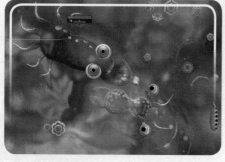

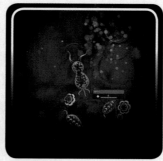

When you start this stage, areas of the water you're swimming in are blurred out, but as you progress, your field of vision expands and you can see a wider area. Because you're really only looking for objects to smash, food to eat, and predators to avoid, this isn't an issue.

CAUTION Beware! If you decide to make your creature blind, your field of vision suffers considerably. However, it is possible to complete this stage without eyes if you make your cell extremely defensible and speedy!

Health

Your cell, and all other cells you encounter have a Health Bar; your cell is dispatched when the Health Bar runs out.

Missions

An Information Bar in the screen's top-left (picture 1) reveals a number of different Missions in this, and every stage to come. Simply follow the instructions to complete the Mission (picture 2), and you're awarded a prize!

Interactive Objects: Edible

The first oceans teem with unfamiliar flotsam and jetsam, and it's your cell's job to differentiate interesting or useful matter from other, potentially dangerous ones. Here's a list of delicious foodstuffs on your floating fun-ride:

Small Green Plant Matter

First Located: Level 1
Notes: Edible with Filter Mouth or Proboscis

For non-carnivorous life, these floating plants, which come in a variety of chunks and circular shapes, are the key to life. Eating these (by running your Mouth part into a plant section) increases your DNA Points and fills your Progression Bar; the key to evolving! If you've chosen the carnivorous Jaw, attack the cells feeding off the plants instead.

NOTE Plant matter becomes available in larger single sections as your cell's body grows, too. "Small Green Plant Matter" refers to any green material floating about, unattached, either in small clusters or singly.

Large Green Plants

First Located: Level 2.5
Notes: Edible with Filter Mouth

Sporting a variety of tendrils and tips, larger sections of seaweed-like ferns and similar plant life also provide sustenance to herbivorous and omnivorous creatures. Eating the small, green food matter attached to the edge of a Large Green Plant increases your DNA Points, and fills your Progression Bar.

CAUTION Clusters of larger plants are often where groups of herbivorous feeders come to graze, and also where predators lurk, so be careful! If you've chosen a carnivorous creature, then try to **be** that predator!

TIP Stay in the area of a Large Green Plant if you're about to grow in size, as Large Green Plants become Small Green Plant Matter after you double in size, under some circumstances, and provide a quick source of nearby food.

Meat Chunks

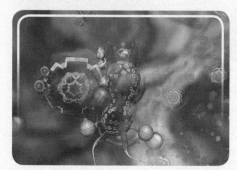

First Located: Level 1

Notes: Edible with Jaw only

When another cell has been defeated, either by your attacks or wounds inflicted by another, it explodes into Meat Chunks, which appear mainly in small pieces. At higher levels, these pieces are larger. Eating these Meat Chunks with the Jaw increases your DNA Points, and fills your Progression Bar. This is the food of carnivorous cells only.

TIP Large Meat Chunks are usually too big to consume at your current size. Either grow to the next level (or "half" level), or break large Meat Chunks into smaller pieces by hitting them with a Jaw or Spike.

NOTE The Proboscis cannot consume "chunks" of meat, only living cells. See below.

Living Food

First Located: Level 2

Notes: Edible with Proboscis only

As your cell expands in size, other beings that were your size previously stay smaller, and are now "Prey sized." Refer to the size chart at the end of each level to see which cells are considered "Prey," and slurp them with your Proboscis. Slurping Living Food with the Proboscis increases your DNA Points, and fills the Progression Bar of omnivorous cells.

NOTE You can wolf down entire critters using this Mouth part, so try a still-wiggling meal rather than a recently deceased one, or your Proboscis ignores the floating Meat Chunk.

Eggs (Small and Large)

First Located: Level 5

Notes: Small: Edible with all Mouth types

Notes: Large: Not edible

As your primordial swim reaches a nearby beach, another cell begins to deposit large, sac-like Eggs. These spawn tiny cells called "Junior." Before they hatch, you can eat small Eggs using any Mouth type. However, you can't eat larger Eggs (the Proboscis is useful for vacuuming up a hatched cell if you're too late to the Egg meal).

NOTE A cell named "Junior" hatches from Eggs. A cell named "Maa" leaves Eggs behind if defeated.

Food Types

Type of Food	DNA Points Gained	Filter Mouth	Jaw	Proboscis
Small Green Plant Matter	1	✓	✗	✓
Large Green Plant (Attached Matter)	1	✓	✗	✓
Meat Chunk (Small)	1	✗	✓	✗
Meat Chunk (Large)*	N/A	✗	✗	✗
Living Food	1	✗	✗	✓
Egg (Small)	1	✓	✓	✓

NOTE * = Large Meat Chunks must be broken down (by Spikes or Jaws) into Small Meat Chunks.
You can gain a maximum of 65 DNA Points before you can evolve legs and move to the next stage Combined with the 35 you already begin with, you have a total of 100 DNA Points.

TIP Remember that Living Food usually flees your presence, so even though there is more value per eat, you may spend more time catching up to your food.

Interactive Objects: Scenic

The next set of obstacles vying for space in this undersea world are objects that are too tough to strike, can bounce you around, or will provide a period of discomfort if you touch them. Beware of these when you're out and about:

Unbreakable Objects

Crystals

Debris

Shells

First Located: Level 1

Threat Level: ●●○○○

Each level has a variety of unbreakable objects floating around, and all are variations of the three types shown. These simply act as floating barriers; swim around them, or hit them so they move away from you.

Air Bubbles

First Located: Level 1
Threat Level: ●○○○○

Pockets of air can be found in bubble form throughout the levels of this stage, and such bubbles come in a variety of sizes, and all can be popped.

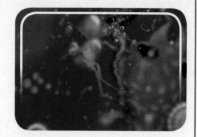

Flow Field

First Located: Level 1
Threat Level: ●●○○○

Although not completely visible, ripples of current in the water show these fields, which are randomly scattered throughout each level. You swim faster when you "go with the flow," and slower when against it. Don't get trapped near a dangerous cell and swim against a Flow Field; see where it takes you!

Poison Cloud

First Located: Level 2
Threat Level: ●●●○○

If you encounter an enemy cell that's armed with a Poison part, you'll see a dangerous cloudy trail emitting from it. Swim into this trail and you suffer damage. Counteract this by avoiding the trail, or equipping the Poison part yourself, rendering you immune.

Meteor Blocks

First Located: Level 3
Threat Level: ●○○○○

Always be on the lookout for these specific types of rocky blocks, because they contain new Cell Body Parts. Ram into a block as soon as you see it, and claim the part; optionally enter the Creator and equip it immediately!

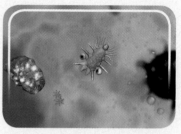

> **NOTE** Find out more about the contents of Meteor Blocks in the section entitled "Cell Parts."

Cell Parts

While eating to increase your DNA Points is the first plan in Cell Stage, the second (and just as important) plan is to locate the remaining Cell Body Parts, which are then added to your cell throughout the stage to create a more versatile or deadly creature. The following information shows how this is accomplished.

Gold Shields

First Located: Level 1

These shield-like icons are the avatars for each Body Part you'll discover. There are six to find (as you begin this stage with six Body Parts already in your collection). Remember to claim each Gold Shield by swimming into it. Find a shield using one of three methods (shown in order of appearance):

Method #1: Defeat Rival Cells

First Located: Level 1.5

This is the preferred method of locating Gold Shields. Below is a complete list of Body Parts you don't have access to at the start of this stage, and what creatures "drop" the part after you defeat them. Do this whether or not you're going to eat the meat afterward.

TIP Hover your mouse over a rival or enemy cell to see if it has a Gold Shield icon to the right of its name. If so, defeating the creature will unlock the Gold Shield.

TIP It is safer to attack "Prey" and "Peer" sized creatures for Body Parts. It is unwise to try tackling anything larger! Use your Jaw, Spike, Poison, or Electric parts to attack each creature. Damage ratings are shown later in this chapter.

Method #2: The Meteor Block

First Located: Level 3

These blocks are big and occur in the later levels of this stage, and contain only parts that you may have failed to find in earlier levels (by using Method 1 or 2). Crack these open immediately because they are sure to give you a part you're missing.

Entering the Creator

First available: Level 1

You can access the Cell Creator by pressing the Call Mate button in the center of the bottom of the screen. Follow the cooing sound of an amorous fellow cell, and swim up to it to enter the Cell Creator.

Call a mate to enter the Cell Creator!

Body Parts to Collect

 Filter Mouth
First Located: Start

 Jaw
First Located: Start

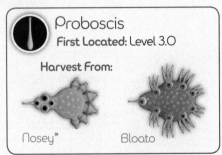 Proboscis
First Located: Level 3.0

Harvest From:

Nosey*   Bloato

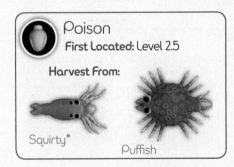 Poison
First Located: Level 2.5

Harvest From:

Squirty*   Puffish

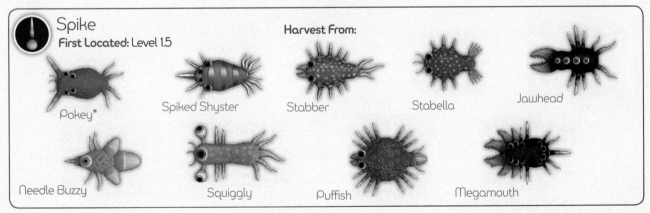 Spike
First Located: Level 1.5

Harvest From:

Pokey*   Spiked Shyster   Stabber   Stabella   Jawhead

Needle Buzzy   Squiggly   Puffish   Megamouth

Electric
First Located: Level 4.0
Harvest From:

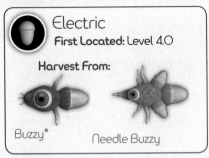

Buzzy*   Needle Buzzy

Cilia
First Located: Level 3.0
Harvest From:

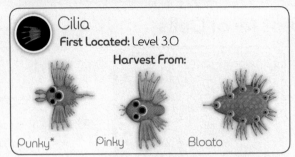

Punky*   Pinky   Bloato

Flagella
First Located: Start

Beady Eye
First Located: Start

Stalk Eye
First Located: Start

Button Eye
First Located: Start

Jet
First Located: Level 2.0
Harvest From:

Booster*   Nosey   Jetster   Paa   Snorf

NOTE * This is usually the first cell you encounter with a specific Body Part you want, and is therefore the optimal one to defeat.

NOTE For the different abilities that each Body Part possesses, see the Ultimate Cell Creator section.

NOTE The first time you defeat a cell equipped with a specific part, you usually get that part.

NOTE Some cells do not drop parts.

Health and Damage

It is important to remember how much punishment cells can handle. This is shown below:

Cell	Health Points
You	6
Rival Cells	6

NOTE † = This damage is inflicted on you.

* = This damage is inflicted on the specific cell mentioned, if you equip this part. If a cell isn't listed, you cannot harm it with a particular part.

Cell Size / Body Part	Damage Inflicted
Epic	6 (you are defeated instantly)†
Predator	3†
Peer	2†
Spike	1 (to Predator-sized cell)*
Jaw	3 (to Peer-sized cell) *
Spike	3 (to Peer-sized cell) *
Poison	3 (to Peer-sized cell) *
Electric	3 (to Peer-sized cell) *
Jaw	6 (Prey-sized cell defeated instantly)*
Spike	6 (does not affect Prey-sized cells)*
Poison	6 (Prey-sized cell defeated instantly)*
Electric	6 (Prey-sized cell defeated instantly)*

Levels: Introduction

There are five "epochs" (known as levels) in the Cell Stage, from the time you wiggle out of your extraterrestrial rock, to the moment you evolve legs and swim to land. The following section shows general information about levels.

Five Levels, Ten Stages

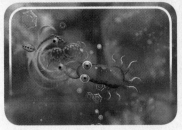

Within each level are two sections (Level 1 for example, has 1.0 and 1.5). The "half" level marks your creature's growth spurt (see both pictures for a before and after), occurring midway through the level.

Prey, Peer, and Predators

Each level has a variety of cells swimming about (revealed previously). However, they come in different sizes (the exact size for each cell is shown in the specific

level tactics to come). The first size is "Prey." These cells are much smaller than you and can easily be eaten or defeated for meaty food. The second (picture 2) are "Peer" cells, which are around the same size as you. You can battle them (as long as you find their weaknesses) relatively easily. The third (picture 3) are "Predator" cells, usually much larger than you, and able to bite or spike you to death with a single hit. Beware of Predators!

Epic Cells

From Level 2.5 onward, you may encounter a species of cell that is tremendously bigger than you. These are Epic cells, and they can only be defeated by exploiting their individual secret weaknesses. They are the most feared of all cells, so give them a wide berth.

Missions

As previously mentioned, the Cell Stage has Missions to optionally complete. These occur semi-randomly depending on where you're swimming and what you've encountered. Your Mission instructions are shown in the screen's top-left corner. Here are tactics for the available Missions:

Mission: Eat
Consume five pieces of food

Available: Start
Difficulty: ●○○○○
Reward: DNA Points

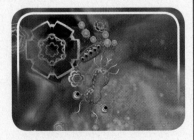

As soon as you begin, chow down on five foodstuffs to claim your first batch of DNA Points and increase your Progression Bar. If you've equipped the Filter Mouth, eat Green Plant Matter. If you've chosen the Jaw, charge and defeat any nearby cells, and eat the Meat Chunks of their remains.

Mission: Collect
Unlock Cell Parts

Available: Level 1.5
Difficulty: ●●●●○
Reward: Additional Body Parts (up to six)

This is the main Mission for almost the entirety of this stage. Locate six Gold Shields and complete your collection of Body Parts. Find Gold Shields in other cells (check that they have a Gold Shield after their name, then use Spikes to defeat them), or Meteor Blocks (if you didn't track down enemies).

cell levels: tactical advice

The last part of this chapter concerns specific tactics for surviving each of the stage's levels. Our own created cell, Lumpy, is shown to give one example of how to play through each section. Each time we added parts to Lumpy, we showcase the new look. There's also information on what to look out for, and the types of cells you encounter.

Cell Level 1: Ice

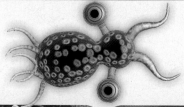

Lumpy: Level 1.0. Lumpy has just escaped from a crystalline rock meteor.

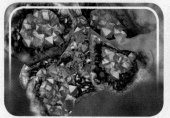 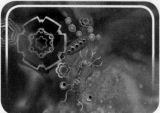  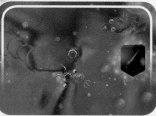

In the Beginning: Your cell hatches from a tiny particle of a fallen meteorite.

Chow Down: Begin the "Eat" Mission, following the advice on-screen. Eat five Green Plants (with the Filter Mouth) or Meat Chunks (with the Jaw) to complete this Mission.

Poking Pokey: If you have a jaw, seek and destroy the nearest Pokey, and claim the first of six Body Parts; the Spike! This is an easy dispatch because Pokey isn't aggressive.

The Chowing Chomper: If you spend your time eating instead, as soon as you grow and reach Level 1.5, a Chomper automatically eats a Pokey, revealing the Spike Gold Shield. Swim into it.

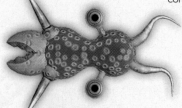

Lumpy: Level 1.5. Lumpy acquires a taste for meat, changes to a Jaw, and adds Spikes for protection.

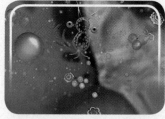

Food, Glorious Food: Continue to Level 2.0 by eating more of your favorite food, whether it is meat or plant materials.

TIP Enter the Cell Creator as soon as you have enough DNA Points for additional parts; don't wait!

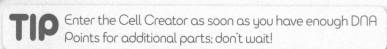
TIP You're wise to invest in Spikes. Place them near your mouth to help defeat opponents you ram into.

Cell Level 2: Rock

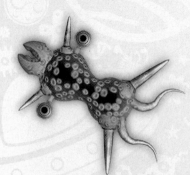

Lumpy: Level 2.0. Additional Spikes are added to fend off Predators attacking from behind.

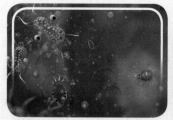 

Send in the Clones: You first encounter the same species of cell as your own during this level. You can't damage or be damaged by them; they simply dart about on their own.

Booster Jets: This is your first opportunity to collect the Jet part, once you dispatch your first Booster. Because Boosters are Predator-sized, you may wish to wait until Level 2.5 to challenge them.

Poison Clouds: After you reach Level 2.5, you can challenge a Squirty and claim the Poison Body Part.

Additional Sustenance: You first encounter Large Green Plants with smaller food at their tips from this point onward.

Stabber: You encounter your first Epic creature: a Stabber. Avoid it at all costs!

Lumpy: Level 2.5. Poison sacs are added on either side of the Jaw to stun food.

TIP Remember that you can tackle any enemy cell with a part you want; not the first type you encounter.

TIP As you collect more DNA Points, you can add multiple Flagella, Poison, and Jets to increase your speed or poison potency. Similarly, you can keep adding Spikes to ward off attacks from every direction.

Cell Level 3: Plant

Seeking the Cilia: Search out a Pinky or Punky and secure a Cilium to help you turn 180 degrees quickly.

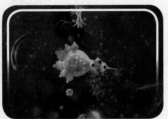

Nosey Parker: Locate and ram a Nosey for your first attempt at securing the Proboscis, the penultimate Body Part.

Lumpy: Level 3.0. A quick dispatch of Blooty yielded some booty. Cilia are added!

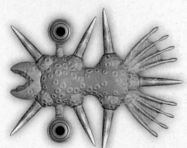

Lumpy: Level 3.5. Poison sacs were dispatched in favor of more Spikes. Nearby cells need to watch out!

Keep on Chomping: Continue to feed on plant or meat products until you grow to Level 4.0.

TIP As DNA Points become available (or if you redesign your cell), add more Cilia if you want more pronounced turning.

TIP Add more Spikes if you want a cell that is difficult for others to attack.

TIP Add more Flagella for extra speed; however, it is better to replace Flagella for Jets as soon as your DNA Points allow.

TIP Add more Poison parts to increase the potency and range of your automatically discharged clouds.

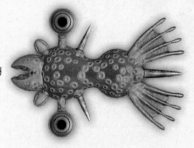

Cell Level 4: Water

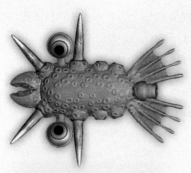

Lumpy: Level 4.0. A thicker midriff, Spikes, and a Jet mean Lumpy isn't to be messed with!

A Bright Spark: The search for the final Body Part begins. Locate either Buzzy type, and defeat it to claim your final part!

TIP As always, try different cell combinations, based on the tactics shown in the Ultimate Cell Creator (previously detailed in this chapter).

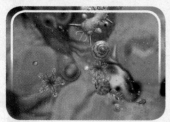

Snack Food: Continue to munch on plants, meat, or prey; easy takedowns are available near the Large Green Plants.

Lumpy: Level 4.5. Lumpy changed his hue to blend in with the sand of a prehistoric beach.

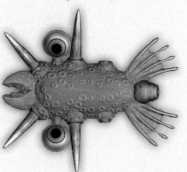

TIP The Electric Body Part jolts an enemy cell, allowing you to finish it off easily. This is a great tactic if you're vicious! Add more Electric Body Parts to reduce the charge time (which starts at 5-10 seconds). Only the Buzzy carries the Electric Body Part, so make sure to find one to defeat.

Cell Level 5: Beach

Cracking Eggs: As you continue to suck DNA from food matter, locate your first Eggs.

Cracking Eggs Part 2: Destroy them for DNA, or wait for them to hatch, and defeat the Junior cell that hatches.

Lumpy: Level 5.0. Lumpy sports thick Cilia for powerful swimming, and a Proboscis for sucking down foes!

Lumpy: Level 5.5. Now with a lighter tone, and back to being a herbivore, Lumpy evolves to a Poison-emitting speed demon!

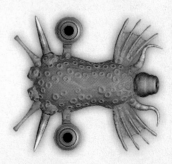

Almost Evolved: Continue your merry way, bopping floating shells, and collecting 65 DNA Points to the end of this stage.

TIP If you want to create more cells, call a mate and access the Cell Creator.

End Game: Evolution

As soon as you finish this stage, a chart listing your major accomplishments (shown) is revealed. You can look back at the decisions you made, and which trait you ended up in. This is important, because each trait awards you with a number of specific skills, as follows:

Trait	Creature Skill	Tribe Skill	Civilization Skill	Space Skill	Superpower
Herbivore	Siren Song	Refreshing Storm	Healing Aura	Social Suave	Return Ticket
Omnivore	Summon Flock	Flying Fish	EMP Bomb	Gentle Generalist	Cash Infusion
Carnivore	Raging Roar	Traps	Invulnerability	Power Monger	Raider Rally

Read up about these skills in the appropriate chapter, under Legacy Traits. Now enter the Creature Creator, and scramble up onto your first continent.

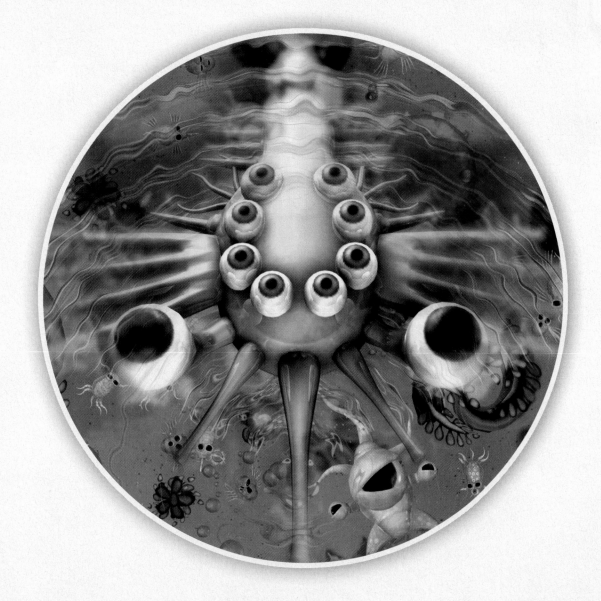

🐾 creature stage

Your Evolution Continues

Welcome to the **Creature Stage** of *Spore*, where your evolved cell scrambles up from the ocean and treads, slithers, or staggers onto land for the first time. Before you reach your nest, the hub of your over-world activities, you are encouraged to create and texture your own first creature, courtesy of the in-game Creator. Remember that this has only Cell Body Parts (and three legs) to choose from, but these parts now have brand new values. As you explore the Creature Stage, you gradually unlock more and more of the main Creature Creator (the full extent of which is shown in the next section). In this book, two Creature Creator plans are showcased: the first to construct your initial creature, and the second to show off a variety of creatures that should help you imagine your own creations. Finally, a walkthrough of the Creature Stage is shown, along with all the excitement to expect and tactics to try.

NOTE The Body Parts you collect throughout the Creature Stage are semi-randomized. In this chapter, we show you how to unlock all these parts, and we'll give each part's statistics. In addition, a complete list of all the available Body Parts (and their usefulness for each skill) in this stage and the next appears in the next section of this guide.

Initial Creature Creator
flumpy
(Duos Crur Terra Rostrum)

The Birth of Flumpy: Behold this feeble-armed monstrosity! Flumpy, named after the waddling walk it makes when investigating the new continent, has some of the most important Body Parts from Lumpy the Cell, but has a completely redesigned body and a pair of sturdy legs, ending in some gigantic feet! Investigating the world soon yielded additional parts, but here's what we started with.

Mouth: Jaw
Flumpy leapt from the water with a taste for meat, and this Jaw is the most "animal" like. He soon changed his carnivorous ways....

Eyes: Stalk Eyes
Two bulbous pupils at the end of sinewy stalks give Flumpy a slightly comical look, as if he's permanently worried.

Propulsion: Cilia
We positioned these fin-like appendages near where Flumpy will grow his arms, to keep with the theory of evolution. Now Flumpy can jump.

Legs: Thundercalf
With the most muscular of the three Leg types, Flumpy now has +1 to speed and can walk on dry land.

Propulsion: Flagella
Although shrunken into Flumpy's back end to act as a double tail, this Cell remnant helps with sneaking.

Weapons: Poison
Flumpy needed an additional weapon, and a Poison sac is a perfect tail, allowing another attack: the Spit.

Weapons: Spike
Although the two Spikes are on Flumpy's back, they still give you a Charge attack. The second Spike is just for looks; it isn't stackable.

Statistics

Carnivore

primagames.com

Body Manipulation

Creating Flumpy was a simple, but multi-step process:

1. On a seabed near the beach rests an odd-shaped body. We removed all aspects of the cell named Lumpy, and adjusted the body.

2. After noticing that the Cell Body Parts now have different functions, we first anchored Flumpy to the ground with some Thundercalf legs.

3. We next concentrated on the face. Each mouth gives Mating Call, Bite, and Sing, but we kept Lumpy's carnivorous Jaw.

4. Next were the Stalk Eyes, which gave Flumpy the startled look we were after. We used the Circle and Ball tools to adjust the direction.

5. After shrinking the eyes slightly to bring them into proportion, we began to decorate Flumpy's spine, setting on a Spike...

6. ...or two! Remember that the second Spike doesn't affect the statistics, and you can shrink or grow each Body Part using the mouse wheel.

7. Next on Flumpy's prehistoric body was a large Poison sac, allowing a Spit combat move. The sac was shrunk to appear in proportion.

8. To finish the tail, and add another remnant of Flumpy's former existence, two Flagella were added on either side of the Poison sac.

9. Almost done! At the shoulder, we added the closest part to a hand, the Cilia, which will evolve into something more useful later on.

10. A final critter created, we pressed each ability button to see his combat and social animations. Then we gave him this terrible skin condition...

11. ...which we quickly changed to Lumpy's original look, and tweaked the color slightly. Then we sent him to explore this brave new world....

NOTE Remember to place Body Parts in the middle of the creature unless you want two identical parts shown. Unlike the Cell Stage, there is no statistical improvement if you place multiple parts on a creature, but it can look impressive, frightening, or simply groovy!

NOTE You're likely to change Body Parts constantly throughout the Creature Stage, so don't worry too much about how your initial creature looks, or follow the examples to come. It is better to "de-evolve" your cell by taking off all the parts and adjusting the body instead of adding legs to your cell. Otherwise, your creature may look overly odd (and not in a good way).

Remember that you can extend the creature's body, and use the mouse wheel to inflate and deflate the different sections. This way you can begin creating featureless "heads" (by inflating the top end of your body, and deflating the third or fourth "vertebrae" to act as a neck). Experiment with this, so that your creatures aren't a series of balls connected by overly stretched skin.

Try keeping your creature tall if you're an omnivore or herbivore, because this helps it reach food from taller trees.

stage start: creature creator

Unlike the Cell Stage, once you reach dry land, you can find up to 228 Body Parts, allowing for an even more diverse number of creatures, and strengthening your creature's abilities. Use **the Tribal Outfitter later in this guide**, to figure out the best Body Parts to place on your creature as you progress through this stage, assuming you find the Body Parts in question. In this section, we show you the exact improvements each Body Part gives your creature when choosing from the initial list, and give advice on maximizing your creature's different attributes.

NOTE No Body Parts from this point on are "stackable." However, Body Parts you find during the Creature Stage have a greater value than the current selection (which only give a level of 1), so always check the statistics if you select a new part.

NOTE The pictures of the different creatures are for illustrative purposes only. You may (or may not) have enough DNA Points to construct creatures exactly like the ones shown.

TIP It is very important to note that the type of Cell Body Parts you affix to your creature affects the likelihood of receiving particular Body Parts. Two large charts later in this section show this information in great detail.

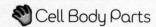 Mouths

Your creature can eat either fruit (herbivore), other creatures (carnivore), or both fruit and other creatures (omnivore).

🖐 Cell Body Parts

Filter Mouth	Jaw	Proboscis
🎲 15	🎲 15	🎲 25
Other Skills:	**Other Skills:**	**Other Skills:**
🔊 Mating Call	🔊 Mating Call	🔊 Mating Call
🦷 Bite Level 1	🦷 Bite Level 1	🦷 Bite Level 1
🎵 Sing Level 1	🎵 Sing Level 1	🎵 Sing Level 1
Your creature eats fruit.	Your creature eats other creatures.	Your creature eats both fruit and other creatures.

Design Hints: Check the guide's tactics on surviving while eating fruit, creatures, or a mixture of both, and then choose the Mouth parts that are right for your creation. As each of the different mouths give you the same Attack and Socialize skills, you have four options. You can place one or more of a single type of mouth on your entity, or you can go with a single Proboscis. Or, you can create an omnivore, but place a Filter Mouth and Jaw instead of a Proboscis. Mouths are great at the top of a herbivorous creature, so it can reach high fruit.

 # Abilities

The parts you choose give you special advantages.

Mating Call

Call to locate your mate and your nest, but beware of alerting nearby predators.

Cell Body Parts

Filter Mouth

 15

Other Skills:
- Bite Level 1
- Sing Level 1

You can sing, shout, or screech a Mating Call with this mouth.

Jaw

15

Other Skills:
- Bite Level 1
- Sing Level 1

You can warble, waffle, or roar a Mating Call with this mouth.

Proboscis

25

Other Skills:
- Bite Level 1
- Sing Level 1

You can create murmured or melodious Mating Call music with this mouth.

Design Hints: All mouths provide a Mating Call during this stage, so any mouth will do. Therefore, think about other Body Parts that can help you return to a mate safely. Consider adding attack-related Body Parts, such as the Spike and Poison, to help you return to your nest with a minimum of savaging.

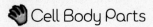 Jump

Jumping allows access to hard-to-reach areas. Higher levels increase the height of your jump.

Cell Body Parts

Cilia

15

Jump Level 1

Other Skills:
None

This is the only Body Part (to begin with) that allows jumping.

Design Hints: This is a very useful ability as it allows you to leap up steeper hills and across chasms and valleys more easily. Give your creature long and mobile legs, and make it as tall as you can for additional reach.

Sneak

Sneak up on unsuspecting creatures or evade attackers. Attacking a creature while sneaking gives a bonus to the attack.

Cell Body Parts

Flagella

15

Sneak Level 1

Other Skills:
None

This is the only Body Part (to begin with) that allows sneaking.

Design Hints: Adding this part is another no-brainer. Employ this on your starting creature, because it helps you on your way back to mate, when you're exploring, and when fighting is called for. Add it easily to your starting creature, but perhaps not in as lavish a display as this particular critter!

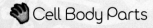 Sprint

Sprint allows for a quick burst of speed. Higher-level Sprint parts found during this stage extend the duration.

Cell Body Parts

Jet

25

Sprint Level 1

Other Skills:
None

This is the only Body Part (to begin with) that allows sprinting.

Design Hints: Although the DNA cost is 10 more than for other Abilities-based skills, this allows you to traverse the vast landscapes faster. This is handy if you're trying to outrun a pack of carnivorous pursuers that are more evolved (and therefore more dangerous) than you.

Sight

Your creature needs eyes to see clearly in the world.

Cell Body Parts

Beady Eye
 5

Other Skills:
None

Attach these to see what's going on.

Stalk Eye
5

Other Skills:
None

Fit these to spot fiends and friends.

Button Eye
5

Other Skills:
None

Place these and check out the new continent.

Design Hints: The type of eyes you choose and size you make each eye is irrelevant; it comes down to personal tastes. Fit more than a pair onto your critter only if you're going for a "looker," both metaphorically and physically.

Attack

Add Bite, Strike, Charge, and Spit parts to attack other creatures. Strike skill is currently unavailable.

Bite

This quick attack damages a single target in close range.

Cell Body Parts

Filter Mouth
15
Bite Level 1

Other Skills:
Herbivore
Mating Call
Sing Level 1

You can maul, munch, and mangle with this mouth.

Jaw
15
Bite Level 1

Other Skills:
Carnivore
Mating Call
Sing Level 1

You can chew, chomp, and bite down hard with this mouth.

Proboscis
25
Bite Level 1

Other Skills:
Omnivore
Mating Call
Sing Level 1

You can snap, grab, and devour with this mouth.

Design Hints: You cannot leave the Creature Creator without first fixing one or more mouths to your specimen. As you might be able to tell by now, mouths are an excellent return on your DNA investment, and any of the mouths give you the same Level 1 Bite attack. Placing more than one identical mouth on your creature doesn't give additional bonuses, so one mouth is all you need. Multiple mouths certainly look fearsome though!

Charge

The Charge attack intercepts a single target from a distance and stuns upon contact.

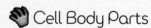 Cell Body Parts

Spike
10
Charge Level 1

Other Skills:
None

After a run-up, a nasty Spike causes a good deal of hurting to your adversary.

Design Hints: You'd be foolish **not** to fit a Spike to your chosen creature, as the benefits are immense. You gain a long-range attack, meaning you can target an enemy, then start a Charge attack and have your creature storm in without tricky, manual maneuvering. The DNA cost is excellent, too! Don't miss this chance to strengthen your offensive.

Spit

This quick attack spits projectiles at a single target.

Cell Body Parts

Poison
15
Spit Level 1

Other Skills:
None

After engaging in combat and backing up, spit on your adversary with noxious vapors.

Design Hints: The Spit attack is another excellent skill for your initial creature to possess. It does damage over time, so it is good to reapply. You should be roaming this continent with the most skills possible, and this allows a third attack type, which is great when your others (Bite and Charge) are recovering.

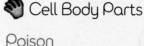

prima games.com

 # Socialize

Add Sing, Dance, Pose, and Charm parts to socialize with other creatures. Dance and Pose skills are currently unavailable.

Sing

Sing to befriend creatures who like to vocalize.

Cell Body Parts

Filter Mouth	Jaw	Proboscis
15	15	25
Sing Level 1	Sing Level 1	Sing Level 1

Other Skills:

Herbivore	Carnivore	Omnivore
Mating Call	Mating Call	Mating Call
Bite Level 1	Bite Level 1	Bite Level 1

You can warble, waffle, and wail with this mouth.

You can chirp, chirrup, and chat with this mouth.

You can screech, soliloquize, and sing with this mouth.

Design Hints: The final skill of the multi-talented mouths allows rudimentary singing, which is the basis of a good communication between yourself and a strange wild creature you're attempting to befriend. The three initial mouths all give you the same skill at Level 1, so choose based on style rather than function.

Charm

Creatures with many Detail parts can be charmed with this Social skill.

Cell Body Parts

Electric

 25

Charm Level 1

Other Skills:
None

Instead of zapping a foe with electricity, your nodule has evolved as a real talking point!

Design Hints: Although it is easier to begin your Creature Stage as an aggressive carnivore, in order to gain pack members from other creature types, you'll need a wide variety of Social skills, and it's preferable to have both types available at the start. Use this to win over the first few creatures you come across, in conjunction with singing.

Speed

Add faster feet to increase speed!

Legs

Brawnysaurus	Phatella	Thundercalf
50	50	50
Speed Level 1	Speed Level 1	Speed Level 1

Other Skills:
None

Other Skills:
None

Other Skills:
None

This poorly defined fat leg has prehistoric overtones.

This leg has more of a pronounced knee, but is less defined than the Thundercalf.

Here's a more muscular leg with definition. Any leg will do, though!

Design Hints: Three sets of legs are now available, and all three offer the same skill: a Level 1 Speed boost. Pick the one you like the look of the most. Be aware that it's the foot itself that gives you the bonus; you can remove it and have a "leg" appendage (which you can add other parts to, as in the examples to come). Or, you can go with a single, hopping leg or three pairs of legs, but the more legs you add, the more DNA it costs, leaving you less to spend on other parts. Ideally, stick with two legs, and keep the feet on the end of them!

 Health

Each brain level upgrade adds to your health. You can also buy armored parts to help you survive in combat.

Design Hints: Adding health parts gains you Health Points. For every Health Point you have you gain 2 HP. First, consult the Tribal Stage chapter's Creature Creator to find the best armored parts (flagged with "Health") that you can. But before then, make sure your creature has all the abilities listed previously in this section; if it has the biggest variety of skills, it can survive the largest number of threats. This "alpha" type critter with every possible ability is a good example.

creature examples (various styles)

Finally, here are a few of the billions of different creatures you could create, revealing just how advanced the specimens are that you could bring onto the land. All of them were created in the initial Creature Creator. For more complex Creature examples, using a choice of the 228 Body Parts you find during this stage, consult the **Creature Creator** at the end of the Creature Stage chapter.

NOTE Because we've already shown a great example of a creature created to maximize the starting set of skills (in conjunction with Health advice, see previously), we've split the following creatures into three different groups. The first are Personality-based. The second show Earth influences.

Style 1. Personality-Driven

Terrain Spawn

Key Characteristics: Filter Mouth, Jaw, Flagella
Other Characteristics: Cilia

Created by unspeakable entities deep beneath the waves, the Terrain Spawn seeks to commit unspeakable acts before fleeing to the stars, enslaving races it can't drive insane, and becoming the stuff of nightmares. At the moment however, it showcases how Body Parts can be used in different ways, for example, Jaws as hands, Flagella and Filter Mouths as face tentacles, and Cilia as feet!

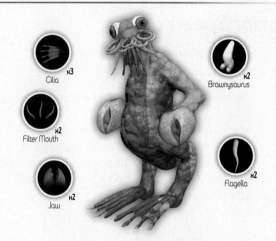

Cilia x3
Brawnysaurus x2
Filter Mouth x2
Flagella x2
Jaw x2

Trass of Thun

Key Characteristics: Spikes
Other Characteristics: Jaw

The primitive form of an evolutionary predator, Trass of Thun would soon evolve into one of the galaxy's most feared, warlike races. For now though, Trass of Thun is content with being the dominant aggressor thanks to an incredible display of body adornments (call the weapons, in fact). Notice how the size of the Jaw makes Trass even more imposing. Also of note are Trass's nostrils: actually two Jets placed under its giant eye!

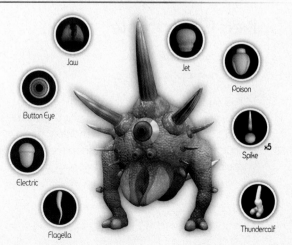

Jaw
Jet
Poison
Button Eye
Spike x5
Electric
Flagella
Thundercalf

Grunt Mite

Key Characteristics: Jet
Other Characteristics: Poison

A relatively simple creature, the Grunt Mite gets its name from its small size and the mighty noise it makes when it attacks, propelling noxious a cloud from its Poison sacs and using a circle of Jets to gauge range as the spittle flies from its Proboscis. This shows the type of elements you can use in places on a creature you normally wouldn't think of. Plus, the circle of Jets look like the casings around a gun barrel.

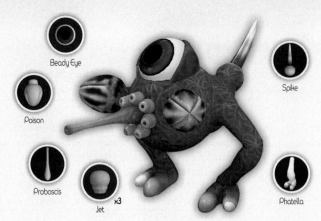

Beady Eye
Spike
Poison
Proboscis
Jet x3
Phatella

EyeVorr

Key Characteristics: Button Eyes
Other Characteristics: None

When you concentrate on cloning one particular Body Part, the results can be interesting, or in this case, truly frightening! EyeVorr skulks about on its darkened gloomworld, using many of its ocular senses to seek out prey. Each eye is covered in a tough membrane, which repels most attacks. Although not practical in most situations, EyeVorr shows just how many single items you can affix to your critter.

Button Eye x12
Jaw
Thundercalf

Junior Speedo

Key Characteristics: Thundercalf, Spikes
Other Characteristics: None

The primitive form of the alpha predator known as Senior Speedo, this mini-crustacean shows off what three sets of legs can be used to create, in this case, a pair of feet and four thrashing arms, each with a deadly set of Spikes at the end. Bulky, muscular beasts are just as easy to create as blobs; simply work out your body shape before adding other Body Parts.

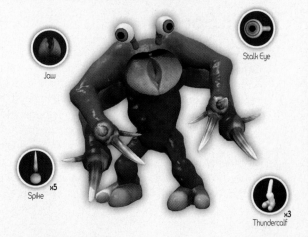

Jaw
Stalk Eye
Spike x5
Thundercalf x3

Spiked Gentrifugle

Key Characteristics: Spikes
Other Characteristics: None

This atrocity of flailing limbs and odd-shaped appendages actually has a laid-back personality thanks to its posture, and it showcases just how outlandish you can make your basic creature. The body shape is important, as is positioning parts so they don't appear to be humanoid in any way whatsoever. What a looker!

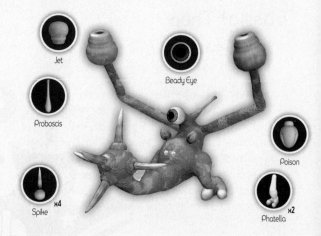

Jet
Beady Eye
Proboscis
Poison
Spike x4
Phatella x2

Style 2. Earth-Influenced

Elepottimus

Key Characteristics: Thundercalf, Brawnysaurus, Cilia
Other Characteristics: None

A skittish but lumbering fruit-picker, the Elepottimus is one of many examples of a creature that looks reasonably like an earthbound animal, but with a Sporish twist! In this case, five legs (two pairs and a single) are used, with the fifth forming the creature's trunk. Meanwhile, Cilia were spread around the creature's neck to act like a mane, although two could be employed as ear-shaped protrusions.

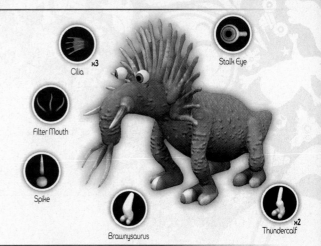

Wormin

Key Characteristics: Spikes
Other Characteristics: Cilia

Invertebrates were never meant to wander around standing up, but this is exactly what the plague-afflicted Wormin has managed, thanks to some toughened hindquarters and careful balancing. Showing that legs are not mandatory, and not every creature needs to be rotund, the Wormin features a pair of Flagella and a Jet that act like a tripod, making this creature's posture more believable.

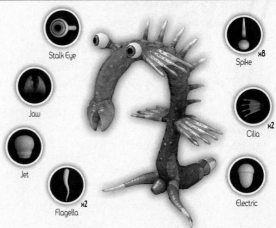

Spiny Tussler

Key Characteristics: Spikes
Other Characteristics: Brawnysaurus

Part porcupine, and all adorable, this little fellow may look cute, but he certainly makes sure his prey is dispatched. He rolls over it using his Spikes to chop it into manageable pieces. Although simple, this shows how to use Cell parts in ways you might not have thought of, such as making an Electric snout and Filter Mouth tufts above the eyes.

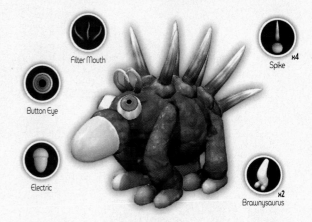

Six-legged Slurper

Key Characteristics: Phatella
Other Characteristics: Proboscis

No burrows are safe from the Slurper, an omnivore adept at fruit sucking and small animal dessication. Based loosely on an anteater, this creation uses the Proboscis as a main functional part, and attempts to make an overly large number of legs look as cute as possible. The colors used also create some major differences in how your critter looks.

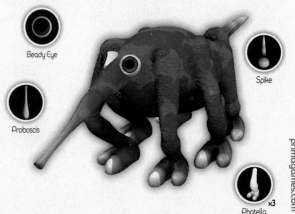

Tusked Scuttler

Key Characteristics: Phatella
Other Characteristics: Button Eyes

Attempting to create something fearsome with as many legs as possible led us to attempt an arachnid-based life form. Although not sporting the perquisite number of legs, the Tusked Scuttler still has the look of a frightening creepy-crawlie, thanks to the leg joint placement at the top of the body, the two sets of Button Eyes, and some nasty-looking tusks behind the Filter Mouths.

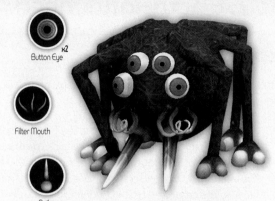

Button Eye x2

Filter Mouth

Spike

Phatella x3

Piltdown Golem

Key Characteristics: None
Other Characteristics: None

Said to be created by the wizard lords of Banthos VII, this primitive humanoid figure proves that odd and bulbous beings with giant beady eyes are but one of the billions of creature types you can create, even at this early stage. This pitiful creature has Spikes for eyebrows, Flagella for hair, and a backward Button Eye for a mouth. The less said about the Poison sacs, the better!

Beady Eye

Button Eye

Cilia x2

Flagella

Thundercalf

Spike

Proboscis

Poison

Jet

creature stage advice

Up from the Depths....

Struggling up and out of the water, a small pride of your chosen creatures waddle, stagger, and meander onto dry land, and a large, unexplored continent

Introduction

Welcome to the Creature Stage. This is a three-dimensional exploration of your planet's massive continent, with a series of "brain expanding" levels to reach and master. Your objectives are slightly more complicated than before; although you must eat to survive, you must also begin to collect a variety of Body Parts to "upgrade" your creature's different skill-sets, and these skills—mainly the combat and social aspects—are the key to thriving. You must befriend and/or butcher the other creatures residing on this rock, continue to uncover more Body Parts, and grow your creature into a well-rounded entity that eventually learns the secrets of fire and tribal life!

TIP Refer to the previous Creature Creator for information on the different Body Parts and their specific advantages in this stage.

TIP Refer to the Parts List in this chapter to show how all these parts unlock.

TIP Consult the Creature Creator (prior to the Tribal Stage chapter's Walkthrough section) for tips on creating creatures with a specific skill-set or personality.

Plans of Progression: Socializing and Combat

This wilderness teems with interesting, cheerful, frightening, and monstrous denizens that are finding their own way through life. Meet, greet, or beat them for a variety of rewards; this is the crux of the Creature Stage.

Plan #1: Socializing

If you're the social type, when you first encounter a new entity, you can attempt to befriend it. Bring up your Social skills from the on-screen tab, and click to target your first would-be chum. Social progression involves becoming friendly with other creatures by responding to their Social abilities with your own:

Singing: A chirrup, squawk, or friendly bellow comprise plan A.

Dancing: Create some fancy, quick, or nimble footwork for plan B.

Charming: Emphasizing your cute playful exterior is plan C.

Pose: Striking just the right kind of posed affectation forms plan D.

TIP Use the following tactics when attempting to impress, befriend, and ally with another creature:

- Click on the creature you want to interact with to target it, then select your stance (social or combat) and click again to take action. Try to Sing first.
- Watch the creature; it will attempt one of the four plans.
- Match the plan, and raise your Social Meter.
- Continue until both meters meet in the middle, or to one side if your Social abilities are superior.
- You must match skills. If a creature strikes a pose, you should too, as quickly as possible!
- If you fail, try again. If you fail a second time, return to your nest, edit your creature, then try again.
- If you fail, you can also try combat options instead!

- The larger the creature and the more Body Parts it has, the more of the four different Social skills you'll need.
- When you first see a creature, click on it, and view it in the Sporepedia. Its Social skills are likely the ones you need to befriend it (usually at or above the creature's levels).
- The larger the skill level, the quicker you fill your Social Meter, and the easier it is to befriend more complex creatures.
- Consult the next chapter for making the "ultimate" social creature, and to learn which Body Parts offer Level 5 Sing, Dance, Charm, and Pose skills.

Plan #2: Combat

If you crave the demise of a particular species after initial contact, you can begin to battle it. Bring up your Attack skills from the on-screen tab, and target your first fodder. Simply defeat enough of a particular species so they become extinct, and optionally feast on their still-twitching corpses!

Bite: Quickly bite down hard at your foe with your mouth. This attack is the quickest of all, but it doesn't dish out much damage. Employ this constantly during close combat, as you wait for other attacks to recharge.

Charge: Running into your enemy to stun them is plan B. Target a foe from range, and your creature dashes in and strikes. This is the perfect way to wound a foe as you close. Don't activate it from too far away, or you may miss!

Spit: Projecting a fast-acting poison from a body sac at distant enemies is plan C. An excellent long-range attack, Spit is perfect for pinpointing a single foe and damaging it severely before it closes. This allows you to stay at range and not get hurt, while your pack attempts close combat.

Strike: Slash at your adversary *and* inflict secondary damage to nearby enemies. Strike is a very strong attack that also wounds nearby enemies on either side and behind your target. It has a long recharge, though. It's arguably the best attack, and there's nothing better when tackling a number of foes at once.

TIP Consult the Creature Creator for making the "ultimate" combat creature, and to learn which Body Parts offer Level 5 Bite, Charge, Strike, and Spit skills.

Skill (and Level)	Damage (Health Points)	Duration (in secs.)	Recharge (in secs.)
Spit Level 1	2	6	3
Spit Level 2	3	6	3
Spit Level 3	4	6	3
Spit Level 4	5	6	3
Spit Level 5	6	6	3
Charge Level 1	1	1.5	12
Charge Level 2	1.5	1.75	12
Charge Level 3	2	2	10
Charge Level 4	2.5	2.25	8
Charge Level 5	3	2.5	6

Skill (and Level)	Damage (Health Points)	Recharge (in secs.)	Area-of-Effect Damage (Health Points)*
Strike Level 1	3	4.5	.8
Strike Level 2	4.5	4.5	1.1
Strike Level 3	6	4.5	1.5
Strike Level 4	7.5	4.5	1.9
Strike Level 5	9	4.5	2.3
Bite Level 1	1	1.5	—
Bite Level 2	1.5	1.5	—
Bite Level 3	2	1.5	—
Bite Level 4	2.5	1.5	—
Bite Level 5	3	1.5	—

NOTE * Only available with the Strike skill, this inflicts the damage shown in a small cone to either side and behind the enemy you're attacking, allowing multiple enemies to be struck.

Plans of Progression: Other Accessible Skills

On your display, under your Social or Attack tabs, is a set of five buttons, ready to be activated when you equip a creature with Body Parts that allow you other skills. Because you press a button to use them, they are known as "accessible" skills.

Mating Call

This is always in the middle of the five-button area, and activating it causes you to locate your nest to mate. See further into this chapter for additional information.

Glide

This allows you to float above the ground for a time. It's excellent for crossing rough or dangerous terrain.

Jump

This enables you to leap into the air, allowing you to cross rough ground.

Sneak

This turns you semi-transparent and is excellent for maneuvering through dangerous nest areas without being spotted.

Sprint

This doubles your regular speed, allowing you to cover ground quickly. Use this when traveling long distances.

NOTE The decisions you make effect what kind of consequence ability you receive. For more on what consequence abilities are available to you see the Consequence Abilities section on page 54.

	Level 1 (Skill)	Level 1 (Recharge)	Level 2 (Skill)	Level 2 (Recharge)	Level 3 (Skill)	Level 3 (Recharge)	Level 4 (Skill)	Level 4 (Recharge)	Level 5 (Skill)	Level 5 (Recharge)
Maximum time skill can be used before recharge										
Skill										
Glide	2 flaps	1 sec.	4 flaps	1 sec.	6 flaps	1 sec.	8 flaps	1 sec.	10 flaps	1 sec.
Jump	5 ft.	.5 sec.	7 ft.	.5 sec.	10 ft.	.5 sec.	14 ft.	.5 sec.	20 ft.	.5 sec.
Sneak	5-16 meters	25 sec.	4-12 meters	25 sec.	3-8 meters	25 sec.	1.5-4 meters	25 sec.	.75-2 meters	25 sec.
Sprint	10 sec.	120 sec.	15 sec.	105 sec.	20 sec.	90 sec.	25 sec.	75 sec.	30 sec.	60 sec.

Plans of Progression: Other Inaccessible Skills

The so-called "inaccessible" skills are granted by Body Parts, but you don't need to "activate" them. They are automatically added to your creature's abilities and are permanent until removed. Weigh the benefits of each skill before you equip.

✚ Health

Health is very important to your creature. The more Body Parts you activate with high Health Levels, the more additional Health Points your creature receives. Gauge how well you fight before adding higher Health Level parts, because you may not need them. If you're fighting an Epic or very high-level creature, you will, though!

	Level 1	Level 2	Level 3	Level 4	Level 5
Health	+10 HP	+15 HP	+25 HP	+40 HP	+100 HP

⇒ Speed

Speed is the other important inaccessible skill, as it quickens your creature's pace automatically. Not only can you cover distances more swiftly, but you can outrun enemies. If foes are chasing and tackling you, check their Speed Level on the Sporepedia, and find a Body Part that makes you faster. Or, employ the Sprint skill.

Plans of Progression: Bone Stomping and Shield Collecting

Almost as important as challenging or chatting with all your continent's wildlife is a series of foraging attempts to collect Gold Shields. These are the same as the shields you first saw during the Cell Stage, and they offer brand-new Body Parts. Counting all three categories of mouths (herbivore, carnivore, and omnivore) and the smattering of initially available parts, there are 228 parts to collect in total. Collect these Body Parts so you can select them and add them to your creature. Enter the Creature Creator by mating at your nest (detailed later in this chapter).

Method #1: You can find Gold Shields if you dig through fossil piles. The bigger the fossils, the more advanced the parts.

Method #2: Socialize with, or defeat another creature with the prefix "alpha" in its name.

NOTE Place your cursor over a group of creatures to locate the leader, or "alpha" one. These are usually the biggest. Engage it first, because defeating or socializing with it influences the rest of the same creature type. You'll learn what Socialize skills you need, or if the creatures back off or swarm you (if you're using Attack skills).

TIP Also remember that stronger creatures (shown by their general size and Health Points) unlock better Body Parts.

Plans of Progression: Body Parts Charts

You should, at the beginning of this stage, have some idea of what skills you'd like your creature to excel at. In this section, we show you the specifics of unlocking a particular part, and run through the Body Part evolutions that are available. Check the Creature Creator at the end of this chapter for advice on outfitting your creature with specific and complementary parts.

Chart 1 of 2: Unlockables

First, some sage advice: The 12 Cell parts you placed on your initial creature affect the multitude of Creature parts you find during this stage. The following chart shows you the Cell part, the "base" Body Parts the Cell part unlocks 100 percent of the time, and the two "random" selections of "base" parts, either (but not both) of which are unlocked. This assumes, of course, that you find a Gold Shield with the appropriate icon.

Choose a Cell part for your initial creature. In this example, we chose the Beady Eye. Check the chart below: Beady Eye unlocks certain "base" Senses and Details. Begin the Creature Stage.

Locate your first sets of bones. Smash them. Assuming you receive a Shield with the Senses or Details icon on it, you have a 100 percent chance of unlocking the Coygamine or the Felizard (both are "base" Mouths).

NOTE If you *didn't* receive a Shield with a Senses or Details icon, it's because one of your **other** Cell parts unlocked, instead.

After you've collecting the Coygamine and Felizard, subsequent Gold Shields unlock either the set of four base Senses (Selection 1 in the chart), or eight base Details (Selection 2 in the chart).

TIP Do you want to unlock the Toucan't mouth (for example)? Then you *must* equip your initial creature with the Proboscis! If you want to unlock a specific Body Part, you must begin the Creature Stage with a particular Cell part!

TIP What are "base" Body Parts? Check the Statistics Chart for all the information.

Cell Part	**Filter Mouth** Unlocks Mouths, Weapons, and Details			**Jaw** Unlocks Mouths, Weapons, and Details				**Proboscis** Unlocks Mouths, Weapons, and Details			
100% chance of unlocking	Mollratt	Swillson	Cantovis	Gobsterclaw	Manglerfish	D'orca		Leeyotch	Simperton	Sauroclod	Toucan't
Selection 1	Gobstalker	Pediculous	Scimitard	Heycorn	Pomp Pom	Sporesalfin	Featherbluster	Heycorn	Pomp Pom	Sporesalfin	Featherbluster
	Maceball	Keratinhorn	Hockitlauncher	Grasstachio	Whipwhick	Shellshard	Bonekneepad	Grasstachio	Whipwhick	Shellshard	Bonekneepad
Selection 2	Heycorn	Pomp Pom	Sporesalfin	Gobstalker	Pediculous	Scimitard		Pediculous	Scimitard	Maceball	
	Featherbluster	Grasstachio	Whipwhick	Maceball	Keratinhorn	Hockitlauncher		Keratinhorn	Gobstalker	Hockitlauncher	

Cell Part			Cell Part			Cell Part		

Spike
Unlocks Weapons only

Poison
Unlocks Weapons only

Electric
Unlocks Weapons only

100% chance of unlocking

Spike:
Pediculous, Keratinhorn

Poison:
Gobstalker, Hockitlauncher

Electric:
Maceball, Scimitard

Flagella
Unlocks Feet, Graspers, Details, Arms & Legs

100% chance of unlocking
Deltroid, Cankle, Stompbottom, Ostrichopath, Nubknuckle, Trapfist, Palmwalker, Suctoped, Grasstachio

Selection 1
Sporesalfin, Antisoptera

Selection 2
Slackwrist, Meekling

Cilia
Unlocks Feet, Graspers, Details, Arms & Legs

100% chance of unlocking
Deltroid, Cankle, Stompbottom, Ostrichopath, Setaetarsal, Butterbib, Bonestickler, The Geckonator, Stumplestilt, Webwaddle, Antisoptera

Selection 1
Slackwrist, Meekling

Jet
Unlocks Feet, Graspers, Details, Arms & Legs

100% chance of unlocking
Meekling, Cankle, Stompbottom, Ostrichopath, Grubbygrabber, Phatlanges, Stubbtoe, Twopaw, Clippity, Sporesalfin

Selection 1
Slackwrist, Deltroid

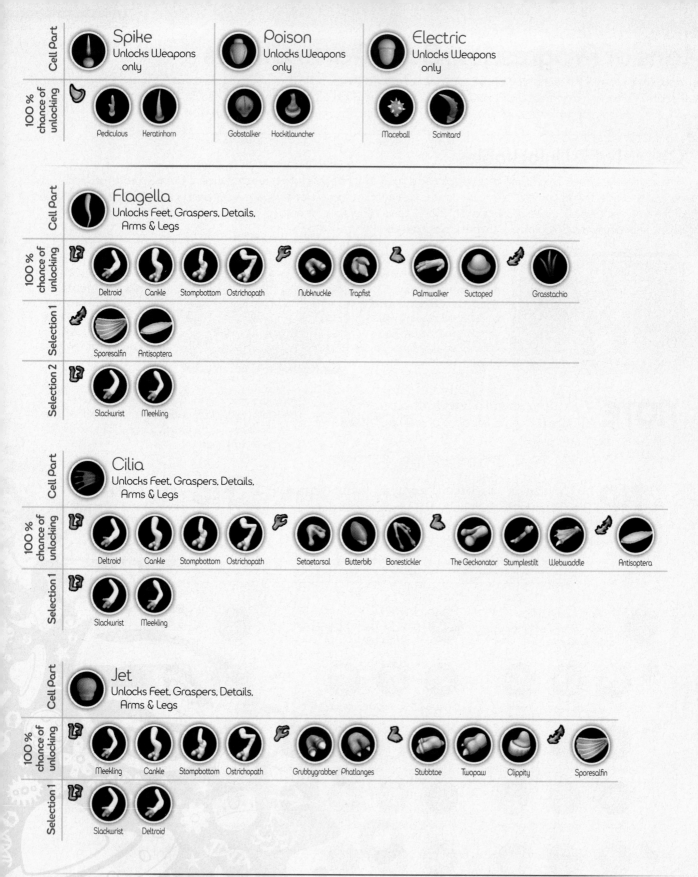

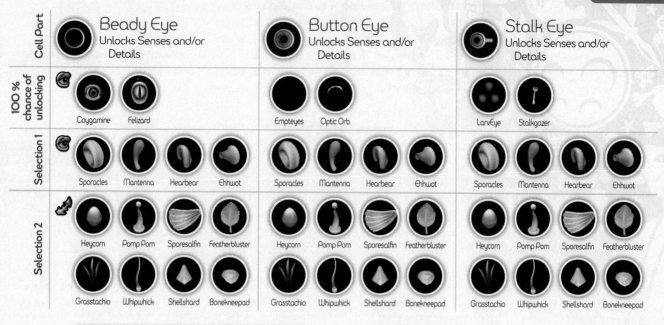

Cell Part	Beady Eye — Unlocks Senses and/or Details				Button Eye — Unlocks Senses and/or Details				Stalk Eye — Unlocks Senses and/or Details			
100% chance of unlocking	Coygamine	Felizard			Empteyes	Optic Orb			LarvEye	Stalkgazer		
Selection 1	Sporacles	Mantenna	Hearbear	Ehhwot	Sporacles	Mantenna	Hearbear	Ehhwot	Sporacles	Mantenna	Hearbear	Ehhwot
Selection 2	Heycorn	Pomp Pom	Sporesalfin	Featherbluster	Heycorn	Pomp Pom	Sporesalfin	Featherbluster	Heycorn	Pomp Pom	Sporesalfin	Featherbluster
	Grasstachio	Whipwhick	Shellshard	Bonekneepad	Grasstachio	Whipwhick	Shellshard	Bonekneepad	Grasstachio	Whipwhick	Shellshard	Bonekneepad

TIP The total number of base Body Parts is shown in the next chart.

TIP Your choice of arms and legs do not affect or unlock any Base Body Parts.

Unlocking All Base Parts

Now that you know what Cell parts unlock base Creature parts, you can pick which ones you want to try unlocking. This is achieved by placing every single Cell part onto your creature at the start of this stage. Because the number of DNA Points is high, forgo high-priced appendages, such as arms and legs, and "grow" them once you begin the stage. Also compare the elements of this previous chart, and you'll see some overlap.

Do you need the Cell weapons? After all, they only unlock two base parts. If you're playing a more social game, then no. However, because the Cell weapons unlock only two base weapons, they are easily unlocked. Plus, carnivores need these Cell parts when fighting, unless you're relying on just your Bite skill!

NOTE Remember that you don't need to unlock every single part. You can unlock just the ones you deem most useful or aesthetically pleasing.

Chart 2 of 2: Statistics

Now that you've uncovered just what Cell parts are needed to unlock your favorite Creature Body Part, check out the following statistical chart. It shows the 63 base parts, and what "Better," "Even Better," and "Best" Body Parts you can unlock as you progress through the Creature Stage. To unlock the more advanced parts, you need to use a base part and unlock more Gold Shields.

NOTE We segmented the 63 "base" parts as follows: 10 Mouths, 10 Eyes & Senses, 12 Arms & Legs†, 7 Graspers, 8 Feet, 6 Weapons, and 10 Details

NOTE † The Legs have three base appendages that you are given at the start of the Creature Stage, and another three that can be unlocked if you begin with specific Cell propulsion parts.

For example, let's assume you've unlocked the Leeyotch Mouth part, and you want to get the "best" version of it. First, you have to use it in the Creature Stage. Affix it to your creature, go off adventuring, and use the skills the part possesses (mainly Bite or Sing).

When you uncover bigger bone piles, or dispatch or befriend an alpha creature, you're very likely to obtain the "better" Body Part—in this case, Gnathognasher. Check your Body Part inventory, then go back to your nest and mate, and attach this part. Continue, locate an even bigger bone pile, and unlock the "even better" and "best" mouths (Saginaughty and Dietrap, in this example).

If you're "collecting" Body Parts in this stage, you need to swap them out each time the "best" one is found, and start again with another one. Or, you can concentrate on using the "best" Body Parts instead, and make your creature incredibly adept at a particular skill. With the Dietrap, for example, your creature has the most ferocious Bite possible, a Level 5 attack!

Here's another example. Say you want to make a creature with the best Singing skill possible. You cross-reference this chart, and find that four "best" mouths offer a Level 5 Singing skill. They are the **Amphibitude**, the **Whalephant**, the **Haunchface**, and the **Grubblemaw**. So you'd look to see whether any of the "base" mouths related to any of those four have been unlocked, and use them, working through the "better" and "even better" mouths until you unlock the "best" one.

TIP For more advanced players, the secondary skills offered by each mouth would also be a factor. For example, if you're interested in a toughened creature that can sing, you'd use the **Grubblemaw**, because this mouth also gives you Level 3 Health Points. The "base" mouth is the **Cantovis**, so you'd want to use this consistently. Remember though, you need to know which Cell part unlocks the Cantovis, so check the previous chart, first! The Cell mouth in question is the **Filter Mouth**. Phew!

TIP Now for the mind-boggling part: Because none of these skill levels are "stackable," you'd use this chart to see what other parts offer the best Health Points. Although the **Grubblemaw's** Health bonus is at Level 3, the **Triterraflops** is an example of a part that offers Level 5, so you might want to choose a different mouth instead (such as the **Haunchface**, with a Level 3 Charge). The Creature Creator tactics splits the skills out so that you can quickly check all the Body Parts that are associated with a specific skill. This helps you locate your key skills, and therefore your key parts.

NOTE Important! Some Body Parts, such as Eyes & Senses and Arms & Legs, aren't necessarily "better" than the base version, nor do they offer any skill improvements. However, they are unlocked in the same way.

What are "best" Body Parts and what skills are unlocked when you use them? Check the following for all the information:

🦖 Mouths

Base Part	Better Part	Even Better Part	Best Part
D'orca — Mating Call, Bite Level 2, Sing Level 1 — 25	**Terrorpin** — Mating Call, Bite Level 3, Sing Level 1 — 75	**CrocKisser** — Mating Call, Bite Level 4, Sing Level 2 — 150	**Shortensnout** — Mating Call, Bite Level 5, Sing Level 3 — 250
Gobsterclaw — Mating Call, Bite Level 2, Sing Level 1 — 25	**Handibles** — Mating Call, Bite Level 3, Sing Level 1, Health Level 1 — 75	**Handtennae** — Mating Call, Bite Level 4, Sing Level 1, Health Level 2 — 150	**Pincernaut** — Mating Call, Bite Level 5, Sing Level 1, Health Level 3 — 250
Manglerfish — Mating Call, Bite Level 2, Sing Level 1 — 25	**Slagjawed** — Mating Call, Bite Level 3, Charge Level 1, Sing Level 1 — 75	**Barracutie** — Mating Call, Bite Level 4, Charge Level 2, Sing Level 1 — 150	**Carcharebear** — Mating Call, Bite Level 5, Charge Level 3, Sing Level 1 — 250
Toucan't — Mating Call, Bite Level 1, Sing Level 1 — 25	**Buzzbeak** — Mating Call, Bite Level 1, Sing Level 2, Health Level 1 — 75	**Buzzmuzzle** — Mating Call, Bite Level 2, Sing Level 3, Health Level 2 — 150	**Skexybeast** — Mating Call, Bite Level 3, Sing Level 4, Health Level 3 — 250

Base Part	Better Part	Even Better Part	Best Part
Sauroclod — Mating Call, Bite Level 1, Sing Level 1 — 25	**Grinnace** — Mating Call, Bite Level 2, Sing Level 2 — 75	**Vermillips** — Mating Call, Bite Level 3, Sing Level 3 — 150	**S'gnarly** — Mating Call, Bite Level 4, Sing Level 4 — 250
Simperton — Mating Call, Bite Level 1, Sing Level 2 — 25	**Rostrum** — Mating Call, Bite Level 1, Sing Level 3 — 75	**Worrybeak** — Mating Call, Bite Level 1, Sing Level 4 — 150	**Amphibitude** — Mating Call, Bite Level 1, Sing Level 5 — 250
Leeyotch — Mating Call, Bite Level 2, Sing Level 1 — 25	**Gnathognasher** — Mating Call, Bite Level 3, Sing Level 1 — 75	**Saginaughty** — Mating Call, Bite Level 4, Sing Level 1 — 150	**Dietrap** — Mating Call, Bite Level 5, Sing Level 1 — 250
Mollratt — Mating Call, Bite Level 1, Sing Level 2 — 25	**Laardvark** — Mating Call, Bite Level 1, Sing Level 3 — 75	**Ruminanteater** — Mating Call, Bite Level 2, Sing Level 4 — 150	**Whalephant** — Mating Call, Bite Level 3, Sing Level 5 — 250
Swillson — Mating Call, Bite Level 1, Sing Level 2 — 25	**Ungulot** — Mating Call, Bite Level 1, Charge Level 1, Sing Level 3 — 75	**Soundersnout** — Mating Call, Bite Level 1, Charge Level 2, Sing Level 4 — 150	**Haunchface** — Mating Call, Bite Level 1, Charge Level 3, Sing Level 5 — 250
Cantovis — Mating Call, Bite Level 1, Sing Level 2 — 25	**Splatypus** — Mating Call, Bite Level 1, Sing Level 3, Health Level 1 — 75	**Snapgator** — Mating Call, Bite Level 1, Sing Level 4, Health Level 2 — 150	**Grubblemaw** — Mating Call, Bite Level 1, Sing Level 5, Health Level 3 — 250

🐾 Eyes and Senses

Base Part	Better Part	Even Better Part	Best Part
Optic Orb — 10, Sight	**Ocubulge** — 10, Sight	**Eyebissed** — 10, Sight	**Scrutineyes** — 10, Sight
LarvEye — 10, Sight	**Seeodesic** — 10, Sight	**Eyelien** — 10, Sight	**Stemma-addict** — 10, Sight

Base Part	Better Part	Even Better Part	Best Part
Empteyes — 10 — Sight	Occulus — 10 — Sight	Wide Eyed — 10 — Sight	Neo-teeny — 10 — Sight
Coygamine — 10 — Sight	Grumpeye — 10 — Sight	Furtive — 10 — Sight	Evil Eye — 10 — Sight
Felizard — 10 — Sight	Wizened — 10 — Sight	Saurian — 10 — Sight	Boneye — 10 — Sight
Stalkgazer — 10 — Sight	Meanstalk — 10 — Sight	Periscoptic — 10 — Sight	Peducledunk — 10 — Sight
Sporacles — 10	Chuffle — 10	Snuffle — 10	Snortle — 10
Mantenna — 10	Feelyfrond — 10	Segmentenna — 10	Ant-ler — 10
Hearbear — 10	Kitty — 10	Elfinmagick — 10	Gettineerful — 10
Ehhwot — 10	Overhear — 10	Panhear — 10	Batboy — 10

Arms & Legs

Base Part	Better Part	Even Better Part	Best Part
Slackwrist — 50 — Graspers	Python — 50 — Graspers	Doubelbow — 65 — Graspers	Wizardsleeve — 65 — Graspers
Meekling — 50 — Graspers	Flextor — 50 — Graspers	Burly — 50 — Graspers	Bulgo — 65 — Graspers
Deltroid — 50 — Graspers	Cutty — 50 — Graspers	Skrappy — 65 — Graspers	Gunnshow — 65 — Graspers

Base Part	Better Part	Even Better Part	Best Part
Brawnysaurus † 🧬50 ➡ Speed Level 1	Cankle 🧬65 ➡ Speed Level 1	Broncosaurus 🧬65 ➡ Speed Level 1	Steatopiggy 🧬65 ➡ Speed Level 1
Phatella † 🧬50 ➡ Speed Level 1	Stompbottom 🧬65 ➡ Speed Level 1	Callypigeon 🧬65 ➡ Speed Level 1	Yumstick 🧬65 ➡ Speed Level 1
Thundercalf † 🧬50 ➡ Speed Level 1	Ostrichopath 🧬65 ➡ Speed Level 1	Thighstrider 🧬65 ➡ Speed Level 1	Qopazcoati 🧬65 ➡ Speed Level 1

NOTE † These legs are available between the Cell and Creature Stages, in the initial Creature Creator.

Graspers

Base Part	Better Part	Even Better Part	Best Part
Setaetarsal Graspers Pose Level 2 🧬25	Amphibigrab Graspers Pose Level 3 🧬75	Amphibigrip Graspers Pose Level 4 🧬150	Croak Masseur Graspers Pose Level 5 🧬250
Nubknuckle Graspers Strike Level 1 Pose Level 1 🧬25	Lockpicker Graspers Strike Level 1 Pose Level 2 🧬75	Opposabubba Graspers Strike Level 2 Pose Level 3 🧬150	Monstrumtalon Graspers Strike Level 3 Pose Level 4 🧬250
Trapfist Graspers Strike Level 1 Health Level 1 🧬25	Succulenders Graspers Strike Level 2 Health Level 2 🧬75	Snatchengrabben Graspers Strike Level 3 Health Level 3 🧬150	Dexterrorous Graspers Strike Level 4 Health Level 4 🧬250
Bonestickler Graspers Strike Level 1 Pose Level 1 🧬25	Torsionwrencher Graspers Strike Level 2 Pose Level 2 Health Level 1 🧬75	Prongripper Graspers Strike Level 3 Pose Level 2 Health Level 2 🧬150	Tearerwrist Graspers Strike Level 3 Pose Level 3 Health Level 3 🧬250
Phatlanges Graspers Strike Level 1 Pose Level 1 🧬25	Badgerbear Graspers Strike Level 2 Pose Level 1 🧬75	Ultrarolfer Graspers Strike Level 3 Pose Level 2 🧬150	Metacarnal Graspers Strike Level 4 Pose Level 3 🧬250

Base Part	Better Part	Even Better Part	Best Part
Grubbygrabber — Graspers, Strike Level 2 — 25	**Velocigrasper** — Graspers, Strike Level 3 — 75	**Hookencrook** — Graspers, Strike Level 4 — 150	**Horrorthumbs** — Graspers, Strike Level 5 — 250
Butterbib — Graspers, Pose Level 1, Health Level 1 — 25	**Mitzy** — Graspers, Pose Level 2, Health Level 2 — 75	**Classic Minion** — Graspers, Pose Level 3, Health Level 3 — 150	**Ectoknight** — Graspers, Pose Level 4, Health Level 4 — 250

👣 Feet

Base Part	Better Part	Even Better Part	Best Part
Stubbtoe — Sprint Level 2, Dance Level 1, Speed Level 2 — 25	**Scareclaw** — Sprint Level 3, Dance Level 2, Speed Level 3 — 75	**The Clawman** — Sprint Level 4, Dance Level 3, Speed Level 4 — 150	**Dirtchargers** — Sprint Level 5, Dance Level 4, Speed Level 5 — 250
Twopaw — Sprint Level 1, Dance Level 2, Speed Level 2 — 25	**Threepaw** — Sprint Level 2, Dance Level 3, Speed Level 3 — 75	**Fourpaw** — Sprint Level 3, Dance Level 4, Speed Level 4 — 150	**Morepaw** — Sprint Level 4, Dance Level 5, Speed Level 5 — 250
Webwaddle — Jump Level 1, Charge Level 1, Speed Level 2 — 25	**Backskritcher** — Jump Level 2, Charge Level 2, Speed Level 3 — 75	**Elevatorclaws** — Jump Level 3, Charge Level 3, Speed Level 4 — 150	**Raptorclaws** — Jump Level 4, Charge Level 4, Speed Level 5 — 250
Palmwalker — Sneak Level 2, Dance Level 2, Speed Level 1 — 25	**Underhanded** — Sneak Level 3, Dance Level 3, Speed Level 2 — 75	**Hombrenid** — Sneak Level 4, Dance Level 4, Speed Level 3 — 150	**Sassyquatch** — Sneak Level 5, Dance Level 5, Speed Level 4 — 250
Clippity — Sprint Level 1, Charge Level 2, Speed Level 2 — 25	**Cloppity** — Sprint Level 2, Charge Level 3, Speed Level 3 — 75	**Hoppity** — Sprint Level 3, Charge Level 4, Speed Level 4 — 150	**Hippoty** — Sprint Level 4, Charge Level 5, Speed Level 5 — 250
Stumplestilt — Jump Level 1, Dance Level 1, Speed Level 1, Health Level 1 — 25	**Buckfoot** — Jump Level 2, Dance Level 2, Speed Level 2, Health Level 2 — 75	**Slasherknight** — Jump Level 3, Dance Level 3, Speed Level 3, Health Level 3 — 150	**Scarmaker** — Jump Level 4, Dance Level 4, Speed Level 4, Health Level 4 — 250

Base Part	Better Part	Even Better Part	Best Part
Suctoped — Sneak Level 1, Charge Level 1, Dance Level 1, Speed Level 1 — 25	**Sugerefoot** — Sneak Level 2, Charge Level 1, Dance Level 1, Speed Level 2 — 75	**Suctopod** — Sneak Level 3, Charge Level 2, Dance Level 2, Speed Level 3 — 150	**Suctofleur** — Sneak Level 4, Charge Level 3, Dance Level 3, Speed Level 4 — 250
The Geckonator — Jump Level 2, Dance Level 1, Speed Level 1 — 25	**The Geckoning** — Jump Level 3, Dance Level 2, Speed Level 2 — 75	**The Froggening** — Jump Level 4, Dance Level 3, Speed Level 3 — 150	**The Toadening** — Jump Level 5, Dance Level 4, Speed Level 4 — 250

🐚 Weapons

Base Part	Better Part	Even Better Part	Best Part
Pediculous — 25, Charge Level 2	**Fawninatrix** — 75, Charge Level 3	**Ultramegadeer** — 150, Charge Level 4	**Elkegent** — 250, Charge Level 5
Keratinhorn — Charge Level 1, Health Level 1 — 25	**Narwhalicorn** — Charge Level 2, Health Level 2 — 75	**Cornutopia** — Charge Level 3, Health Level 3 — 150	**Rammer** — Charge Level 4, Health Level 4 — 250
Gobstalker — Spit Level 1, Health Level 1 — 25	**Phlegmthrower** — Spit Level 2, Health Level 2 — 75	**Problem-Solvent** — Spit Level 3, Health Level 3 — 150	**Spraypalm** — Spit Level 4, Health Level 4 — 250
Hockitlauncher — 25, Spit Level 2	**Spraybuchet** — 75, Spit Level 3	**Ziggur-hat** — 150, Spit Level 4	**Porcupain** — 250, Spit Level 5
Maceball — Strike Level 1, Health Level 1 — 25	**Stessball** — Strike Level 2, Health Level 2 — 75	**The Tauntlet** — Strike Level 3, Health Level 3 — 150	**SlimSlam Kablam** — Strike Level 4, Health Level 4 — 250
Scimitard — 25, Strike Level 2	**Toxic Telson** — 75, Strike Level 3	**Reapermantis** — 150, Strike Level 4	**Spurprise!** — 250, Strike Level 5

Details

Base Part	Better Part	Even Better Part	Best Part
Heycorn — 25, Charm Level 2	**Nurple** — 75, Charm Level 3	**Jellybutton** — 150, Charm Level 4	**Mackne** — 250, Charm Level 5
Pomp Pom — 25, Charm Level 2	**Springle** — 75, Charm Level 3	**Wrottontail** — 150, Charm Level 4	**Fleurbine** — 250, Charm Level 5
Derma Bark — Charm Level 1, Health Level 1, 25	**Baublewarts** — Charm Level 2, Health Level 2, 75	**Jemite** — Charm Level 3, Health Level 3, 150	**Stealing Crystals** — Charm Level 4, Health Level 4, 250
Featherbluster — Jump Level 1, Charm Level 1, 25	**Marshcara** — Sneak Level 1, Charm Level 2, 75	**Peacrock** — Sprint Level 1, Charm Level 3, 150	**Featherferns** — Charm Level 5, 250
Grasstachio — Sneak Level 1, Charm Level 1, 25	**Coverleaf** — Sneak Level 2, Charm Level 2, 75	**Branch Deco** — Sneak Level 3, Charm Level 3, 150	**Florsage** — Sneak Level 4, Charm Level 4, 250
Whipwhick — 25, Charm Level 2	**Protubers** — 75, Charm Level 3	**Hairlagmites** — 150, Charm Level 4	**Crestacean** — 250, Charm Level 5
Shellshard — 25, Health Level 2	**Osteoflippy** — 75, Health Level 3	**Hydroxylappetite** — 150, Health Level 4	**Triterraflops** — 250, Health Level 5
Bonekneepad — 25, Health Level 2	**Knurl Down** — 75, Health Level 3	**Bone Tablets** — 150, Health Level 4	**Rockne** — 250, Health Level 5
Sporsalfin — Sprint Level 1, Charm Level 1, 25	**Icky-osaur** — Sprint Level 2, Speed Level 1, 75	**Finneas** — Jump Level 1, Sprint Level 3, 150	**Pool Party-Foul** — Sneak Level 1, Sprint Level 4, 250
Antisoptera — Jump Level 1, Glide Level 2, 25	**Fauxry Wings** — Jump Level 1, Glide Level 3, 75	**Megachiraptora** — Jump Level 1, Glide Level 4, 150	**Cassoworry** — Jump Level 1, Glide Level 5, 250

Obtaining DNA Points

Searching for the best Body Parts is all well and good, but they cost a lot (up to 250 points) to use. So you don't run out, employ the following techniques to increase your DNA Points, so you have more than enough when you want to mate and retool your creature:

- Search for bone piles.
- Defeat an enemy creature.
- Befriend another creature.
- Make an enemy species extinct.
- Ally with another species.

- Ally with a mini-epic creature.
- Defeat a mini-epic creature.
- Follow your species to a new nest when they migrate.
- Finish any of the Missions (detailed later in this chapter).

Plans of Progression: Nesting

The nest is the hub of activity for your group of creatures, and you'll return to it often. Initially, it's by the shore where you evolved from. However, as you progress through the levels, you will migrate to new nesting grounds. Here's some nesting advice:

You can heal while you are standing near or on your base. If you're coming back from a failed raid, or enemy creatures are attacking, run here for immediate Health Point improvement.

TIP If you have befriended another creature to the point that you are allies, you can use its nest to heal, too. Remember this if you're attacked, and this second nest is closer than your home nest.

Your mate always waits at your nest. A mate is a creature of your exact size and species, with a head swirling with love hearts. Mate to enter the Creature Creator.

If you expend all your Health Points during an exploration and are dispatched, you hatch again at the nest. There is no penalty for this.

You are wise to fan out around your nest, covering the nearby territories (hills, valleys, woods, beach) first, because the farther you are from your nest, the more dangerous and difficult your environment becomes (mainly due to a more fearsome population of critters).

Later in the stage, your creature species migrates across the landscape to a new nesting position. Be sure to travel to this new location for additional DNA Points (locate it with the mini-map or Mating Call if you're lost).

Plans of Progression: Mating and Creature Creator

To use the Body Parts you're uncovering across the continent, you must return to your mate and start a mating dance. This is the key to increasing important abilities and skills.

Mating: Move back to your nest, and locate the creature from your species with the hearts revolving around its head. Click on it to begin a slow mating dance and ritual.

Entering the Creator: You lay an egg, and you're transported into the Creature Creator. The Cell Body Parts are now no longer available (although they're still attached to your creature), but the choice has widened.

NOTE Locate all the different bonuses for each Body Part you can collect by using the Creature Creator section. Remember to compare the stats increase your current Body Part has over a new one, if you value skill improvements over creating a specific look (although you can do both).

New Skills: When you exit the Creator, all of your species are outfitted with the Body Parts you chose, and your specific creature hatches from an egg. Now is the time to learn any new abilities.

The Hatching Mimicry: If you've learned a new Attack or Social interaction, or one you've already learned has increased a level, you must activate this skill after watching a fellow creature perform it. This demonstration and mimicry continues until all new skills are learned.

Choosing the Correct Diet

Aside from exploration and collection, the third important aspect of life roaming around as a creature is the constant search for food. As with the Cell Stage, there are three choices, and each provides a different type of sustenance and way to play.

🐾 Herbivore

Pick a mouth that allows you to eat only plant matter. This allows you to eat the following:

Fruit lying on the ground.

Fruit on small, low-level bushes.

Fruit on larger trees. Add graspers to reach higher fruit.

TIP Making your creature very tall helps you grab some of the fruit on the larger trees, but adding graspers or Body Parts that allow you to jump or glide also helps you grab hard-to-reach fruit. However, there's usually an abundance of fruit, so you shouldn't starve.

ᕓ Carnivore

Pick a mouth that allows you to consume only meat. This allows you to eat the following:

Meaty chunks from a recently slain creature.

TIP Being a carnivore can be very rewarding; you can attack a nearby creature, slay it, and then immediately feast on its carcass. This gives you instant Health Points, and is easier than backing away and finding a fruit tree!

TIP Remember you can also return to your nest to quickly regain Health Points.

ᕓᕓ Omnivore

Pick a mouth that allows you to devour both fruit and meat. This allows you to eat the following:

Fruit, from the various locations detailed previously.

Meat, from the recently slain. Basically, if it's fresh and you can eat it, do so!

When to Eat

Keep track of your Health and Hunger Bars (in the bottom right of your screen). Make sure they are topped up before you engage in battle.

If your creature shows a thought bubble about eating, locate the nearest food immediately. Failure means your creature begins to lose Health Points until death occurs. You can heal at a nest, but that doesn't cure your hunger. Go chomp on some delicious fruit or freshly slain carcass, pronto!

NOTE Eating the "wrong" type of food is possible, but it can make you sick. If you're a herbivore, don't chow down on an animal carcass, or you'll get a very unhappy tummy!

Cartographical Evidence: The Mini-Map

As you venture out from your first nest, the mini-map, in the screen's bottom-left corner, is very helpful for exploration. Be sure to use the map's many useful tools when negotiating the countryside.

Other nests show up as a green "?" if they are unexplored. They change to gray nests if you've already been to this nest area—mouse over them to see which species calls them home. A red skull and crossbones shows a nest of an extinct creature (dispatched by you). A "house" icon indicates your home nest. As you progress through the Creature Stage levels, the mini-map displays migration paths, dotted lines that you can follow to your new nest, or use as relatively safe and flat ground to walk on.

Adversaries, Allies, and Epics: Other Creatures

You'll soon discover you're not alone on this continent. The place is teeming with wildlife, and some of these primitive creature types can end up being strong allies, your next feast, or both! Here are the main creature types, and generally how to deal with them:

Curious Creatures

Curious creatures allow you to approach them and their nest. They are usually open to Social advances. They are easy to spot and they have a neutral icon near their name if you click on them.

Aggressive Creatures

More aggressive creatures are easily spotted because they attack you as soon as they see you. Approach their nest at your own risk, or face a fight; sometimes with a swarm overwhelming you!

Mini-Epic Creatures

There's a third type of creature, known colloquially as a "mini-epic." These creatures are larger and stronger than average, are encountered on their own, and (although imposing) allow you to socialize with them...as long as your Social skills are good enough!

Epic Creatures

Beware of the great behemoths! You won't miss these massive and imposing beasts, and they are almost always angry. However, they tend to guard a few sets of very large bone piles (which can be snagged for a powerful Body Part or two).

Plan #1: Your first tactic, which can be easier, is to snag the Epic's bone piles by sneaking (either using the skill, or when the Epic's back is turned) to each pile, smashing it, and fleeing before the Epic realizes the pilfering has occurred!

Plan #2: Epics can't be reasoned with, so another (much more dangerous) plan is to attack. Begin with long-range spitting, then charge in, and be sure you have the maximum number of pack members with you (and a mini-epic creature helping, if possible). With luck and high level Attack skills (Level 4 or 5 Bites, Charges, Strikes, and Spits), you may fell this giant, but be ready to run if things go badly for you!

CAUTION Epic Fail: One wrong move or launching an attack without pack back-up results in a swift and embarrassing battering by this titan!

Plans of Progression: Levelling Up Your Brain

Before our example of a Creature Stage begins, there's a last part of the stage to detail: actually completing each level and finishing this chapter of your evolution. Below is information on exactly what you need to do and what occurs at each of the four levels of the stage.

Progression Bar: Brain Detail

The Progression Bar at the foot of your screen shows you how much of the stage you've completed. This particular bar shows your brain level. Your brain increases in size when you gain DNA.

History: Game Detail

You can access the History whenever you like. It shows your progress throughout this stage, including the parts you've unlocked, species slain or socialized with, and edits you've made to your creature, as well as the type of creature: herbivorous, omnivorous, or carnivorous.

Levels: Building a Pack

The size of your brain (and therefore your level) determines how many creatures can follow you around in a pack (also called pack). These are shown on the right side of your screen. Your pack follows you wherever you go, and sometimes helps with specific Missions. They act independently and don't need to be controlled. They are perfect to bring along when you're tackling a pride of vicious rival creatures that must be defeated!

Level	Number of Possible Pack Members
1	0 (start)
2	1
3	2
4	3
5	3 (immediately enter Tribal Stage)

Fellow Creatures of Your Species

Pack members are beckoned into service using your Social techniques, in exactly the same way as you would befriend a curious herd of creatures. There are three types of pack members:

These are the easiest ones to coax. Simply click on them, and beckon them with a Social skill. They have the same attacks as you do.

Allied Creatures

Use a variety of Social techniques. You need to have already allied with a creature before it will agree to come with you.

TIP This is a key technique for the more pacifist player. Instead of slaying a powerful pride of more complex creatures, employ high-level Social skills to ally with them. Then, once you have a pack, these act as your "bodyguards," fending off aggressors.

Mini-Epic Creatures

If you find a mini-epic creature that's large and imposing but isn't squishing your head into the dirt with a mighty stomp, try befriending it instead of attacking. It can be a faithful pet, and great in combat situations!

Consequence Abilities

If you're playing each stage in turn, and have completed the Cell Stage with your chosen creature, it begins with one of the following special "super" Consequence Ability or trait! Each attack is very powerful, but has a long recharge.

Herbivorous Cell Player: Siren's Song

If you finished the Cell Stage as a herbivore, you can stop nearby aggressive creatures from attacking you for a limited time by singing at them.

Omnivorous Cell Player: Summon Flock

If you completed the Cell Stage as an omnivore, you can summon a small collection of critters to fly in and help you either attack or befriend during an encounter with another group of creatures.

Carnivorous Cell Player: Raging Roar

If you were triumphant in the Cell Stage as a carnivore, you can emit a mighty bellow. Any nearby creatures become afraid of you and run away.

NOTE Continue to play through this stage, checking your History so you know what type of play style you're employing, and you receive more Consequence Abilities that unlock at the beginning of the Tribal Stage.

The Three Play Styles

Social: Gain the majority of your DNA through Social abilities and you will gain related traits.

Adaptable: Balance your play style and gain different traits than playing at either extreme.

Predator: Progress by primarily killing creatures and aggression will only become easier.

Oddities

While Flumpy and his friends stretch their legs in preparation for their epic explorations to come, there's just room to mention some of the oddities you might encounter during this stage. They include (but aren't limited to):

Landmarks

The landscape is dotted with odd-looking hillocks and dells. Some have strange structures; the remnants of a past civilization?

Steaming Vents

If you want to go gliding without wings, seek out these rare vents in the ground; step onto them and you're shot high into the air, offering a great view. The descent is almost never fatal....

Extraterrestrial Objects

Among the landmarks, there are sometimes large rocks with their own crater or furrow; evidence of outer-space bombardment like the one that gave your own creature life. Did you find the rare bones near the object?

Meteor Shower

Incoming! The sky is filled with fiery debris raining down from the heavens! Seek a healing nest immediately, or face some nasty extraterrestrial damage!

UFO Abduction

While more evolved creatures might think this is simply an alien species completing Space Missions to make an alliance, you and your of primitive critters are freaked by the giant shiny thing sucking up various unlucky animals for otherworldly experimentation....

creature levels: the flight of flumpy

An Exploration in Five Parts

The last part of this section concerns examples of a particular experience throughout this stage. Our own created creature, Flumpy, is shown to give one of the billions of examples of how you might play through each level. Each time Flumpy's appearance and statistics changed, we reveal it.

◉ Level 1: Brain Size: Pea (approximate)

As dawn breaks, Flumpy and his youngster waddle from the nest to complete the first Mission; collecting a part from a bone pile.

Flumpy: Level 1.0. Moments after waddling ashore from the ocean.

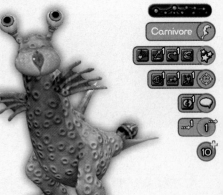

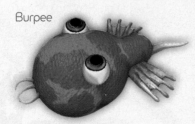

Shortly afterward, Flumpy finds a deceased Burpee on the grass. Fortunately, due to Flumpy's Jaw, the meat is both edible and delicious!

Burpee

With two Missions complete in as many minutes, Flumpy confidently strides southward. Some Gom are transfixed by Flumpy's Siren Song Consequence Ability!

Flumpy has crushed more than a dozen bone piles by the time he finds his next nest. He impresses a Batzu and they're now friends!

Gom

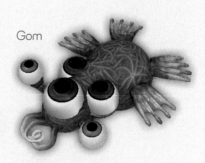

Batzu

Flumpy can't find two more Batzu to ally with, so Flumpy crushes more bone piles.

Flumpy heads north. Because he didn't kill the dead Burpee he feasted on, he can still befriend the alpha Burpee. This gains him a great Body Part!

Two more Burpees are impressed, and the first alliance is formed! With more bones crushed, Flumpy returns to the nest and mates.

Hatching from the egg, baby Flumpy learns how to Spit and Charge before growing to full-size. The brain is almost ready to grow, too!

Trotting southwest, Flumpy enters a grassy plain, and stumbles into an Octilon nest. He makes short work of the alpha Octilon...

Flumpy: Level 1.5. Flumpy sports a change in diet, the first real arms, a height increase, and a slightly furry coat. Only the Flagella remain from Flumpy's Cell incarnation.

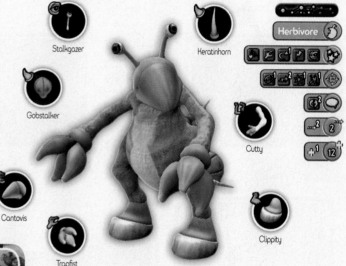

Stalkgazer

Gobstalker

Cantovis

Trapfist

Keratinhorn

Herbivore

Cutty

Clippity

Octilon

... before barfing up its remains into the nest! Flumpy forgot he's changed his diet to fruit-only, so he heads to the forest for a feast.

With a full tummy, Flumpy returns to the Octilon area, and begins a beatdown; he feels funny after making them extinct. Is this regret?

Of course not! It's Flumpy's pea-sized brain evolving to Level 2! He can now hunt with a friend and really begin to explore!

Flumpy: Level 2.0. A slight change of mouth makes Flumpy take a turn for the fearsome! He's back to eating meat, and now has antler-like protuberances.

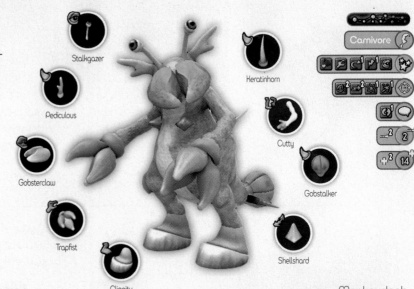

Stalkgazer

Pediculous

Gobsterclaw

Trapfist

Clippity

Keratinhorn

Cutty

Gobstalker

Shellshard

Carnivore

Flumpy's also been spending time collecting more Gold Shields from bone piles. He races back to the nest and mates again.

After some social Singing with another of Flumpy's kind, both trot back and eradicate the Gom, then feast on their flesh (Flumpy's mouth is now carnivorous).

Cracking more bone piles as they go, Flumpy and friend hunt Monkeydoobs; Flumpy Spits from range while his pal charges in for close combat!

Monkeydoob

Flumpy's long-range plan is an astounding success and is thoroughly recommended!

As dawn breaks, Flumpy begins to devour four Doofnits! Defeating the Doofnits is a little trickier, as these slightly more enhanced creatures require four deaths to become extinct. To victory!

Ignoring the opportunities to change appearance, Flumpy continues into the woods, and deals exotic spittle death to an alpha Octavius and his minions! Soon after, brain-swelling evolution occurs!

Doofnit

Heading straight back for some mating, Flumpy uses his Sprint ability, allowing much faster movement. He also grabs a few shells to decorate the nest.

Octavius

Level 3: Brain Size: Satsuma (approximate)

Flumpy: Level 3.0. A fishy appearance, some brand new peepers, improved graspers, faster feet, and a growth spurt make Flumpy more freakishly ugly than ever! Flumpy's Flagella finally fall off, too!

After Flumpy's new and more monstrous form hatches, the nest moves, and a sing-song allows Flumpy's pack to expand to two.

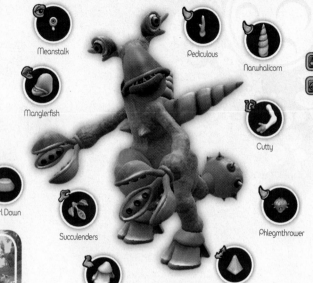

Meanstalk
Pediculous
Narwhalicorn
Manglerfish
Cutty
Knurl Down
Succulenders
Phlegmthrower
Cloppity
Shellshard

Carnivore

The Migrate Mission begins. Flumpy pauses to smash a few more bone piles, then follows the migratory path into parts unknown.

The trail continues to a new nest, which is claimed for Flumpykind. A good-sized DNA Point bonus is awarded.

Celebrations come to a swift end as night falls, and Flumpy tries some fruit lying on the ground; vomiting promptly ensues!

Another trek around this new nest begins, and an increasingly hungry carnivorous Flumpy spots a mini-epic Doltasaur. His pack attacks!

Doltasaur

The Doltasaur could have been a great pack member, but Flumpy lacks social graces, is starving, and wanted to complete the hunt goal.

A vicious fight breaks out as five Boyards scuttle into combat. Flumpy shoots spittle from range, and challenges the alpha leader to battle!

Boyard

This seven-creature fight ends with a pack member taking a critical wound, but the sacrifice is worth it. Flumpy's brain expands again!

Flumpy returns to the nest to heal an injured pal, then trots toward the woods. Checking the Boyard's stats confirms that these beasts are cruising for a bruising!

Level 4: Brain Size: Blood Orange (approximate)

Flumpy: Level 4.25. The first of four Flumpys in this long level has a longer neck, impressive horns, and a new mouth. Some rocky appendages and a new coat finish this striped look!

With an excellent pair of Elkegents to show off, Flumpy summons a friend and heads north into a hillside. Ahead, something monstrous stirs!

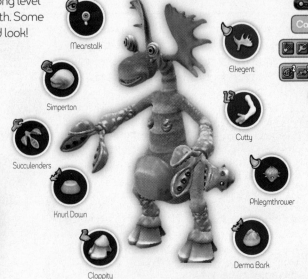

Carnivore

Meanstalk

Simperton

Succulenders

Knurl Down

Cloppity

Elkegent

Cutty

Phlegmthrower

Derma Bark

Guarding two gigantic bone piles is a huge beast: an Epic version of a creature known as Thistles! Flumpy dashes for the first bone pile...

Thistles

...and is promptly stomped on, hard! This is Flumpy's first brush with death; there's a new dominator on planet Ravian! Flumpy hatches back at the nest, and summons a pack!

Learning a lesson, Flumpy skirts the grassy plains where Thistles roams, waits for him to move away, then sprints to Thistles's two bone piles!

Flumpy is distracted by a large furrow nearby. On closer inspection, there appears to be a strange craft crashed into the ground! Flumpy grabs the unearthed bone pile, pronto!

Oh no! Flumpy's spent too long gazing at the shiny object in the furrow, and Thistles has spotted them! Combat lasts longer, but Flumpy suffers the same fate!

Flumpy: Level 4.5. Flumpy cheers up with a brand new bill, and some fancy new feet. Not only that, but he's adorned with a pair of brand new details, too!

Flumpy decides to leave Thistles alone, and heads east toward the woods, bringing three friends. He passes through a Batzu nest without a problem; they're still allies, after all.

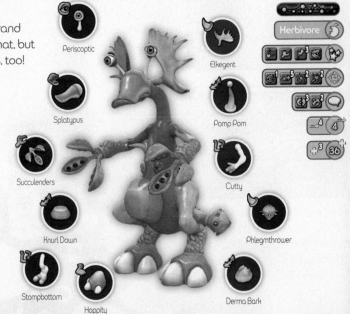

Herbivore

Periscoptic

Splatypus

Succulenders

Knurl Down

Stompbottom

Hoppity

Elkegent

Pomp Pom

Cutty

Phlegmthrower

Derma Bark

60

Bimingo

A woodside wander at dawn is rudely interrupted as a flock of Bimingoes ambush the pack! Fortunately, they're all squawk and no bite!

After some more bone pile hunting, Flumpy spots a massive tree on the horizon, so the pack swims to investigate. More bone piles are found, so it's time for a change!

The Flumpy clan is looking healthier than ever, and ready for a final expedition. Flumpy sings to three pack members, and the final walkabout begins!

Periscoptic

Mollratt

Herbivore

Succulenders

Cutty

Pomp Pom x2

Knurl Down

Phlegmthrower

Stompbottom

Hoppity

Derma Bark

Flumpy: Level 4.75. He's taller, sports yet another mouth type, and enjoys additional appendages on the tail. This is Flumpy's penultimate form!

Heading eastward to a hilly range, Flumpy uses Sneak and Sprint to work around to higher ground, before launching long-range spittle at an out-matched Singtoo!

Singtoo

After dominating and finally felling the last Singtoo, Flumpy inspects every nearby bone pile, then gambols over to a fruit tree for some delicious food.

Continuing across the hillside, Flumpy and friends stumble on a Chuchoko's nest. These feathered fiends aren't too friendly, so they're swarmed by the Flumpy pack immediately.

After Chuchoko extinction is assured, Flumpy hikes to the lush grasslands on the other side of the hill. There are two strange landmarks in the distance...

Chuchoko

...the first is a steam vent, blowing warm air from deep underground. Stepping on it, Flumpy is propelled sky high!

After a soft landing, Flumpy and crew skedaddle over to a large crater with a strange space rock in it. The creature it hit yields a major Body Part.

Bigger mistake! The Catfish Bandits are set upon by the Flumpy pack, and all are slain. This feat of strength causes massive brain inflation! Yippee!

Emerging from the crater, Flumpy goes fruit-searching. Big mistake! A nest of Catfish Bandits stun and swarm him, butting him with their pointy horns.

Catfish Bandit

Level 5: Brain Size: Large Grapefruit (approximate)

Flumpy: Level 5.0. Behold the evolution! Flumpy sports a bigger frame, a better mouth, fewer extraneous details, and a longer neck. This is his ultimate form, and now he wants to known be known as Clumpy!

Once the Flumpy pack returns triumphantly to the final nest, Clumpy is born! He spends some more time crushing more bone piles and chatting and attacking nearby entities.

Finally, at the end of this stage, Clumpy discovers the wonders of fire, and the stick he was holding is transformed to a Chieftain's staff! Let the Tribal Stage begin!

Meanstalk

Keratinhorn

Laardvark

Succulenders

Skrappy

Springle

Hoppity

Ostrichopath

Herbivore

TIP At the end of this stage, the "Evolve to Tribe" button becomes available. Press this to enter the Tribal Stage, and begin to outfit your creature. If you want to explore more, or make adjustments to your creature, do this before you enter the Tribal Stage.

🐾 creature creator

Say hello to my little friend: Fully Evolved Creature Creating. Just before the **Tribal Stage** of *Spore*, you can conjure an infinite variety of beings and beasties, all created via the **Creature Creator**. These are more comprehensive than those you built during the Creature Stage (all parts are available if you're creating from scratch, while Body Parts you collected during the Creature Stage are available if you're attempting this during the Creature Stage. You can also access a creature, (either new or previously designed) after selecting a planet from the main menu, choosing its Theme, and selecting Tribe Assets. This takes you into the **Sporepedia**, where you can access your favorite creatures, or create one from scratch. The following section showcases the creation of a sample creature, along with advice on all the different appendages you can select. After this comes a wealth of example creatures to aid in your own activities. The time has come to get fully evolved!

clumpy
(Levidensis inconcinnus-pedis)

The Birth of Clumpy: Say hello to Clumpy, a skittish, bipedal herbivore with a long neck to reach the high fruit, vicious arm pincers to stop angry enemies on the ground, clip-cloppety feet for dancing, romancing, and crushing, and (more importantly) a heart of gold! He may lack an array of fearsome fins, or a jagged maw brimming with pointy teeth, but he's got moxie. He's also an excellent example of a beast that is relatively straightforward to create but brings a lot of character to a game; this is important if your fellow *Spore* players are going to select him. Over the next few pages, we show you plans and problems we had while creating Clumpy, which in turn allows you many shortcuts and advantages to creating your own precious little monsters!

> **NOTE** Clumpy is an evolution of the creature created at the start of the Creature Stage. Refer back to this previous chapter if you want the basic Body Parts to select and initial plans on creature creation.

Mouths: Laardvark

With a nasty, but not overly dangerous Bite ability, the Laardvark mouth allows your critter to Sing loud and proud; perfect for befriending neighborly types! This mouth allows for Herbivorous eating only.

Eyes and Senses: Meanstalk

Not as elaborate as the long Periscoptic, this still gives Clumpy the gift of sight.

Graspers: Succulenders

In keeping with Clumpy's oddness, we chose sucker-like pincers that deliver a nasty nip in combat, but also help him gesticulate wildly to other critters; hopefully resulting in gifts, not bloodshed!

Arms and Legs: Skrappy Ostrichopath

Clumpy likes to use his nasty pincer-like graspers in a fracas, so we chose a sinewy, but not overly meaty arm. The legs needed to be thin, but very powerful, and bendy in all the right places!

Weapons: Keratinhorn x3

Only one Keratinhorn is needed to add a bonus to Clumpy's Charging ability, but we added three; the remnants of Clumpy's defenses many generations ago, during his Cell Stage.

Feet: Hoppity

Clumpy is most proud of his feet, not only because of the clippety-clop sound they make, but also the tremendous combat Charge, faster Sprint, and even Dance prowess!

Details: Springle

Adding a fancy tail with a Springle attached to the end finishes the ensemble, and allows Clumpy even more confidence and Charm. He'll get a big box of gifts in no time!

primagames.com

building character

In this section, we reveal exactly how we attached the various appendages to Clumpy, along with advice on making similar — or wildly different — creatures.

To help you design something a little more specific to your gaming needs, this guide segments the different styles of creatures into one of three types. Concentrate on one (or more) of the types when creating your creature for best results. The types are:

Style 1. Personality-Driven

This beast may not be the best at befriending or attacking.

These creatures simply look cool. Ignore elements relating to Attack, Social, or Movement scores, and make something that is truly beautiful or frightening, one that exudes charm or menace, or one that in some way captivates an audience.

Then augment it with additional parts if you think it's too weak!

Style 2. Function-Based

The very definition of a social butterfly, this creature was designed to make friends and influence people.

These are the opposite of personality-driven creatures. Here, you've increased certain statistics on to provide critters for a particular type of gamer. Although these can look cool, they are primarily built around one or two key attributes; such as a "combat" monster, a "social" butterfly, or a "speed" demon.

Style 3. Earth-Influenced

Half cute, and half carnivorous, this gray bear is based in reality, but with the *Spore* "look."

The third main type should be an attempt to put your own design stamp on a creature that already exists. Perhaps it's a gorilla with pink fur, or a particularly large platypus. Locate appendages that fit well together and have names that refer to pre-existing creatures, and group them together. Perhaps refer to a photo of the beast you're trying to recreate, too.

Clumpy was created with personality in mind. These three style types allow you to focus on creating the creature you imagine. Remember that you can have creatures with multiple styles, as the many creature examples at the end of this chapter show.

NOTE After we've built Clumpy, we demonstrate multiple examples of creatures that fall primarily into one of these three stylistic categories, to aid your creativity and imagination. But first, let's go through the many stages of Clumpy creation!

the creation of clumpy

Here's what we learned during the creation of Clumpy. Put these ideas and plans into practice, and heed our hints when you begin to craft your own cool critter!

Overview

Building a creature involves using this menu system. Below are pointers detailing what each area does, and how to best use it.

1 Body Part Menu: This is where all the different part types are chosen, from the seven submenus: Mouths, Eyes & Senses, Arms & Legs, Graspers, Feet, Weapons, and Details.

4 This shows the Hammer (Building), Paw-Print (Test Drive), and Paint Brush (Coloration) part of the Creature Creation.

7 This is an important area. From top to bottom, it shows your creature's Complexity Meter, Abilities, Attacks, Social skills, Speed, Health, and any warnings (a red "!" telling you to add a mouth or other vital Body Part).

2 Body Part Selection Area: When you've picked a Body Part from the menu, the available parts are shown. Grab and drag the parts you want onto the creature to the right. Select a Body Part, and its statistics are shown. If a Body Part has red statistics, your creature is too complex for the part to be added; finish your creature without this part, or remove or adjust other parts first.

8 This is where you can Save, Exit, or remove what you've built if you don't like it, and start anew.

3 This shows (from left to right): the Galaxy button (access to the Options menu that has the *Spore* Guide), the Sporepedia button, and the DNA Budget window for your creature.

5 This is where you name, describe, and create Tags for your creature. Tags are important once you publish a creature, because others can focus on your creature's best elements ("Flying," "Combat," etc.), but only if you've applied the proper Tags to your creation!

6 Creature Plinth: This is where you mold and build your fine creature creation.

TIP For additional information on creating creatures, including copying and editing Body Parts, consult the in-game *Spore* Guide.

NOTE If you press one of the buttons near area 7, such as the "Bite" button in the "Attack" area, your creature demonstrates this ability or skill. Also note that if the Complexity Meter turns red, you are almost full of parts, so choose wisely.

NOTE Make a change you're unhappy about? Click the undo button at the bottom of the screen. Unhappy about your undo? Click the redo button next to it.

Body Manipulation

1. Start: Each time you create a creature, you start with a randomly colored amorphous blob, like this purple specimen here.

2. Body Shaping: This is where the body shape is molded. Remember to use the mouse wheel to inflate or deflate each section of spine.

See Note at bottom of page

3. Mouth: The mouth is a good place to begin. As with all Body Parts, click to shrink, grow, or manipulate the mouth shape.

4. Eyes: We added the eyes, and made slight adjustments to the spine area near the head so all the Body Parts merged well.

5. Legs: Adding legs allows you to pinpoint the creature's eventual height. Leg joint adjustments can now be made.

6. Arms: We determined where the neck began, and planted arms before adjusting and inflating the joints.

7. Graspers: We fitted a nasty pair of hands to Clumpy. As with many parts, you can rotate graspers around, as well as enlarging or shrinking them.

8. Feet: We grabbed a great foot, enlarged it, and manipulated it so the toenails were huge. We also made some minor joint adjustments.

9. Weapons and Details: We finished off Clumpy with a pretty flower on his tummy, which was removed later on. Instead, we used a Detail part to create a tail.

10. Clumpy needed a bit of toughening up, so we added three Weapon parts to his back, to help him in a scrap!

11. Markings: Happy with Clumpy's basic appearance, we began to color him. The first attempt looked a little sickly...

12. ...so we went for a brighter, almost scaly texture, with darker markings for the lower arms and legs.

NOTE* Click on the body to show the arrows, and pull them to increase the number of spinal pieces at either end.

NOTE Use Tab for additional manipulation options, and Alt to copy a Body Part you already have placed on your creature.

TIP Remember you can manipulate your overall color, or the base, coat, and detail color separately. You can even choose and import the color of a previously designed creature (if you're creating a sub-species, for example).

Completion: Let there be life!

After a couple of minor tweaks, which included moving the leg and shoulder joints to a slightly more comfortable-looking position, we took Clumpy for a Test Drive. Here, you can choose a background, and make your beast dance, growl, or cower; there are 24 different movements to try! We also hatched some young, and then we finally named and described Clumpy, and created some Tags. Finally, we published him, and began a Tribe game where Clumpy was (eventually) able to reign supreme!

TIP Make sure your Tags cover the elements your creature has. For example, Clumpy has a "long neck," "eye stalks," "hooves," is "skinny," and has "claws" for hands, and a "curly tail."

body parts: characteristic improvements

In this section, we detail the exact improvements each Body Part gives your creature, and offer advice on maximizing your creature's potential for every different attribute. Remember that all Body Parts are not "stackable," so the creature examples show the variety of Body Parts you can try; you don't need to copy them directly.

NOTE To see a chart showing the total number and type of skills each Body Part has, consult the "Chart 2: Statistics" in the previous section.

Diet-Related

Add Carnivore, Herbivore, and Omnivore mouths to eat different types of food. Mouths are required for survival in the world.

Mouths

Carnivorous

D'orca | Terrorpin | CrocKisser | Shortensnout | Gobsterclaw | Handibles | Handtennae | Pincernaut | Manglerfish | Slagjawed | Barracutie | Carcharebear

Omnivorous

Toucan't | Buzzbeak | Buzzmuzzle | Skexybeast | Sauroclod | Grinnace | Vermillips | S'gnarly | Simperton

Rostrum | Worrybeak | Amphibitude | Leeyotch | Gnathognasher | Saginaughty | Dietrap

Herbivorous

Mollratt | Laardvark | Ruminanteater | Whalephant | Swillson | Ungulot

Soundersnout | Haunchface | Cantovis | Splatypus | Snapgator | Grubblemaw

Design Hints: A good rule to follow is that an Attack-heavy creature should be carnivorous, and a Social creature herbivorous, but in the Tribe game, it is easier to find food if you're omnivorous. However, worry about maximizing other characteristics first. Or select both carnivorous *and* herbivorous mouths!

The parts you choose give you abilities. Evolve!.

Mating Call

Call to locate your mate and your nest, but beware of alerting nearby predators.

Mouths

 D'orca   Terrorpin   CrocKisser   Shortensnout Gobsterclaw Handibles Handtennae Pincernaut

 Manglerfish Slagjawed Barracutie Carcharebear   Toucan't Buzzbeak Buzzmuzzle Skexybeast

Sauroclod Grinnace Vermillips S'gnarly Simperton   Rostrum   Worrybeak   Amphibitude   Leeyotch Gnathognasher Saginaughty Dietrap

Mollratt Laardvark Ruminanteater Whalephant Swillson Ungulot Soundersnout   Haunchface   Cantovis   Splatypus Snapgator Grubblemaw

> **Design Hints:** Only mouths can make a Mating Call, so any of them will do; focus your attention on other improvements.

Jump

Jumping allows access to hard to reach areas. Higher levels increase the height of your jump.

Feet

 Webwaddle +1 Backskritcher +2 Elevatorclaws +3 Raptorclaws +4 Stumplestilt +1 Buckfoot +2 Slasherknight +3

Scarmaker +4 The Geckonator +2 The Geckoning +3 The Froggening +4 The Toadening +5

Details

 Featherbluster +1   Finneas +1   Antisoptera +1   Fauxry Wings +1

Megachiraptora +1 Cassoworry +1

> **Design Hints:** Start your creature off with webbed toes if you want the highest Jump possible; Level 5 The Toadening is the best Jump Body Part to affix. For less impressive (but also useful) leaps, try one of the Details listed here.

✅ Graspers

Pick up and use objects in the world.

✋ Arms & Legs

Slackwrist Python Doubelbow Wizardsleeve

Meekling Flextor Burly Bulgo Deltroid Cutty Skrappy Gunnshow

Design Hints: You automatically gain this characteristic when you add an arm or a grasper. Remember, you can add graspers to legs (as shown) instead of feet; arms aren't mandatory.

✊ Graspers

Setaetarsal Amphibigrab Amphibigrip Croak Masseur Nubknuckle Lockpicker Opposabubba Monstrumtalon Trapfist Succulenders

Snatchengrabben Dexterrorous Bonestickler Torsionwrencher Prongripper Tearerwrist Phatlanges Badgerbear Ultrarolfer Metacarnal Grubbygrabber

    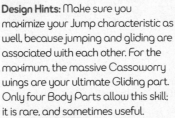
Velocigrasper Hoolencrook Horrorthumbs Butterbib Mitzy Classic Minion Ectoknight

✈️ Glide

Wings allow your creature to flap its wings to fly. Higher levels can fly farther.

🪶 Details

Antisoptera +2 Fauxry Wings +3 Megachiraptora +4 Cassoworry +5

Design Hints: Make sure you maximize your Jump characteristic as well, because jumping and gliding are associated with each other. For the maximum, the massive Cassoworry wings are your ultimate Gliding part. Only four Body Parts allow this skill; it is rare, and sometimes useful.

🐾 Sneak

Sneak up on unsuspecting creatures or evade attackers. Attacking a creature while using the Sneak ability gives a bonus to the attack.

👣 Feet

Palmwalker +2 Underhanded +3 Hombrenid +4 Sassyquatch +5 Suctoped +1 Sugerefoot +2 Suctopod +3 Suctofleur +4

🍃 Details

Marshcara +1 Grasstachio +1 Coverleaf +2

Branch Deco +3 Florsage +4 Pool Party-Foul +1

Design Hints: If you want your creature to skulk about without being spotted, you can't do better than the Sassyquatch; it's the only Body Part that gives you a maximum in this ability. Usually, Detail parts (especially the Florsage) are used, with a foot choice saved for a different skill. Such Details are seen on the under-bellies, knees, or elbows of the creature.

Sprint

Sprint allows for a quick burst of speed.

Feet

| Stubbtoe +1 | Scareclaw +2 | The Clawman +3 | Dirtchargers +4 | Twopaw +1 | Threepaw +2 |

| Fourpaw +3 | Morepaw +4 | Clippity +1 | Cloppity +2 | Hoppity +3 | Hippity +4 |

 Details

| Peacrock +1 | Sporesalfin +1 | Icky-osaur +2 | Finneas +3 | Pool Party-Foul +4 |

Design Hints: Sprint is useful for both Social- and Attack-based creatures. The easiest way to maximize your Sprint ability is to choose one of the two foot types that give you the maximum bonus (in this case, Level 4; you can't reach Level 5 with this skill). Or, try the Pool Party-Foul if your feet are being used to augment another skill.

Sight

Your creature needs eyes to see clearly in the world.

Eyes & Senses

| Optic Orb | Ocubulge | Eyebissed | Scrutineyes | LarvEye |

| Seeodesic | Eyelien | Stemma-addict | Empteyes | Occulus | Wide Eyed | Neo-teeny | Coygamine | Grumpeye |

| Furtive | Evil Eye | Felizard | Wizened | Saurian | Boneye | Stalkgazer | Meanstalk | Periscoptic | Peduncledunk |

Design Hints: Because sight isn't measured in levels from one to five, any number of eyes (one or more) instantly gives you this characteristic. Eyes are usually, but not exclusively, placed on the beast's head. Remember that they can go in a number of other interesting places, depending on how weird you want to be!

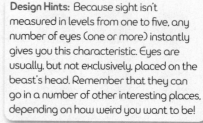

Attack-Related

Add Bite, Charge, Spit, and Strike parts to attack other creatures.

Bite

A quick attack that can damage a single target at close range.

Mouths

 D'orca +2
 Terrorpin +3
 CrocKisser +4
 Shortensnout +5
 Gobsterclaw +2
 Handibles +3
 Handtennae +4
 Pincernaut +5
Manglerfish +2
Slagjawed +3

 Barracutie +4
 Carcharebear +5
 Toucan't +1
 Buzzbeak +1
Buzzmuzzle +2
Skexybeast +3
Sauroclod +1
Grinnace +2
Vermillips +3
S'gnarly +4

 Simperton +1
 Rostrum +1
 Worrybeak +1
 Amphibitude +1
Leeyotch +2
Gnathognasher +3
Saginaughty +4
Dietrap +5
Mollratt +1

 Laardvark +1
 Ruminanteater +2
Whalephant +3
Swillson +1
Ungulot +1
 Soundersnout +1
 Haunchface +1
 Cantovis +1
Splatypus +1
Snapgator +1
Grubblemaw +1

Design Hints: Bites are available only from Mouth parts, so to maximize, choose one of the four +5 mouths, or think about a creature with multiple heads (if you want a high Sing skill, too). Remember that mouths can be hands, and arms can function as necks for two or three-headed creatures.

Charge

An attack that intercepts a single target from a distance and stuns upon contact.

Mouths

 Slagjawed +1
 Barracutie +2
 Carcharebear +3
 Ungulot +1
 Soundersnout +2
Haunchface +3

Design Hints: If you're creating an Attack monster, you're wise to choose your +5 Charge by placing an Elkegent on your creature, and then choosing a +5 Level Bite mouth. Although Hippity offers +5, other feet can be chosen to maximize different skills, such as Speed. Part of conjuring a creature is knowing the best combo of parts for the greatest number of +5 levels.

Weapons

 Pediculous +2
 Fawninatrix +3
 Ultramagadeer +4
 Elkegent +5
 Keratinhorn +1
 Narwhalicorn +2
 Cornutopia +3
 Rammer +4

Feet

 Webwaddle +1
 Backskritcher +2
 Elevatorclaws +3
 Raptorclaws +4
Clippity +2
Cloppity +3

 Hoppity +4
 Hippity +5
 Suctoped +1
Sugerefoot +1
Suctopod +2
Suctofleur +3

Spit

A quick attack that spits projectiles at range at a single target.

Weapons

Gobstalker +1
Phlegmthrower +2
Problem-Solvent +3
Spraypalm +4

 Hockitlauncher +2
 Spraybuchet +3
Ziggur-hat +4
 Porcupain +5

Design Hints: Only the grotesque and squelchy weapons sacs can spit, and there's none better than the Porcupain for delivering a high dose of deadly poison. They can be placed anywhere on your creature's body, turned into back spines (as shown), or on the backside or end of a tail.

Strike

A devastating attack that can damage multiple targets in close range.

Weapons

 Maceball +1
 Stessball +2
 The Tauntlet +3
 Slim Slam Kablam +4
 Scimitard +2

 Toxic Telson +3
 Reapermantis +4
 Spurprise! +5

Graspers

 Nubknuckle +1
 Lockpicker +1
 Opposabubba +2
 Monstrumtalon +3
 Trapfist +1
 Succulenders +2
 Snatchengrabben +3
 Dexterrorous +4

 Bonestickler +1
 Torsionwrencher +2
 Prongripper +3
 Tearerwrist +3
 Phatlanges +1
 Badgerbear +2
 Ultrarolfer +3
 Metacarnal +4
 Grubbygrabber +2
 Velocigrasper +3
 Hoolencrook +4
 Horrorthumbs +5

> **Design Hints:** Remember that giving your creature more than two arms allows you four (or more) graspers! This means you can share Strike and other characteristics (such as Pose) with different arms. Or, a single pair of +5 Horrorthumbs do the trick! Remember that certain Weapon parts help, too, and these have to be placed on the end of arms or legs like graspers.

Socialize-Related

Add Sing, Dance, Pose and Charm parts to socialize with other creatures.

Sing

Sing to befriend creatures who like to vocalize.

Mouths

 D'orca +1
 Terrorpin +1
 CroKisser +2
Shortensnout +3
Gobsterclaw +1
Handibles +1
Handtennae +1
Pincernaut +1
Manglerfish +1
Slagjawed +1

 Barracutie +1
 Carcharebear +1
 Toucan't +1
 Buzzbeak +2
 Buzzmuzzle +3
 Skexybeast +4
 Sauroclod +1
 Grinnace +2
 Vermillips +3
S'gnarly +4

 Simperton +2
 Rostrum +3
 Worrybeak +4
 Amphibitude +5
 Leeyotch +1
 Gnathognasher +1
 Saginaughty +1
Dietrap +1
Mollratt +2
Laardvark +3

 Ruminanteater +4
 Whalephant +5
Swillson +2
Ungulot +3
Soundersnout +4
Haunchface +5
Cantovis +2
Splatypus +3
Snapgator +4
Grubblemaw +5

> **Design Hints:** Only Mouth parts give you Sing bonuses, so make sure you choose a +5 mouth if all you care about is a pitch-perfect specimen! If you want maximum Bite and Sing characteristics, you'll need two mouths. This results in a freaky, but multi-talented, creature!

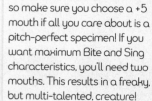

Dance

Dance to befriend other creatures who prefer this social style.

Feet

 Stubbtoe +1
 Scareclaw +1
 The Clawman +1
 Dirtchargers +1
 Twopaw +1
 Threepaw +1
 Fourpaw +2
 Morepaw +2
 Stumplestilt +1
 Buckfoot +2
 Slasherknight +3
 Scarmaker +4

Palmwalker +1
Underhanded +2
Hombrenid +3
 Sassyquatch +4
 Suctoped +2
Sugerefoot +3
Suctopod +4

Suctofleur +5
The Geckonator +2
The Geckoning +3
The Froggening +4
The Toadening +5

Design Hints: Only Feet parts give you the Dance ability, so choose one set of +5 feet for maximum toe-tapping, such as the excellent Sassyquatch, which also gives you a great Sneak level, too. If you want your beast to have the Charge or Speed ability, make your beast four or six-legged.

Charm

Creatures with many Detail parts can be charmed with this social.

Details

 Heycorn +2
 Nurple +3
 Jellybutton +4
 Mackne +5
 Pom Pom +2
 Springle +3
 Wrottintail +4
 Fleurbine +5
 Derma Bark +1
 Baublewarts +2

 Jemite +3
 Stealing Crystals +4
 Featherbluster +1
 Marshcara +2
 Peacrock +3
 Featherferns +5
 Grasstachio +1
 Coverleaf +2
 Branch Deco +3

 Florsage +4
 Whipwhick +2
 Protubers +3
Hairlagmites +4
Crestacean +5
Sporesalfin +1

Design Hints: Charm parts are easy to try out; place one in a crease, flap, under an arm, hanging from an elbow, or as another appendage. Weigh up whether you want Health benefits and a slightly lower level, as some Details provide this benefit, too.

Pose

Poses are popular with other creatures with graspers.

Graspers

 Setaetarsal +2
 Amphibigrab +3
 Amphibigrip +4
 Croak Masseur +5
 Nubknuckle +1
 Lockpicker +2
 Opposabubba +3

Monstrumtalon +4
Bonestickler +1
Torsionwrencher +2
Prongripper +2
Tearerwrist +3
Phatlanges +1
Badgerbear +1

Ultrarolfer +2
Metacarnal +3
Butterbib +1
Mitzy +2
Classic Minion +3
Ectoknight +4

Design Hints: Only graspers increase your Posing capabilities, so add a pair of +4 or +5 graspers if you're also concerned about maximizing your Strike. Doubling the number of arms helps out; that way you can affix another Body Part with a different skill (such as a grasper or weapon with a Strike skill).

Speed-Related

Add faster feet to increase Speed!

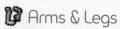 Arms & Legs

 Brawnysaurus +1
 Cankle +1
 Broncosaurus +1
 Steatopiggy +1
 Phatella +1
 Stompbottom +1
 Callypigeon +1
 Yumstick +1
 Thundercalf +1

 Ostrichopath +1
 Thighstrider +1
 Qopazcoati +1

Design Hints: In the same way that you can add graspers to legs, you can also add feet to arms! As usual, if you're after high levels of other skills that feet give you (Health, Dance, and Jump, for example), either place multiple feet on your beast, or (if you want a two-legged creature), choose the Scarmaker, a great all-round foot.

Feet

 Stubbtoe +2
 Scareclaw +3
 The Clawman +4
 Dirtchargers +5
 Twopaw +2
Threepaw +3
Fourpaw +4
Morepaw +5
Webwaddle +2
Backskritcher +3
Elevatorclaws +4
Raptorclaws +5

 Palmwalker +2
 Underhanded +2
 Hombrenid +3
 Sassyquatch +4
 Clippity +2
 Cloppity +3
 Hoppity +4
 Hippity +5
Stumplestilt +1
Buckfoot +2
Slasherknight +3
Scarmaker +4

 Suctoped +1
 Sugerefoot +2
 Suctopod +3
 Suctofleur +4
 The Geckonator +1
 The Geckoning +2
 The Froggening +3
 The Toadening +4

✚ Health-Related

Each brain level upgrade adds to your health, or you can buy armored parts to help you survive in combat.

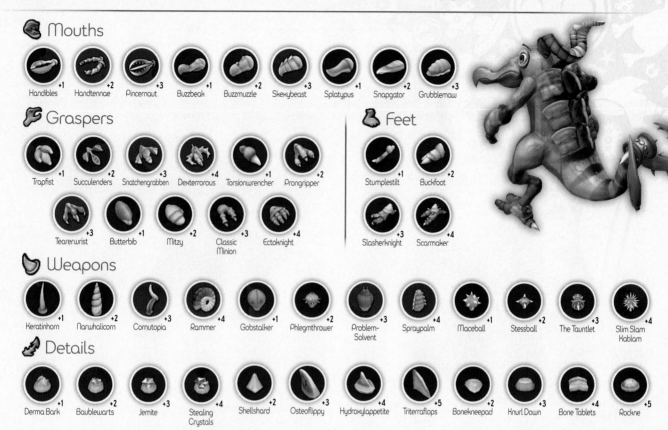

👄 Mouths

| Handibles +1 | Handtennae +2 | Pincernaut +3 | Buzzbeak +1 | Buzzmuzzle +2 | Skexybeast +3 | Splatypus +1 | Snapgator +2 | Grubblemaw +3 |

Graspers

| Trapfist +1 | Succulenders +2 | Snatchengrabben +3 | Dexterrorous +4 | Torsionwrencher +1 | Prongripper +2 |

| Tearerwrist +3 | Butterbib +1 | Mitzy +2 | Classic Minion +3 | Ectoknight +4 |

Feet

| Stumplestilt +1 | Buckfoot +2 |

| Slasherknight +3 | Scarmaker +4 |

Weapons

| Keratinhorn +1 | Narwhalicorn +2 | Cornutopia +3 | Rammer +4 | Gobstalker +1 | Phlegmthrower +2 | Problem-Solvent +3 | Spraypalm +4 | Maceball +1 | Stessball +2 | The Tauntlet +3 | Slim Slam Kablam +4 |

Details

| Derma Bark +1 | Baublewarts +2 | Jemite +3 | Stealing Crystals +4 | Shellshard +2 | Osteoflippy +3 | Hydroxylappetite +4 | Triterraflops +5 | Bonekneepad +2 | Knurl Down +3 | Bone Tablets +4 | Rockne +5 |

Design Hints: If you're playing through the Creature Stage, and only have a few Health Body Parts to choose from, you're better using parts that also have other skills, if you're low on DNA Points. If you've collected more points, or are making a creature from scratch, choose Level 5 Health parts exclusively, such as the Rockne or Triterraflops.

👁 Skill-deficient Body Parts

The following Body Parts do not offer any Stage-specific skill when utilized.

👁 Eyes & Senses

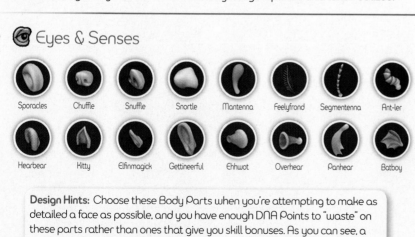

| Sporacles | Chuffle | Snuffle | Snortle | Mantenna | Feelyfrond | Segmentenna | Ant-ler |

| Hearbear | Kitty | Elfinmagick | Gettineerful | Ehhwot | Overhear | Panhear | Batboy |

Design Hints: Choose these Body Parts when you're attempting to make as detailed a face as possible, and you have enough DNA Points to "waste" on these parts rather than ones that give you skill bonuses. As you can see, a variety of odd and frightening visages are possible!

limb and body manipulation

By now, you should have begun to create some truly exciting, frightening, cute, or impressive-looking creatures. Now add a couple of advanced crafting techniques to ensure even more flexibility.

Work That Body

During this and previous Creature Creators, your creations may initially look overly "round" as you inflate the body around the spine pieces, and create something that looks less than impressive, such as the unspeakable thing shown nearby! Stop this by gradually changing the shape of the body at each adjacent spine piece, and you'll end up with a more realistic form.

Here's one of my first creations. It was meant to be an imposing scaly beast from the deep, with a head full of tentacles! This embarrassment was put out of its misery quickly!

Here's a later attempt at a similar type of creature; I learned to form the body properly, and use body parts for a variety of purposes to create something a little more impressive.

Body Part Art

When you've made a few creatures, you should begin to experiment with the different Body Parts (particularly the Senses, Weapons, and Details) to make "special" appendages. These give your creation a unique look. Stretch or contract each part to the desired dimensions to add additional character and turn objects you haven't used in the past into ones you can use again and again. A keen imagination is all you need!

This tentacle-faced Star Spawn is a good example. Cornutopia (which look like twisted horns) were manipulated to create a mouth full of tendrils!

In this example, a single Soundersnout mouth, and another pair of Soundersnouts forms the base of this Cerberus dog, and the body was curved into a tail with a Reapermantis at the end of it!

Extraordinary Limb Use

The final part of this advanced plan in creature creation is to utilize Arm and Leg parts in multiple ways. By now, you should have created a floating creature by placing Grasper parts at the end of its legs. But have you tried placing Weapon or Detail parts at the end of an appendage, or placed an Arm or Leg part to create a different type of limb? The possibilities are endless (using Detail parts to act as ears or nostrils is a good example, as is placing two Knurl Downs on the backside of a baboon-like entity), but here are two main tricks that master creators try again and again:

Does your creature need eyes on stalks, but you don't like any of the original Eye parts? Then place two tiny arms, remove the hand, and add a normal Eye part of your choice, as in this example. Yes, those are arms!

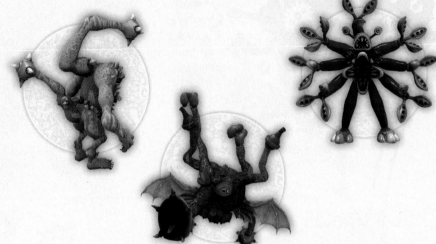

Do you need a sinewy tail with a nasty weapon at the end? Then place some Arms or Leg parts, move them to the middle, and merge them at each joint. You now have another weird limb for your pal to flail with! This is also the way to add certain Weapons (that give a Strike skill) to your creature.

creature examples (various styles)

Finally, here are a few of the billions of different creatures you could create, showing the different ways you can construct your own creature. Critters with personality showcase the wild and varied body styles and part placement. Statistic-heavy monsters showcase the very best in combative or social beasties. Then, we show fiends and furry friends alike, based on real-world entities or monsters from myth, to get your imagination racing. Finally, there are examples Maxis and Will Wright chose specifically for this guide. All have a short invented backstory designed to be placed with each creature's name; remember to write your own, too.

CAUTION Alert! Some of these creatures are very complex and may only be available in later Stages in their current form. Remove one or two body parts as you're building them if their image appears blanked out at the Creature Choice menu. Your Complexity Meter (shown in the top-right corner above your Characteristics) should be just lower than maximum (red) if you want to use a creature in this Stage. These creatures are shown as a primer to creating your own favorite monsters.

Style 1. Personality-Driven

Wild Thing

Key Characteristics: Charge, Pose
Other Characteristics: Strike

This lanky bird-like critter is said to follow a small child with a flute, mesmerized by the lilting sounds. A classic "beast," its understated and mottled plumage allows you to focus on a fabulous mohawk and tail, which is built from Keratinhorns. The shoulders are placed lower from the top of the head to accentuate the large beak and large beady eyes. There's a Bonekneepad behind the eyes, to look like wrinkles, and talon-like hands to gesticulate wildly. An unkempt look was attempted here.

Ocubulge
Keratinhorn x7
Bonekneepad
Toucan't
Skrappy
Hairlagmites
Monstrumtalon
Buckfoot
Yumstick

Omnivore

Star Spawn

Key Characteristics: Bite, Charm, Speed, Health
Other Characteristics: Jump, Glide, Strike, Charge, Spit

A fearsome mass of thick, unspeakable tentacles surrounds a massive central maw, with two side mouths to complete this horrific, and once-aquatic otherworldly beast. Standing in for tentacles are multiple Pincernauts and Cornutopias, manipulated to look very menacing. Servants of an even bigger entity, said to be worshipped deep under the ocean, this Star Spawn has remnants of the sea in its scaly skin and small flapping ears. It can glide too, but it spends most of its time charging in and savaging its prey.

Saurian
Batboy
Spraybuchet
Bone Tablets
Pincernaut x2
Cornutopia x4
Gunnshow
Megachiraptora
Hoolencrook
Qopazcoati
Elevatorclaws

Carnivore

EyeVee

Key Characteristics: Sight
Other Characteristics: Sing, Speed

The word "monstrosity" was never so apt a description! Although it isn't the toughest critter on a primordial planet's surface, it does show what an imagination, and a massive number of Evil Eyes can create! This should set you off into a frenzy of selecting one Body Part and using it multiple times, because although only five different parts are used, the creation still looks fantastic! There is a limit to the number of identical Body Parts you can place though (around 15 for smaller ones). As for EyeVee's combat effectiveness? Let's just say it isn't easily blindsided....

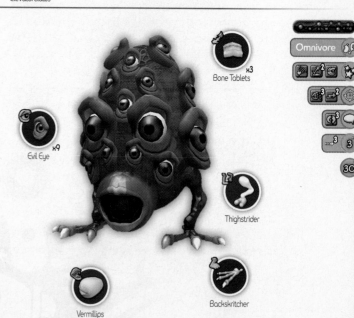

Bone Tablets x3
Evil Eye x9
Thighstrider
Vermillips
Backskritcher

Omnivore

Carnivorous Terror

Key Characteristics: Sneak, Strike, Health
Other Characteristics: Bite, Strike, Dance, Charm

Evolving on a distant and violent lava planet, this brutish monstrosity has a primary urge to bite its prey into small chunky pieces and dance on them. It brings its massively heavy Stessballs down on its foes, striking repeatedly, before trudging away to its next fracas. However, it has the Charm ability, thanks to magical energy stored in the crystals adorning its body. The Carnivorous Terror was built to look mean, and its two Gunnshow arms, which are merged at each joint and fitted onto the beast's back, lend an even more fearsome appearance!

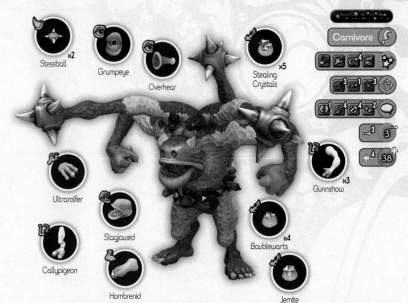

Stessball x2
Grumpeye
Overhear
Stealing Crystals x5
Ultrarolfer
Slagjawed
Baublewarts x4
Callypigeon
Hombrenid
Jemite
Gunnshow x3

Carnivore

Senior Speedo

Key Characteristics: Bite, Strike, Charge
Other Characteristics: Dance, Speed

Although it finds implement-handling something of a chore, Senior Speedo, the big brother of Speedo the bipedal crab monstrosity, usually spends its days rushing around the flood plains and crushing smaller foes with its massive four arms. Instead of graspers, which were removed, it has SlimSlam Kablams. This isn't practical (graspers are more useful), but it looks cooler! Sharp Keratinhorns were added to the back, but the massive eye stalks are actually a pair of Slackwrists with Felizards at the end of them!

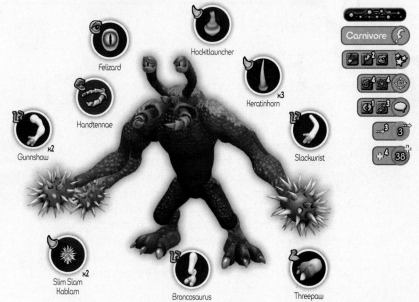

Felizard
Hockitlauncher
Handtennae
Keratinhorn x3
Gunnshow x2
Slackwrist
Slim Slam Kablam x2
Broncosaurus
Threepaw

Carnivore

Greater Koob

Key Characteristics: Sprint, Charge, Strike
Other Characteristics: Spit, Speed

You might think this beast, a slightly larger cousin of the Koob, to be a freak of nature, and you'd be correct. It shows how versatile facial placement can be. A long trunk-like protuberance ends in a mouth and Ant-lers, with primitive Seeodesic eyes at the top. Graspers are ignored in favor of four thin but sinewy arms, each ending in a violent Spurprise! spike wheel, perfect for crushing foes! A single Ziggur-hat is placed where the four legs join, leading to a memorable creature with a hint of elephant about it. Try more trunks out on your own entities!

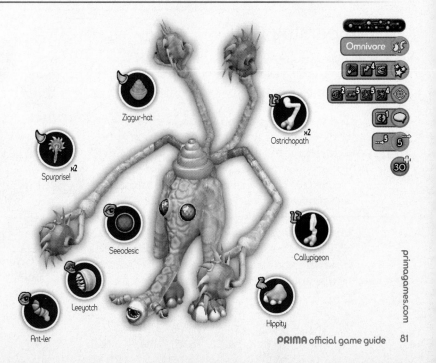

Ziggur-hat
Ostrichopath x2
Spurprise! x2
Seeodesic
Callypigeon
Leeyotch
Ant-ler
Hippity

Omnivore

Style 2. Function-Based

Herboppotimus

Key Characteristics: Jump, Glide, Sprint, Sing, Dance, Charm, Pose, Speed, Charge

Other Characteristics: Bite

Here's a friendly, playful pal who seeks only to befriend other creatures, and munch the alien fruits of alien worlds. "Herby" (to its friends) is the pinnacle of a Social creature's evolution at this point; it has the best set of wings and feet to allow flight and gliding. Specific Grasper and Feet parts are chosen to maximize Social characteristics. Additional Details are added for even more choices at Socializing. Singing, Dancing and Posing are maximized, too. This is a good example of a impressively maneuverable herbivore who loves to socialize.

Peduncledunk · Cassoworry · Whalephant · Python · Croak Masseur · Dirtchargers · Morepaw · The Toadening · Thundercalf ×3 · Coverleaf · Fleurbine

Herbivore

Jass of Thun

Key Characteristics: Sneak, Sprint, Bite, Charge, Strike, Spit, Speed, Health

Other Characteristics: Jump, Dance, Charm

This fine specimen is an example of an ultimate carnivore. It was designed to maximize all the characteristics needed for violent survival, without the creature devolving into some freakish thing. To create something that didn't look overly complex, we used Body Parts relevant to Combat, Speed, and Health. No graspers are employed; instead, striking implements and massive feet cope with attacking. With no natural predators (except Epic versions of themselves), the Jass have conquered the red-rocked tundra of Thun, and now import carnivores from across the galaxy to challenge them in combat!

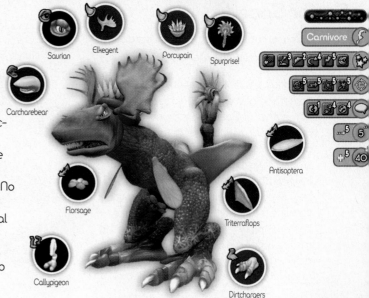

Saurian · Elkegent · Porcupain · Spurprise! · Carcharebear · Florsage · Callypigeon · Dirtchargers · Triterraflops · Antisoptera

Carnivore

Snappersley

Key Characteristics: Bite, Bite, Charge, Strike, Spit, Sing, Charm, Pose

Other Characteristics: Dance, Speed, Health

Snappersley was designed with a two-fold plan: to be the most combat-savvy and social monster in the local spiral arm of this galactic constellation! Flipping fruit or fish from its rear arms, it catches them in two mouths (one at the front, one at the tail) to swallow, and it has evolved a wild set of gesticulations, including slow-dancing and rutting, to communicate with mates and other species. Abilities, Speed, and Health were ignored in favor of attempting to maximize Attack and Social potential, with impressive results, despite parts chosen strictly for their value.

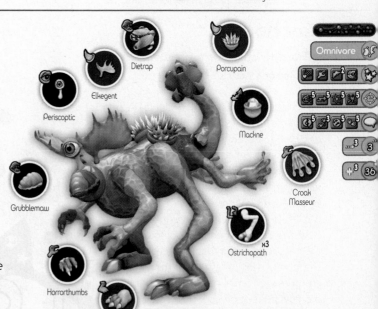

Periscoptic · Elkegent · Dietrap · Porcupain · Grubblemaw · Mackne · Horrorthumbs · Morepaw · Ostrichopath ×3 · Croak Masseur

Omnivore

Little Blue Growler

Key Characteristics: Sprint, Bite, Charge, Spit, Strike, Health

Other Characteristics: Speed, Sing, Pose

Not all highly evolved carnivores need look overly muscular and imposing, like Jass of Thun. The Little Blue Growler is an example of a tiny, vicious, but rather cute meat-eater. Biting the lower legs of its prey, it moves in small herds and has incredible Speed and a thick, sturdy body, resplendent in all manner of spines and armored growths. Ziggur-hats were used in place of ears, and Porcupains as nipples to create a "natural" look to the Growler, but every single part was picked because of its Attack-related bonuses. Ignore the small, and you might fall!

Romuthid

Key Characteristics: Jump, Glide, Sprint, Sing, Dance, Charm, Pose, Speed, Health

Other Characteristics: None

This was another omnivorous creature, but one that could Glide, and had excellent Health and Speed. A unique body shape (it starts as a backward "C") led to some interesting Body Part placement, such as an eye at one end, and a mouth at the other! Just to give a distinctive look, we used mostly Leg parts instead of arms; the two are completely interchangable stat wise. The plan here was simple: this creature mesmerizes its foes with its weird shape and exceptional Social skills, and uses wings (Jump and Glide abilities) to fly to high branches for fruit-picking.

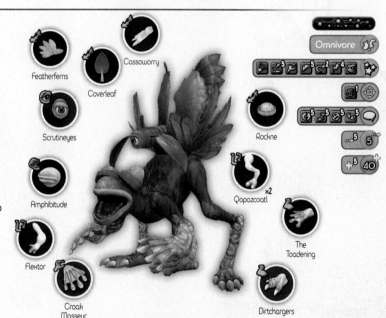

Throkgrunter

Key Characteristics: Sprint, Bite, Charge, Strike, Spit, Health

Other Characteristics: Charm, Sneak, Speed

This creature was designed to see how many different snaking and pointy bits could be attached to a trunked biped, and we came away very pleased with the result. The Throk-grunter, a feared monster with a massive flapping front maw and a huge elongated tail with spines aplenty, can't climb trees, glide, or hold much of a conversation. But it can devour foes in seconds, thanks to its Poison sacs and the weapon-heavy rear end. Also important was Health, and the finished freakshow is both terrifying and adept in combat. Its handshakes are said to be deadly....

Style 3. Earth-Influenced

Tartywoad

Key Characteristics: Sing, Dance
Other Characteristics: Speed, Health

Tartywoads live in the marshy dwellings of Clinkskell, a strange planet in the northern part of the galaxy. They hop with impressive quietness, pausing only to rapidly flee from predators or dance expertly to woo mates as well as other critters. Our take on the toad, this creature has all the necessary Body Parts. After looking at a picture of a real frog for inspiration, we made sure the back legs were stretched while the front ones were tiny, and added as many Heycorns as possible. However, the vivid paint job really finished off the look.

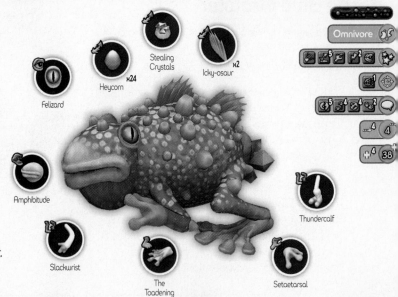

Felizard
Heycorn ×24
Stealing Crystals
Icky-osaur ×2
Amphibitude
Slackwrist
The Toadening
Setaetarsal
Thundercalf

Omnivore

Grizzlebear

Key Characteristics: Charm, Health
Other Characteristics: Bite, Dance, Speed

Locate the correct Body Parts, and you too can create a variation on the bear. Many of the Body Parts are specifically named with bears in mind, but the main plan is to choose a mouth that can be manipulated enough to be stretched into a snout, with a Chuffle to finish the look. After adding a fur-like texture (additional stripes and highlights weren't used to keep a more natural look), we finished off this furry fiend with a set of Nurples and some Rocknes. Our creation shares many characteristics of an Earth bear!

Furtive
Hearbear
Terrorpin
Python
Chuffle
Rockne ×3
Nurple ×4
Wrottintail
Thundercalf
Badgerbear
Threepaw

Carnivore

Killer Gorilla

Key Characteristics: None
Other Characteristics: Dance, Charm, Health

Creating a great ape as the basis of your creature means you need to proportion your body correctly, with a curved spine and a jutting head tapering at the end. Then you can add a Grinnace; the best simian mouth around! To really get a "great" ape look, make sure you select a nose, and place it near the eyes, along with some shrunken ears. When dealing with arms, make the front ones massive and powerful, and the back ones small but sinewy. Then add Underhanded to both arms and legs; it makes for a realistic ape walk! Finally, add two Knurl Downs for a baboon-like bottom!

Furtive
Gettineerful
Snortle
Knurl Down
Grinnace
Bulgo
Nurple
Yumstick
Underhanded ×2

Omnivore

Ryger

Key Characteristics: Sing

Other Characteristics: Dance, Speed

If you're using a tiger as your source of inspiration, try a couple of additional tricks besides raiding all the vaguely feline Body Parts! First though, manipulate the Soundersnout so the bottom lip horn is less pronounced. Make the body thin and lithe, and point it downward toward a tail, which should be made from a fused Leg part! Tigers have lower back legs and massive shoulders, so mimic this with careful attention to each leg. Our Ryger has rather scary eyes; you might want to swap them for something less fear-inducing!

Kitty

Felizard

Chuffle

Soundersnout

Threepaw ×2

Brawnysaurus

Cankle ×2

Herbivore

Batty

Key Characteristics: Glide, Charm

Other Characteristics: Strike, Sing

Although it's likely to come off second-best in a Tribe game against most others, the Batty is a great example of how to make a creature that looks like it's constantly flying. Obviously, you need the wings, and we added a small Batboy flap at the back, even though a real bat doesn't have them. A tiny body has a large face, with a Snuffle for that "vampiric" look, and two Kitty ears (ironically, the Batboy ears aren't quite as realistic looking!). Mainly though, have a grasper instead of any type of feet; your creation tends to hover above the ground.

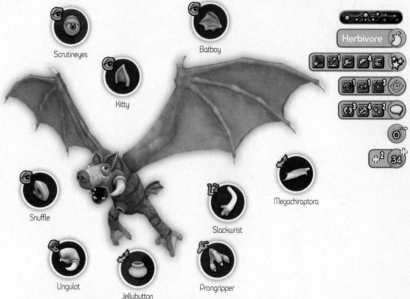

Scrutineyes

Batboy

Kitty

Snuffle

Megachiraptora

Slackwrist

Ungulot

Jellybutton

Prongripper

Herbivore

Sloshi

Key Characteristics: Sing, Health, Dance

Other Characteristics: Bite, Charm

Your creation doesn't need to be influenced only by animals living on this Earth. Look to other sources of inspiration, such as Greek myths (you could construct a fantastic Minotaur or Gorgon!). Or, you could explore other worlds. How about creating a creature from *Mass Effect*? Or even this cute little dinosaur, named Sloshi! He's the best friend of a Spanish carpenter named Miguel. Together they ride around the Ivy Kingdom, searching for the evil Growser the terrapin, and his tortoise minions. Princess Apple must be rescued!

Ocubulge

Rockne

Shellshard

Vermillips

Jellybutton

Slackwrist

Brawnysaurus

Setaetarsal

Sugerefoot

Omnivore

🔥 tribal outfitter

Socialize, Hunt, Fight, Live.

Welcome to the **Tribal Stage** of *Spore*, where your completed creature creates a small, close-knit village community, complete with a totem and a central Tribal Hut built from the remnants of your old nest. Before you begin to explore the continent you trotted about on during the Creature Stage, and interact with the tribal creatures who've had the same idea as you, you are encouraged to take your creature, enter the hut, and place a number of Tribal Accessories to aid your progress. Remember that some of these accessories only become available later in the stage, and they give you brand-new bonuses, too! In this book, we show the example of Clumpy's initial outfit, along with the best accessories to aim for, before showing some familiar creatures in their new get-ups. Finally, a walkthrough of the Tribal Stage is shown, along with all the cunning strategies to try, and hilarity to expect along the way!

clumpy's outfit
(Fortis sententia)

Accessorising Clumpy: Behold this incredibly fashionable (yet rather gangly and ungainly) fellow! Clumpy's attire was meticulously chosen from the initial lines available within the Tribal Hut menu, accessed once the Tribal Stage started. For this season, we went with a full accompaniment of hats, a mask, and various fabulous accoutrements designed to flatter and shock!

Shoulders: Body Aegis
Clumpy's shoulders aren't his best quality, but you wouldn't know it when two Body Aegis plates are placed there.

Hats: Ultra-Fez
Clumpy is likely to be the talk of the continent with this stylish headgear, specifically designed to be a talking point!

Hats: Dockworka
In a bold statement, Clumpy decided to fit this hat over his entire belly, shielding it from nasty attacks.

Masks: Ayuba Mask
When it comes to facial gear, Clumpy didn't want to cover up his beautiful features, so he wore this as neck gear instead.

Statistics

Herbivore 🍃

 3 ⭐

 2 ⚙

 3 🗨

4 ➡

3 110

Detail: Stickler
Not many can carry off the Stickler, but the tribe went mental for these ornamental horns. A breathtaking spectacle!

Chest: Fanncypack
This screams both "hardworking" and "a real go-getter." It's perfect for the fruit-picking creature on the go!

Symbol: Spore Gears x2
Now into the purely aesthetic additions, Clumpy took a shine to this fabulous half-gear, and had a second made to complete the look.

Accessories Manipulation

Each piece was chosen with statistics in mind, and placing them required additional thought:

1. We begin with one of Clumpy's tribe, already designed. First step is hat placement.

2. First of all, Dockworka was chosen, stretched, flattened, and placed on the belly.

3. Then Ultra-Fez was elongated and shrunk slightly, to fit between Clumpy's eye-stalks.

4. Next was the Ayuba Mask. With a strange mouth, Clumpy instead wore this on his upper chest.

5. The indented lower back was the perfect spot for a Fanncypack, stretched slightly.

6. We then added two Spore Gears to make a whole one, and three different details.

7. Not forgetting the shoulders, we used the advanced tab to maneuver these onto the shoulder joint perfectly.

8. We nixed the Glibia and Bravefeather details, as less can sometimes be more, and finished with two Sticklers.

NOTE As you'll see when you read the next section, most of the items were chosen for purely strategic reasons. If you simply want your entity to "look cool," we've provided some familiar sample creatures afterward, along with a host of different ways to wear your gear with pride!

tribal stage start: tribal outfitter

Unlike your previous Creature Creators, the Tribal Outfitter simply adds accessories onto your chosen character; you don't actually change Body Parts. However, it is important to note that Tribal Accessories add particular bonuses to your creature's skills that occur specifically in this stage. Therefore, it is imperative to choose the correct outfit pieces for your play style.

NOTE No accessories are "stackable." However, only half of the Tribal Accessories are available at the start of this stage. The "Better" (and more powerful) accessories are unlocked in the same way as Body Parts were in the Creature Stage; you choose a "base" accessory, and check back after each level to see if your style of play has unlocked the "Better" version. A chart later in this chapter reveals all this information.

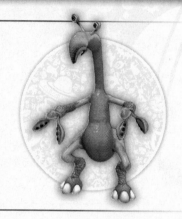

The following information shows the accessories (including all the ones unlocked during this stage) that add bonuses to certain skills. They were all placed on the same **Demoling**, the example creature (shown here).There are still more accessories, but they are available only at the beginning of the Civilization and Space Stages.

NOTE Tribal Accessories pick up the color of the Detail layer of your creature. To change or enhance the color of your newly selected accessories, go to Paint mode, selet Partial styles, choose the Detail layer, and select from the color palette.

Gathering

These accessories aid in adding food (fish and fruit).

Hats

Body Wok	Tierdrop	Bakerwear	El Graucho	Floronet	Aloe Haira
20	30	15	30	15	30
Gathering Level 2	Gathering Level 2	Gathering Level 3	Gathering Level 4	Gathering Level 2	Gathering Level 2
Other Skills:	Other Skills:	Other Skills:	Other Skills:	Other Skills:	Other Skills:
Social Level 2	Social Level 4	None	Social Level 2	Combat Level 1	Combat Level 4

Chest

Fanncypack	Charm Plate
15	25
Gathering Level 3	Gathering Level 5
Other Skills:	Other Skills:
None	None

Design Hints: If you're mostly concerned about fruit-picking and fishing, by far the best idea is to place a Fanncypack on your creature. This gives the maximum Gathering (Level 3) for a "base" accessory, and once you unlock the related "Better" Charm Plate, your team of gatherers become incredibly adept at their work. Add a few other accessories too, like the Bakerwear hat (that unlocks El Graucho) to maximize the chance of upping your level.

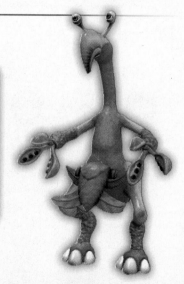

Combat

These accessories increase the damage you do in combat.

Hats

Plundercap
 30

Combat Level 2

Other Skills:
Health Level 4

King Bling
30

Combat Level 2

Other Skills:
Social Level 4

Floronet
 15

Combat Level 1

Other Skills:
Gathering Level 2

Aloe Haira
 30

Combat Level 4

Other Skills:
Gathering Level 2

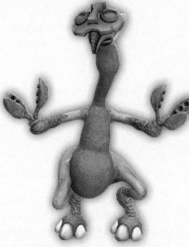

Masks

Apelious
 10

Combat Level 1

Other Skills:
Social Level 1

Kofi Kete
 30

Combat Level 3

Other Skills:
Social Level 3

Ayuba
 10

Combat Level 2

Other Skills:
None

Oba Shaka
25

Combat Level 5

Other Skills:
None

Design Hints: Although a wide variety of accessories add to your Combat potential, the Ayuba Mask (which unlocks the Oba Shaka Mask shown in the picture) is the most proficient at raising this skill. If your creature has a longer face and the mask looks a little strange on it, change the mask to a brooch pendant or small carving; the effect is still the same. The Floronet Hat (unlocking the excellent Aloe Haira) is another good choice. You can also extend a number of shoulder plates (as shown) to complete a military look; it's more stylish, but doesn't give any more bonuses.

Chest

Featherkilt
 5

Combat Level 1

Other Skills:
None

Philamore Kilt
 15

Combat Level 3

Other Skills:
None

Shoulders

Shellshopped
 10

Combat Level 1

Other Skills:
Health Level 1

Kharmadillo
20

Combat Level 3

Other Skills:
Health Level 1

Social

These accessories increase the odds of impressing other tribes during Social interactions.

Hats

Body Wok
 20

Social Level 2

Other Skills:
Gathering Level 2

Tierdrop
 30

Social Level 4

Other Skills:
Gathering Level 2

El Graucho
30

Social Level 2

Other Skills:
Gathering Level 4

Ultra-Fez
 15

Social Level 3

Other Skills:
None

King Bling
30

Social Level 4

Other Skills:
Combat Level 2

Masks

Apelious
 10

Social Level 1

Other Skills:
⊕ Combat Level 1

Kofi Kete
 30

Social Level 3

Other Skills:
⊕ Combat Level 3

Khwame
 10

Social Level 2

Other Skills:
None

Tiki Gamba
 25

Social Level 5

Other Skills:
None

Chest

Thorsbjerg Tunic
 5

Social Level 1

Other Skills:
None

Tunic of Virtue
 15

Social Level 3

Other Skills:
None

Shoulders

Crown Shoulder
 10

Social Level 1

Other Skills:
⬡ Health Level 1

Metal Pleats
 20

Social Level 3

Other Skills:
⬡ Health Level 1

> **Design Hints:** Here's another huge number of accessories to choose from. Pick the Khwame Mask if you're after the best Social skill in this stage, because the unlockable Tiki Gamba Mask (shown) takes you to the pinnacle of interaction. The Body Wok (unlocking the Tierdrop) or the Ultra-Fez (unlocking King Bling) are another two possibilities. Note that our socially acceptable example creature is using two Tierdrops as chest plates; you don't have to place an accessory on the area of the body it was originally designed for!

⬡ Health

These accessories increase the number of Health Points your tribe member has.

Hats

Dockworka
 15

Health Level 3

Other Skills:
None

Plundercap
30

Health Level 4

Other Skills:
⊕ Combat Level 2

Chest

Leaf Camouflage
5

Health Level 1

Other Skills:
None

Singuard
25

Health Level 5

Other Skills:
None

Shoulders

Crown Shoulder
10

Health Level 1

Other Skills:
◯ Social Level 1

Metal Pleats
 20

Health Level 1

Other Skills:
◯ Social Level 3

Shellshopped
 10

Health Level 1

Other Skills:
⊕ Combat Level 1

Kharmadillo
 10

Health Level 1

Other Skills:
⊕ Combat Level 3

Body Aegis

🏆 10

Health Level 2

Other Skills:
None

Warplating

🏆 20

Health Level 4

Other Skills:
None

Design Hints: Although the mustache and horns are optional, our example showcases an extremely well-armored creature, thanks to the use of the Singuard, a large plate that gives the maximum available (Level 5) protection. Usually, creatures using Health accessories are going to need Combat help too, so split your points up between these two. Also place the Body Aegis on your creature, because the unlockable Warplating offers exceptional protection. As before, shoulder plates are excellent for plating one on top of the other, creating an "armored" look.

Accessories Unlockables

The second, "Better" column of accessories unlocks in a similar way to the Body Parts of the creature you created. Simply choose the "base" accessory, and wear it as you begin the Tribal Stage. During the stage, perform a function that uses the skill the accessory gives a bonus to (or, in the case of accessories without bonuses, check after each level is reached). Your "Better" accessory is likely to be unlocked.

TIP Confused? Don't be. Here's another way to read this chart and learn exactly what is available to you:

1. Choose an initial accessory for your creature. In this example, we chose the Ayuba Mask, as we wanted Combat bonuses.
2. Check the chart below: The Ayuba Mask is the "base" mask. Continue the Tribal Stage.
3. After engaging the enemy, we checked back, and the "Better" mask had unlocked.
4. The Oba Shaka Mask offers better Combat bonuses, so we used it as soon as it was unlocked, to the end of the stage.

TIP Accessories that offer skills bonuses unlock after you attempt a plan involving those skills. In the previous example, we fought some wild animals, then checked the Tribal Outfitter, and the Oba Shaka was ours!

TIP If you're focusing on a particular skill (such as Combat), place two or three different accessories on your creature. This gives you a better chance to unlock one of the "Better" versions.

🎩 Hats

Base Part	Better Part
Dockworka	Plundercap
Body Wok	Tierdrop
Bakerwear	El Graucho
Ultra-Fez	King Bling
Floronet	Aloe Haira

🍃 Detail

Base Part	Better Part
Stickler	Trophybuck
Mustache	Hearty
Glibia	Prongalong
Bravefeather	Tufted Stalk
Ring	Skull

👹 Masks

Base Part	Better Part
Apelious Mask	Kofi Kete Mask
Ayuba Mask	Oba Shaka Mask
Khwame Mask	Tiki Gamba Mask

Shoulders

Base Part	Better Part
Crown Shoulder	Metal Pleats
Shellshopped	Kharmadillo
Body Aegis	Warplating

Chest

Base Part	Better Part
Fanncypack	Charm Plate
Leaf Camouflage	Singuard
Thorsbjerg Tunic	Tunic of Virtue
Featherkilt	Philamore Kilt

Symbol

Base Part	Better Part
Stunrise	Spideycrest
Gleeclipse	Geltbuckle
Spore Gears	Stauros

accessories examples (various styles)

Here are a few creatures that we already created during the Enhanced Creature Creator section of this guide. We focused on two types of accessories—those initially available, and those available after being unlocked—so some creatures chose only base accessories, while others picked from everything currently available. The results are the height of fashion!

NOTE There are two more columns of accessories to unlock. The first occurs at the start of the Civilization Stage, and the last at the start of the Space Stage. Check these chapters out for more stylish ensembles!

Warlord Specimen of the Demolings

Key Characteristics: Gathering, Health
Other Characteristics: Social, Speed

Ruling a typical tribe, the Warlord known as "Specimen" uses a base mask to hide the eyes and appear more frightening. An Ultra-Fez worn atop the head props the mask up, and two Prongalongs make great horns. Two types of shoulder armor complement each other down each arm, and for a more primitive look, a few skulls adorn the Warlord's midriff.

Apelious Mask
Charm Plate
Ring
Skull x2
Ultra-Fez
Crown Shoulder
Warplating
Prongalong x2
Spore Gears x2

Wilder Thing

Key Characteristics: None
Other Characteristics: Gathering, Health

Accessorizing the Wild Thing allowed us to position a base mask on the beak and really cover up the eyes well, so the mask looks real. The Floronets look like hair, while the Dockworka is stretched out to resemble a shield. The chest pieces create a "belt"-like line around the beast's lower torso. The symbol is flipped using the tab function, and merged to create a "star"-like design. Feathers adorn the back.

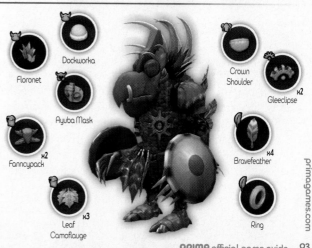

Floronet
Ayuba Mask
Fanncypack x2
Leaf Camoflauge x3
Dockworka
Crown Shoulder
Gleeclipse x2
Bravefeather x4
Ring

Arch Spawn

Key Characteristics: None
Other Characteristics: Speed

Leading the charge against the forces that would dispell darkness is Arch Spawn, recognizable due to a variety of odd glyphs adorning its body, and a strange, cap-like helmet where power is focused. A collection of large and shrunken skulls are sewn into the scaly flesh pieces of this unspeakable beast, while its main and gigantic maw of a mandible receives a ceremonial piercing.

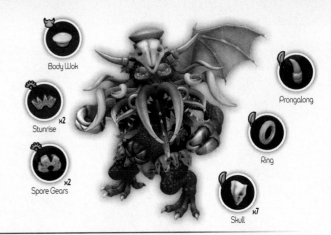

Body Wok

Stunrise x2

Spore Gears x2

Prongalong

Ring

Skull x7

EyeVee the Seer

Key Characteristics: None
Other Characteristics: Gathering, Speed

By the Tribal Stage, certain members of the EyeVee tribe can conjure elemental forces from the skies, and are known colloquially as Seers. This particular one has decided that a base mask will fit over one pair of its eyes, while chest tunics are used to detail another eye in the same area. The legs are well-protected, as is the top of the giant head, thanks to a similar-looking hat and details.

Bakerwear

Khwame Mask

Tunic of Virtue x2

Shellshopped

Glibia

Sergeant Speedo

Key Characteristics: Combat, Health
Other Characteristics: Speed

Speedo doesn't have the face for a mask, so it was positioned as a chest plate to instill fear into Speedo's enemies while still providing the skills benefits. Prongalongs echo the spikes on Speedo's back, and each of his shoulder and knee joints receive shoulder pad protection for the confrontations to come. As for the kilt? It covers Speedo's unmentionables, and links his armored sections together.

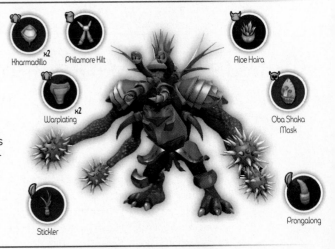

Kharmadillo x2

Philamore Kilt

Warplating x2

Stickler

Aloe Haira

Oba Shaka Mask

Prongalong

Greater Shaman of Koob

Key Characteristics: Social, Speed
Other Characteristics: Combat

This is an example of a creature that looks incredibly different once accessories are placed on it. The Koob's relatively long face makes mask-placement simple. Thorsbjerg's Tunic is positioned on the body, while the Tierdrop hat covers the poisonous Body Part the Koob used during the Creature Stage. Koob's mouth at the end of its trunk is the most stylish, with the Gleeclipse symbols surrounding its maw!

Kharmadillo x3

Body Aegis x4

Gleeclipse x4

Skull

Tierdrop

Kofi Kete Mask

Thorsbjerg Tunic x3

Prongalong

Warrior Class of Thun

Key Characteristics: Combat, Health, Speed
Other Characteristics: None

When a behemoth of Jass shock troops aren't enough, the warrior chieftains of Thun call upon their own creations: battle-ready versions of their normal warriors, bred for battle, and using exceptionally strong Oba Shaka Masks as knee pads. The massive legs are covered in segmented plates, and a pair of Prongalongs act as impromptu nose tusks. This is a carnivorous tribe's ultimate member!

Spore Gears · Plundacap · Oba Shaka Mask · Philamore Kilt · Fanncypack · Prongalong · Warplating x3

Little Blue Prowler

Key Characteristics: Gathering, Speed
Other Characteristics: Combat, Health

Lightly armored recon teams of Growlers go by their own moniker, and fit Ayuba Masks while they wait for a more Combat-worthy accessory to be unlocked. As the Growler is vaguely humanoid-shaped, its array of chest accessories is linked by a Geltbuckle to finish off the lower torso. These Prowlers also have a tiny symbol on each wrist; it is said they tell the time with it....

Dockworka · Charm Plate x4 · Shellshapped x2 · Ayuba Mask · Kharmadillo x3 · Geltbuckle · Gleeclipse

Wartson the Tartywoad

Key Characteristics: Social, Speed
Other Characteristics: None

Wartson is a shy little fellow, and his sheer wartiness is a constant source of embarrassment. He copes with this by wearing the Tiki Gamba Mask, as its Social bonuses give him a brand new confidence. He recently went out and had a symbol fitted around his oldest wart ("if you've got it, flaunt it!" he was said to croak), but locals have mentioned his brand new Trophybucks may be taking things a little far....

King Bling · Tiki Gamba Mask · Leaf Camoflauge · Metal Pleats x3 · Trophybuck · Spore Gears x2

Sir Reginald Honeypot: 101st Grizzlebear Reconnoiter Unit (Retired)

Key Characteristics: Gathering
Other Characteristics: Speed

After a distinguished career in the Grizzlebear Military, Sir Reginald (known to the Koob as "Reggie") has set up shop on a distant planet and begun to explore the vast landscapes and delicious nectar located in the forests. He sports some amazing facial hair, which usually frightens away all but the most persistent of foes. His remaining attire, from the floppy hat to the belt pouches, gives him the look of an explorer.

El Graucho · Charm Plate x9 · Mustache · Geltbuckle · Hearty

tribal stage advice

Fire, Friends, and Foes

After your creature rubbed two sticks together and jump-started the next stage of evolution, your tribe's central fire pit is burning merrily away. After some murmuring discussions, your Chieftain emerges with two tribe members from your brand new Tribal Hut, the hub of activity for this coming exploration. Holding the Chieftain's staff aloft, your leader leaps into the air, and your quest for traders and enemies begins.

introduction: taking the village tour

Welcome to the Tribal Stage. This is a three-dimensional social experiment on a part of your planet's massive continent, beginning at where your final creature nest was located. Your plans are three-fold: to conquer or Impress five rival tribes; to hunt, fish, or gather to earn currency; and to purchase tools and musical instruments to increase efficiency. Your biggest challenges are the ways you deal with five rival tribes, all attempting to live off the land like you. Do you trade with or tackle them? Whichever plan you try, your level increases once you ally with or destroy one, three, and finally all five other tribes. The remaining pages of this chapter show the main facets of this stage, and look into specific problems and solutions of this stage as Clumpy tries to lead his merry band to victory.

Clumpytown: Level 1. Just after the Tribal Hut's construction.

TIP If you're having difficulties with the game controls, consult the in-game guide for a refresher on how to group your tribe mates, maneuver the camera, and other basic elements.

Missions

You can attempt various Missions throughout the Tribal Stage, and many are explained elsewhere, or feature tactics that are explained in more detail elsewhere in this chapter. Here's what to look for:

Populate

Simply click on the appropriate button while selecting the Tribal Hut to roll out an egg and watch it hatch. The right side of your screen has icons showing all your tribe members; at the bottom are youngsters, represented by hatching eggs. The eggs gradually disappear from the icons as the youngsters mature. When the egg is all gone, the youngster has grown into an adult. It only takes about 30 seconds—they grow up so fast!

Gather Food

Encountered at the beginning of the stage, this Mission has you collect a specific amount of food. This is the only way to expand your tribe, so locate your nearest food source and bring it back to your food mat as soon as you can. Populate quickly, as the food consumed by each tribe member is far less than the food each member can bring in.

Tame a Wild Creature

When you're wandering through the landscape, there are many varieties of creatures (essentially beasts from the Creature Stage that haven't evolved to Tribal status yet) that you can attack, and gather the meat for food if you're a carnivore and omnivore. However, you can also try taming them by constantly offering them food until they follow you back to the village pen. After that, they supply you with eggs.

Interact

This will have the associated color of the village as the first word. You have three options: to gift, impress, or destroy, depending on whether you're playing a Social or Combat game. The subtleties of diplomacy and rousing combat plans are shown later in this chapter.

Mini-map

This is very important to your coordination when locating tribe members and other tribes too. Other tribe villages appear as house icons, individual tribe members appear as dots, and destroyed villages appear as red crossbones. Fishing holes are also shown, along with how each rival tribe feels about you (the various face icons, which are shown in the in-game guide).

TIP Hover over a rival village icon to gain more information on it. Double-click on a map to whisk the main screen to that location; this enables you to quickly check how other tribes are progressing, or to check on your own village (if it is under attack, or wild animals are stealing your food).

taking a tour of the village

Before you begin to explore, it is important to know everything about your village, including the areas where livestock, food, buildings, and even a running total of your victories are placed. This is your hub, and it changes constantly throughout this stage. Each rival village is set up identically, too.

The Chief's Hut: Carnivore Tribe

Level 1 Start: Basic
Health Points: 500

Level 2 Start: Upgrade
Health Points: 750

Level 4 Start: Upgrade
Health Points: 1,000

The Chief's Hut: Omnivore Tribe

Level 1 Start: Basic
Health Points: 500

Level 2 Start: Upgrade
Health Points: 750

Level 4 Start: Upgrade
Health Points: 1,000

The Chief's Hut: Herbivore Tribe

Level 1 Start: Basic
Health Points: 500

Level 2 Start: Upgrade
Health Points: 750

Level 4 Start: Upgrade
Health Points: 1,000

The largest hut in the village is key to your tribe's evolution. If you hold your mouse's cursor over the building, you can note its name and color (which corresponds to the color on the mini-map), along with how many members are in your tribe, and the Health Points the building has before it is destroyed.

CAUTION Your stage ends if this hut is destroyed (which only occurs if you're attacked by a rival tribe), so keep an eye on it!

Tribal Hut: Other Functions

The Tribal Hut also has two other functions:

First, if you click on the Tools icon, you can purchase a new building or Tribal Accessories.

Second, if you click on the blue circle icon, an egg rolls out of the hut's doorway. It soon hatches, and after a 30-second gestation period, becomes a new tribe member. Each new tribe member costs 10 points to hatch.

Finally, the fenced pen behind the hut is where tamed wild animals are kept for their egg-laying proficiency. This is discussed in greater detail later in this chapter.

TIP If you're inspecting another tribe's village and wish to attempt friendly relations, click on the Tribal Hut and a selected tribe member will bring a gift to the tribe's totem and food mat.

TIP If you're attempting to raze another tribe's village, defeat all the inhabitants first, and then raze the hut. Once this goes, the tribe goes, so you need not destroy any other buildings.

Fire Pit

Level 1 Start: Basic

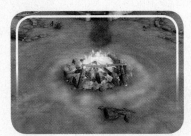

Level 2 Start: Upgrade

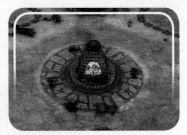

Level 4 Start: Upgrade

In the center of your village is the fire pit. This is the focus of the village, and all buildings surround it. If you click on the fire pit, and have tribe members selected, they will converge on the fire and dance around it. The pit cannot be destroyed. When you have a full force of tribe members, this can be an impressive display, as shown!

Tribal Totem and Food Mat

Level 1 Start: Basic

Level 2 Start: Upgrade

Level 4 Start: Upgrade

On the opposite side of the village from the hut is the tribal totem and food mat.

Two Types of Totem

The tribal totem is currently empty. However, each time you interact successfully with another tribe, a carved figure is added to the totem:

If you defeat a rival tribe by Combat, this totem is created.

If you negotiate a Social outcome and befriend a tribe, this totem is created.

When five of these carvings adorn your totem, you can evolve to the Civilization Stage.

Feeding the Food Mat

Below the totem is a primitive food mat. This is where all three types of food are brought back, and where gifts from other tribes are presented. Meat is placed to the left, fish is in the middle, and fruit to the right.

Throughout this stage, check your Food Points total (in the screen's bottom left), and keep a continuous supply of food coming to this food mat, no matter what type it is. Your tribe's eating habits (discussed later) determine the food you can bring back.

From time to time, rival tribes you haven't encountered yet, or are working on befriending, will bring a gift to this location. If you're playing a Social game, make sure a representative is waiting here to receive the gift, which is always food added to your food mat's pile.

If your tribe members display the Food icon, maneuver each hungry creature to the totem, and right-click on it to tell the selected tribe members to dig in.

If your tribe is away from the village for 30 seconds, wild animals may approach and steal your food! This is an annoyance, so place a single tribe member near the totem to guard it, assuming you can spare one from other tasks.

Building Sites

Level 1 Start: Basic

Level 2 Start: Upgrade

Level 4 Start: Upgrade

Your village has six different building sites, upon which a variety of helpful structures can be instantly created. Simply enter the Tribal Hut, and choose the available buildings. These are unlocked throughout the stage, and the order they are unlocked depends on your style of play, as shown in the chart to come.

structures to build

The following structures (also known as "Tools") are available to build at some point during the Tribal Stage. As you only have six building sites, it is important to determine which buildings are most useful. Again, the chart to come shows you the six buildings that best help your style of play.

TIP As a general rule, employ Food and Healing buildings whether you're playing a Combat or Social game. The other two types are advantageous to build if you're combat-based (Weapons) or like to dance and chat (Musical Instruments).

TIP The higher the difficulty level, the more important and useful these structures, and the augmentations they provide, become.

Food and Healing

Fishing Spears

Fishing Spears allow you to gather food more effectively from nearby fishing holes.

Although herbivores can ignore this option, this is an excellent plan for omnivores or carnivores early in this stage.

Fishing Huts can augment your other sources of food/currency to a great degree. Look on your mini-map and scour the coastline for your nearest fishing hole.

If the fishing hole is much farther away than other food sources, ignore this augmentation.

If the fruit or wild animal situation is plentiful, weigh the options to see which gets you food the quickest.

Other tribes also fish, and may commandeer a fishing hole, so be first, or share resources.

Herbivores commanded to harvest from fishing holes will bring back seaweed piles to eat instead of fish.

Gathering Canes

This tool lets you gather the most fruit possible and harvest from bushes and short trees.

The advantage Gathering Canes have over Fishing Spears is that you're likely to be closer to fruit you can harvest.

The disadvantage is that you're relying on only one food source; so check your fruit supplies if you're an omnivore.

If you're a herbivore, this is a critically important augmentation, and should be employed by all your fruit pickers.

Herbivores should grab this, and gathering accessories, as soon as possible for the ultimate in food-gathering teams.

This knocks down fruit from bushes and short trees, and is particularly useful in more mature fruit forests.

Remember this adds a bonus of currency to each fruit pile you bring back to the food mat.

Healing Rods

Equip your creatures with a shaman staff so they can heal their brethren in the field.

This can be employed by any tribe, no matter the diet they consume.

This augmentation isn't quite as imperative as the main Social, Combat, or Gathering sticks.

Every type of tribe needs this if they haven't maximized their Health through accessories.

The more difficult the game setting, the greater the chance you'll need this.

This is an excellent plan to use on hunting parties; equip one or two "shamans" with this rod.

Then, during fights (especially with groups of foes or Epics), have the shaman heal them.

This leads to an almost invincible army, if you can keep your team from getting hungry!

Musical Instruments

 Wooden Horns

Impress other tribe members with these Wooden Horns!

 Maracas

Impress other tribe members with these Maracas!

 Didgeridoos

Impress other tribe members with these Didgeridoos!

All three musical instruments work in exactly the same way, and are for Social tribes only.

Tribes only concerned with conquering rivals should ignore these three building types and the instruments they provide.

Use the chart in the next section of this chapter to determine how your style of play influences the available buildings.

Consult the information about Social interaction later in this chapter to see how instruments are used.

Weapons

 Stone Axes

Axes are brutally effective against wild creatures and tribes, but are less useful against huts and tools.

These have a cone damage effect that deals damage to adjacent NPCs, which makes a Stone Axe great for fighting groups. Stone Axes also have a triggered whirlwind attack that damages all creatures in the area.

The Stone Axe, coupled with Combat accessories, is the most aggressive and advantageous weapon in this stage.

If you are a carnivore, this is also incredibly important because wild animals are felled much more quickly, speeding up the meat delivery to your food mat.

Although less useful against huts and tools, Stone Axes are still better than unarmed strikes.

Flaming Torches

Flaming Torches destroy tools and huts quickly and are good against creatures.

Flaming Torches have a fire breath attack that stuns other creatures.

If you want to forgo hand-to-hand combat with the enemy, race to the hut with a group of torch-carriers, and burn it before all of you are defeated. This ends the rival tribe.

Otherwise, keep a few of your tribe armed with torches to "mop up" after a strike force with axes.

Throwing Spears

Spears are best used from a distance; they are less useful in melee combat.

This is great for hunting near your own village, as you can catch wild animals quicker, before taking the meat.

You can also tackle an enemy village from a distance, throwing from the grass.

This allows you to wound most of the enemy tribe before they even reach you, making Throwing Spears an excellent alternative to Stone Axes!

Try equipping a couple of shock troops armed with spears to catch a rival Chieftain, then follow up with hand-to-hand shock troops.

Throwing Spears has a charge attack that allows you to run past enemies to gain the distance necessary to make a good throwing attack.

➕ Repairing Buildings

If your village is attacked by another tribe, they may attempt to destroy your buildings. After defeating or driving away your foes, be sure to click on all of your buildings to check their Health. Then select tribe members to repair these buildings. No special tools are needed for this.

Building (Tools) Unlock Chart

The way you play through the Tribal Stage actually influences the type of available buildings that you can construct in each of the levels. The following chart shows what to expect from each rival tribe, based on your style of play:

Creature Play Style	Available Building(s)					
	Phase Start	Tribe 1 (Tutorial)	Tribe 2	Tribe 3	Tribe 4	Tribe 5 (Boss)
Carnivore Aggressive	Gather **Axe** **Didger** Fish Spear Horns Heal Torch Maracas	Gather Axe Didger **Fish** Spear **Horns** Heal Torch Maracas	**Gather** Axe Didger Fish **Spear** **Horns** Heal Torch Maracas	Gather Axe Didger **Fish** Spear Horns Heal **Torch** **Maracas**	Gather **Axe** Didger Fish Spear Horns **Heal** Torch **Maracas**	Gather Axe Didger Fish Spear Horns Heal Torch Maracas
Carnivore Mix	Gather **Axe** **Didger** Fish Spear Horns Heal Torch Maracas	Gather Axe Didger **Fish** Spear **Horns** Heal Torch Maracas	**Gather** Axe Didger Fish **Spear** **Horns** Heal Torch Maracas	Gather Axe Didger **Fish** Spear Horns Heal **Torch** **Maracas**	Gather **Axe** Didger Fish Spear Horns **Heal** Torch **Maracas**	Gather Axe Didger Fish Spear Horns Heal Torch Maracas
Carnivore Social	Gather **Axe** **Didger** Fish Spear Horns Heal Torch Maracas	Gather Axe Didger **Fish** Spear **Horns** Heal Torch Maracas	**Gather** Axe Didger Fish **Spear** **Horns** Heal Torch Maracas	Gather Axe Didger **Fish** Spear Horns Heal **Torch** **Maracas**	Gather **Axe** Didger Fish Spear Horns **Heal** Torch **Maracas**	Gather Axe Didger Fish Spear Horns Heal Torch Maracas
Omnivore Aggressive	Gather Axe Didger Fish **Spear** **Horns** Heal Torch Maracas	Gather Axe Didger **Fish** Spear Horns Heal Torch **Maracas**	**Gather** Axe **Didger** Fish **Spear** Horns **Heal** Torch Maracas	Gather Axe Didger **Fish** Spear Horns Heal **Torch** **Maracas**	Gather **Axe** **Didger** Fish Spear Horns Heal Torch Maracas	Gather Axe Didger Fish Spear Horns Heal Torch Maracas
Omnivore Mix	Gather Axe Didger Fish **Spear** **Horns** Heal Torch Maracas	Gather Axe Didger **Fish** Spear Horns Heal Torch **Maracas**	**Gather** Axe **Didger** Fish **Spear** Horns **Heal** Torch Maracas	Gather Axe Didger **Fish** Spear Horns Heal **Torch** **Maracas**	Gather **Axe** **Didger** Fish Spear Horns Heal Torch Maracas	Gather Axe Didger Fish Spear Horns Heal Torch Maracas
Omnivore Social	Gather Axe Didger Fish **Spear** **Horns** Heal Torch Maracas	Gather Axe Didger **Fish** Spear Horns Heal Torch **Maracas**	**Gather** Axe **Didger** Fish **Spear** Horns **Heal** Torch Maracas	Gather Axe Didger **Fish** Spear Horns Heal **Torch** **Maracas**	Gather **Axe** **Didger** Fish Spear Horns Heal Torch Maracas	Gather Axe Didger Fish Spear Horns Heal Torch Maracas
Herbivore Aggressive	Gather Axe Didger Fish Spear Horns Heal **Torch** **Maracas**	**Gather** Axe **Didger** Fish Spear Horns Heal Torch Maracas	**Gather** Axe Didger Fish **Spear** **Horns** Heal Torch Maracas	Gather Axe Didger **Fish** Spear **Horns** **Heal** **Torch** Maracas	Gather **Axe** **Didger** Fish Spear Horns Heal Torch Maracas	Gather Axe Didger Fish Spear Horns Heal Torch Maracas
Herbivore Mix	Gather Axe Didger Fish Spear Horns Heal **Torch** **Maracas**	**Gather** Axe **Didger** Fish Spear Horns Heal Torch Maracas	**Gather** Axe Didger Fish **Spear** **Horns** Heal Torch Maracas	Gather Axe Didger **Fish** Spear **Horns** **Heal** **Torch** Maracas	Gather **Axe** **Didger** Fish Spear Horns Heal Torch Maracas	Gather Axe Didger Fish Spear Horns Heal Torch Maracas
Herbivore Social	Gather Axe Didger Fish Spear Horns Heal **Torch** **Maracas**	**Gather** Axe **Didger** Fish Spear Horns Heal Torch Maracas	**Gather** Axe Didger Fish **Spear** **Horns** Heal Torch Maracas	Gather Axe Didger **Fish** Spear **Horns** **Heal** **Torch** Maracas	Gather **Axe** **Didger** Fish Spear Horns Heal Torch Maracas	Gather Axe Didger Fish Spear Horns Heal Torch Maracas

Legend

Gather = Gathering Canes

Fish = Fishing Spears

Heal = Healing Rods

Axe = Stone Axes

Spear = Throwing Spears

Torch = Flaming Torches

Didger = Didgeridoos

Horns = Horns

Maracas = Maracas

Gray text = Not Interested

Bold text = Starting Tool

Red text = What your tribe wants

NOTE See the next page for detailed instructions about how to read this chart.

How to read this chart:

Column 1. When you completed the Creature Stage, the game worked out how you played: Aggressively (mainly Combat), Aggro-socially (equally parts Combat and Social), or Socially (mainly Social).

Column 2. This influences the type of building initially available from the start of the Tribal Stage. For example, if you were herbivorous, and played a mainly Social game, your initial available building would be the one housing Maracas.

The table text in **red** shows what your tribe wants to build (as they are most preferable to your play style). For example, an Herbivorous Social tribe wants Gathering Canes, Fishing Spears, Healing Rods, Didgeridoos, and Horns (as it has no need for Combat buildings).

Column 3. When you encounter your first tribe, this is the type of building it has. When you ally with or destroy the rival tribe, this building unlocks and can be built in your village. So, for our Herbivorous Social player, the Gathering Canes building can be constructed at the start of Level 2.

Column 4. When you encounter your second tribe, it not only has additional buildings (shown in black) that become yours once your befriend or destroy Tribe #2, but has a particular instrument they want to hear if you're being Social. In our example, Tribe #2 wants to hear Didgeridoos or Maracas. As the Herbivorous Social tribe started with a Maracas building, this should be an easy alliance!

Columns 5-7. This continues until your tribe completes this stage.

NOTE Remember you can change your style of play at any time! For example, if you began as a Herbivorous Social player, and during the negotiations with Tribe #1 you decided to slaughter them instead, you'd become a Herbivorous Aggressive player, and look across this row at what the next tribe has and wants to hear.

Tribal Outfitter

The other menu inside the Tribal Hut leads you to the Tribal Outfitter. Tactics on choosing your wardrobe are available in the previous chapter.

meat, fish, eggs, and fruit: a new and delicious currency

One of the major additions to this stage is the use of currency. DNA Points are no longer important. When you're dealing with a tribe, or building additions to your village, you must rely on a brand-new method of bartering: food.

Your Food Choices

There are four types of food to consume and/or collect. The majority are deposited by your gatherers, hunters, or fishermen on your village food mat. All are worth the same value, and are used for purchasing. You should also feed hungry tribe members with food.

Fruit

 Fruit is found on bushes and short trees. Carnivores can ignore this because you cannot gather (or even touch) fruit. Wear outfits that favor gathering to boost the number of points each load of fruit gives your tribe.

Fish

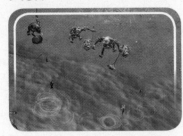

Find fish in the water, where you see them jumping. Also check the mini-map. For much more proficient results (catching fish faster), use a Fishing Spear. All species of creature can fish, but herbivores gather seaweed instead of fish.

CAUTION There are limited stocks of fish, so watch your fishing members closely. If they are taking a long time, there are fewer or no fish jumping out of the water, and Fishing Spears aren't making a difference, you've over-fished. Step back and see if the area gets restocked, or find another fishing hole.

Meat

 Meat is found on the bodies of wild animals (and Epic-sized creatures) you slay. You cannot harvest meat from other tribe members. Use Stone Axes to help defeat animals. Herbivores can also hunt, but cannot harvest meat from the slain bodies of wild animals. Make sure you wear outfits favoring Health and Combat to aid you in hunting, and use Stone Axe tools (and to a lesser extent, Flaming Torches and Throwing Spears) to deal heavier damage.

Eggs

The most tricky of the foodstuffs to collect, eggs are available only after you domesticate a wild animal, place it in the pen behind the Tribal Hut, and wait for it to lay an egg. Afterward, command a tribe member to retrieve the eggs from the pen.

Stealing Food

Although most of the time is spent finding your own fresh food, you can also command tribe members to visit other tribes and steal food from their food mats. This is a sure-fire way to deteriorate a relationship with that tribe. They'll become angry and return to steal from you or engage in combat.

TIP If you're attacking another tribe, and razing their village to the ground, be sure to collect all their fruit, meat, fish, and eggs from the food mat before you return home; it's a Food Points bonanza!

Your Shopping Choices

Obtaining food is critical, because you can "spend" food on the following:

Tools (Buildings)

Discussed previously, they provide rods, poles, spears, torches, and axes that add to a particular tribe skill.

Tribe Members

Check the number of members your current level allows, and hatch members from the Tribal Hut as soon as you can. More members means more food they can collect!

Filling Your Tribe Members' Bellies

Whenever your tribe members come back from hunting, fruit-picking, fishing, or socializing (or fighting) with another tribe, they may start to mention their hunger in a word bubble. Guide them to the food mat, and let them feast.

Domestication

Please feed the animals, especially if you want to tame them! Socialize with a wild animal (any creature not a member of a tribe), and your favorable relationship with them increases at the cost of a bit of food, which is automatically deducted from your food mat. Continue to do this until the relationship is high enough that the animal follows you back to the village, and is placed in the pen behind the Tribal Hut. Over time, your "pet" lays eggs that can be harvested by your tribe from the egg basket attached to the pen. Then bring the egg to your food mat.

Gifts

If another tribe likes or admires you, which occurs with more frequency if you've already attempted Social contact with them (and no violence), they wrap up a gift box and head to your food mat. Use your Social skills to contact the representative at your mat, and accept the food to add it to your total.

meeting your tribe mates

Your tribe members are a motley bunch, and their specific job is shown in their name, and on a specific icon on the screen's right side. Left-click on an icon, or drag your on-screen cursor over a member to select them. You can group them into different parties.

Egg	Youngster	Tribe Member	Fisherman	Farmer

This rolls out of your Tribal Hut, and immediately hatches into a...	...youngster. This tiny creature takes around 30 seconds to grow into...	...an adult. Tribe members are unarmed members of your village.	Equip a tribe member with a Fishing Pole, and it looks like this.	Give a tribe member a Gathering Cane, and this is what it looks like.

Shaman

If you require magical healing in combat, bring a Healing Rod.

Axeling

Should wild animals and creatures require swift dispatch, claim this.

Firestarter

If your main objectives are burning buildings, the torchman is your friend.

Spearman

Do you want to attack from range? Let your tribe member carry this.

Hornist

Should you attempt to appease another village, play a tune on this.

Maracan

Another option are the funky sounds of these rattling instruments.

Aerophonist

For a more down-to-earth feel, blow down these long wooden instruments.

Chieftain

Bigger, sporting more Health Points, and carrying an impressive skull staff, this is your leader.

NOTE The faction icons show which tribe members are selected by highlighting the icon representing that tribe member in yellow.

The tribe member's icon changes to depict what tool they have equipped. It also displays current Health and hunger levels.

NOTE Tribe members with Social tools are grouped into a Social section. Tribe members with Aggressive tools are grouped into a Combat section. Click on the heading of any group (Tribe/Social/Combat) to select all tribe members in that group. Double click on a tribe member to select all tribe members that are equipped with the same tools. Double clicking a tribe member that is not equipped with a tool will select only tribe members that are not equipped with any tools.

Number of Tribe Members (Stage)	
Level (Start)	Maximum Number of Tribe Members
1	5 + Chieftain
2	8 + Chieftain
3	8 + Chieftain
4	11 + Chieftain
5	11 + Chieftain

Large and In Charge: The Chieftain

Of all the different tribe members to keep track of and use, your Chieftain is the most important. Aside from his size, your Chieftain is easily spotted because he carries a staff with a skull on it, and has a unique icon in the party buttons. He has some interesting abilities, too:

Immortal

Although the Chieftain can be defeated, which freaks out your fellow tribe members, he automatically revives in your village after a while.

Tools Are For Fools

The Chieftain can perform almost every action a regular tribe member can, using his staff as a tool.

Combat Hero

The Chieftain dishes out more damage, gathers food more quickly, and has more Health Points than a regular tribe member, so he doesn't really need to carry other tools.

Follow the Leader

If you're playing a Social game, and are using instruments to impress a rival tribe, you need the Chieftain to lead your musicians and act as the go-between and maestro.

Super Powers

The Consequence Abilities or Traits that you received after the Cell and Creature Stages are part of the Chieftain's powers. Here are all the different powers available:

Refreshing Storm

A storm is summoned over the immediate area around the Chieftain. Trees are replenished, and fruit falls from the trees! Harvest this refreshing bounty! Use this on an area you've over-harvested, and have numerous gatherers waiting to go after the rain stops.

Flying Fish

A large sea monster is summoned and does a cannonball into the water, which causes fish to die and fly out of the water to land at your feet. Then the helpful sea monster waves good-bye.

Traps

A keen and adept hunter, the Chieftain drops a trap that has up to three poison triggers in a series. These attract and ensnare wild animals. Bring on the meat feast! Be sure members are waiting to ferry the meat back, or lay traps near the food mat to snare wild animals before they steal your food.

Fireworks

The Chieftain sets off a series of beautiful fireworks that zip and arch with impressive lights and colors. The relationship status with a nearby tribe increases. Use this in conjunction with other Social skills to impress a rival village.

Beastmaster

Using trusted and old shamanic techniques, the Chieftain can enchant nearby animals. This is an excellent way to reduce the time it takes to tame an animal and then harvest the eggs it produces after you lead it back to the pen. The animals don't become domesticated, but they will follow the chieftain for a period of time and aid in combat or social interactions. Beastmaster is just a temporary charm that doesn't affect relationships or domestication.

Firebombs

The Chieftain removes a set of firebombs from his pouch, and drops them around him. This damages creatures, rival tribe members, and nearby structures, but not members of the Chieftain's tribe. Use this to really hammer an enemy tribe you're defeating.

plans of progression: befriending or battling

Now for the main progression path in this stage; you have five levels to complete, and each requires you to either ally with, or destroy, a rival tribe in your area. You can choose any available tribe. More tribes appear the farther through the stage you are.

TIP Your tribe members perform Aggressive or Social actions based on the stance of the tribe. Change the stance to Aggressive (red) or Social (green) using the Stance buttons in the screen's bottom-middle.

Battling: Aggressive Combat-based Interactions

The following actions cause a nearby rival tribe to dislike you more and more until they launch an all-out attack on your village: Get them before they get you!

Action #1: Attacking a Rival Member

Attack a rival tribe member. This can be as they are bringing a gift to you, or if you encounter them fishing or wandering about the landscape. Obviously, the larger your group, and the smaller the rival's group, the better your chances are.

Action #2: Attacking Rivals Inside Their Village

Round up a fighting force and storm into a rival's village, and you're presented with a variety of options. It's best to charge in with overwhelming odds, and then mop up the remaining stragglers before burning down the Tribal Hut.

Plan #1: Take Down the Chieftain

If you want to demoralize a rival tribe, target the Chieftain (move your cursor over the biggest rival to check its name). This causes the remaining members to mill about less effectively than your crack team of bloodthirsty pillagers. It also stops a Chieftain from using his super powers.

Plan #2: Fighting Factions

Your team should be composed of various types of warriors. Don't saunter into a well-defended village with gatherers carrying fruit. Make sure your tribe is outfitted with accessories that favor Health and Combat. Then give them Stone Axes, because this is the most effective weapon against enemies.

TIP **Other Faction Plans**

Spearmen and Axemen: Use a back row of spearmen to throw from far distances, cutting down the enemy. Wait for them to charge you, then start a melee with your axemen.

Torch Bearers and Axemen: Split your crew into two; have the torch bearers circle around the village and attack the Tribal Hut, while your axemen engage the enemies. Even if you're out-numbered, as long as the Tribal Hut falls, you will succeed!

All Spearmen: This interesting plan works if you place two teams of spearmen, one behind the other. Let the closer team throw their weapons, then run away. As the enemies advance, let the second team throw, and retreat. Then start this plan again with the first team, and so on.

All Torch Bearers: Expect some casualties if you attempt to burn down a well-guarded village. A better technique is to wait for little defense (if your rivals are out picking fruit or asleep, for example); then torch the Tribal Hut only. Keep burning the hut, even if you're attacked.

Spearmen and Torch Bearers: For this interesting combination, coax villagers toward the spearmen while the torch bearers sneak around to demolish the Tribal Hut.

Plan #3: Special Attacks

The red "Aggressive" tray at the bottom-middle of the screen activates during battle. When the buttons light up, be sure to use them, allowing your tribe to perform a special attack with each of the three different weapons. This can turn a battle easily!

Plan #4: Overwhelming Odds

Your tribe is at risk if you attempt to fight with only a few of your tribe. The first plan is to stock up on food while hatching the maximum number of members. Then, equip them all with your favored weapon. Finally, storm the rival village with all of them, either in one mass, or in two separate converging teams.

Plan #5: Run Away? No!

Is the attack going extremely badly? You may be tempted to run away, but this isn't a particularly good plan. You're likely to be followed and cut down before you can return to a village that your enemies are likely to set fire to anyway! Let your members continue to the bitter end, while you return to the village to hatch more members and begin to accrue a new crew.

Plan #6: Super Power Slaughter

Don't forget your Chieftain's Consequence Traits. You can further demolish a rival tribe if you launch an aggressive attack while combat is going on. There's nothing better than firebombing a melee fight! Obviously, this means you need to play aggressively in the previous two stages to obtain violent traits.

Plan #7: Send in the Shaman

Remember that a Healing Rod is also key to success. If you're having difficulties, make one or two of your tribe into shamans, following the main members into battle and constantly healing them during a fight. If your team can't die, then your rivals will surely perish!

Befriending: Social, Friendship-based Interactions

The following actions cause a nearby rival tribe to like you more and more until they share the love and become firm friends and great allies. Can't we all just get along? Yes, if you try these actions out:

> **NOTE** The gifting action is only available on tribes that have a negative relationship, and performing is only available on tribes with a neutral or friendly relationship. Gifts will appease angry or hostile tribes, and keep them from attacking or stealing your food, but the effect is only temporary and if the player wishes to remain friends with the tribe they need to impress them with their musical skills.

Action #1: Gift Delivery

Select one of your tribe members, and click on the mini-map to select a rival tribe's main hut. Your tribe member now takes a gift box (which is a donation of food), moves to the tribe's food mat, and places the gift in front of the mat.

Action #2: Gift Receiving

If you've already performed Actions 1, 3, and/or 4 one or more times, you should expect a gift from the tribe you're attempting to befriend. Make sure a member is there to pick up the gift and place it on your food mat.

Action #3: Socializing

Click on one of your tribe members, and maneuver them near a rival member. Then right-click on the rival tribe member and your villager walks over and begins to socialize. This causes the rival to become more neutral, and gradually like your tribe more and more. Keep this up multiple times, and you should soon see a gift coming toward your food mat.

Action #4: A Musical Performance

By far the biggest song and dance you can make is an actual song and dance, thanks to the Musical Instrument Huts that are available during this stage. When you have acquired one or more of these Social tools, and you've checked the **Building (Tools) Unlock Chart** (earlier in this chapter) and selected the instrument, you can perform for a rival tribe.

A Band of Merry Makers

Equip a few tribe members with one of the instruments by selecting them, then right-click on your hut. Remember to select your Chieftain before you leave for the rival tribe's village, because he is needed to conduct your orchestra. You can move to a village (where the majority of your rivals will be listening), or locate one or more rival members elsewhere. Click on one, and your selected musicians and Chieftain move to and begin to play for the selected rival member.

Going Solo

When the music actually begins, watch for the reaction from the rival tribe members. Periodically, a speech bubble will appear over their heads, and this contains the icon of a specific instrument. If one or more of your orchestra is playing this instrument, click on it in the green Social tray, and your musician plays a solo that pleases the tribe to a much greater extent.

TIP To receive the highest rating, bring your entire tribe, use all three instruments, and perform a solo whenever you are asked. Wear socially acceptable accessories, too!

Recital Ratings

You are rated by the listeners at the end of your recital, and given a mark from 1 to 10. You can either begin this again to gradually add more likability to your tribe until the rivals are impressed enough to become allies, or go away and try with a different instrument, or groups of instruments. Once again; remember to **play a solo** to increase your score, and **turn up with the correct instruments**!

Other Entities

There are two other entity types to worry about during this stage, and both may have been spotted during the Creature Stage. Be ready to react to creatures (also called wild animals) and Epics!

Wild Animal Interaction

Any creature that isn't part of a tribe, and is wandering the landscape, is now called a wild animal. You can cut it down with Combat, using any of the techniques employed when fighting tribes.

Or, you can enter a Social stance, and target the animal. You'll automatically feed the animal until it follows you back to your village. It wanders into the pen and begins to produce eggs, another form of currency!

NOTE Your tribesmen don't need to have food in hand to charm the beast, but it makes domesticating the animal that much easier if they do.

Epic Battling

Rarely, you may encounter gigantic lumbering behemoths moving through your continent. They represent a large meat addition to your food mat. Engage them only if you have eight or more members armed with Stone Axes, and a couple of shamans for quick healing. If you slay an Epic near a rival village, the tribe likes you more.

rewards for alliance or victory

Your totem must rise from your food mat to the skies, and claim any combination of five defeated or allied tribes before this stage ends, so you can progress to the Civilization Stage. During this stage, certain elements are unlocked:

Unlockables

Buildings

Every time a rival tribe is defeated or allied with, you can purchase the tools the rival tribe had in their village, dragging them onto one of the six building sites while in the Tribal Planner menu. This is the only way to unlock new tools, and the previous chart shows exactly what to expect based on your style of play.

TIP Remember, if you want Stone Axes (the best tool to defeat wild animals and other tribe members) or other preferred tools, use the mini-map to look at all the villages, then ally with or destroy the nearest one with a tool building that you want.

NOTE You receive a village "upgrade" (your Tribal Hut, grounds, food mat, and totem are improved, as shown previously) at the start of Level 2 and Level 4.

Accessories

As previously mentioned (although this bears repeating, as it is very important to your success), check your Tribal Outfitter after every large Combat or Social interaction, and definitely after each level is completed, to check whether the "Better" accessory has become unlocked. Then add it to your tribe members immediately.

Ultimate Victory (or Defeat)

Victory!

You complete the Tribal Stage if you destroy or befriend five tribes in total. Any combination of destroyed or befriended tribes counts as a winning condition. Once you win, your tribe chats about creating larger housing, and hare-brained schemes for shooting to the stars!

Defeat!

You lose the Tribal Stage if you lose all of your adult tribe members. You are reborn at the last game save. If you have no save assets, the game resets to the beginning of the Tribal Stage.

tribe stage tables

The following information is both interesting and handy for your Tribal Stage adventure, as it shows exactly how many points are needed for a variety of Combat, Social, Gathering, and Health-based aspects to this stage.

Combat Damage
(inflicted on an enemy by your tribe members)

Attack Type	Damage	Recovery Time (secs.)	Range
Unarmed (Member)	Depends on Creature	2	Melee
Chieftain	12	2	Melee
Stone Axes	8	2	Melee
Flaming Torches	6	1.5	Melee
Spears	5	3	Melee
Healing Rod	3	2.5	Melee
Throwing Spears	10	3	Ranged
Chieftain (against buildings)	7	2	Raze
Stone Axes (against buildings)	5	2	Raze
Flaming Torches (against buildings)	9	1.5	Raze
Throwing Spears (against buildings)	4	3	Raze
Healing Rod	3	2.5	Raze
Level 1 Combat Bonus	0.3	—	—
Level 2 Combat Bonus	0.6	—	—
Level 3 Combat Bonus	0.9	—	—
Level 4 Combat Bonus	1.2	—	—
Level 5 Combat Bonus	1.5	—	—

Gathering Bonuses

Gathering Technique	Amount, or Bonus (Currency)
Fruit Food Points (gathered, per trip)	1
Fishing Food Points (gathered, per trip)	1.5
Egg Food Points (gathered, per trip)	1
Gathering Bonus: Fishing Spears	2.5
Gathering Bonus: Gathering Canes	2
Max Carrying Capacity	5
Level 1 max Carrying Capacity with Tool	6
Level 2 max Carrying Capacity with Tool	7
Level 3 max Carrying Capacity with Tool	8
Level 4 max Carrying Capacity with Tool	9
Level 5 max Carrying Capacity with Tool	10

Health Bonuses

Health Description	Health Points
Health Points (Tribe Member)	100-120*
Health Points (Chieftain)	150-170*
Healing Rods (HP Restored)	3 (per second)
Rival Chieftain	150-170
Rival Tribe Member	100-120

*Health Points depend on Creature health parts and armor accessories

Social Rules

Score for Impressing Rival Tribe	Points
Full Correct Match	175
Per Creature	25
Incorrect Match per Creature	5
Per Accessory Level	35
For Animal	25
Points Needed to Ally Early Rival Tribe (Blue Face)	795
Points Needed to Ally Early Rival Tribe (Green Face)	880
Points Needed to Ally Mid Level Rival Tribe (Blue Face)	905
Points Needed to Ally Mid Level Rival Tribe (Green Face)	990
Points Needed to Ally Later Rival Tribe (Blue Face)	1,000
Points Needed to Ally Later Rival Tribe (Green Face)	1,090

Health Points for Tribe Huts

Building Type	Health Points
Hut (Level 1)	500
Hut (Level 2)	750
Hut (Level 3)	1,000
Tools	200

tribe levels: won't you take me to, clumpytown?

An Interaction in Five Stages

The last portion of this chapter reveals specific examples of the Tribal Stage in action, thanks to the ongoing saga of Clumpy, our own created creature. This is one of the infinite examples of a creature, and only one of many possible ways to complete the five levels. Each time Clumpy's village and accessories changed, we reveal it.

Level 1: Getting Down with Brown

Clumpytown: Level 1.0. A simple Tribal Hut and food mat, ready for expansion.

After learning the camera movements and outfitting Clan Clumpy, we realize a rival tribe of Gremlo has formed, and colored themselves brown.

This prompts Clumpytown to go into maximum fruit picking mode. Currency is needed, and the Chieftain isn't above bringing back a plate to the food mat!

Fruit production is thankfully easy due to a large wooded area nearby. Tribe members are quickly born, and the only available building is constructed. Flaming Torches are now available.

Clumpytown has grown to five tribe members and a Chieftain. One member peels off to investigate a nearby nest of Tootsies. He produces a milk bone, and leaves it for a Tootsie to nibble on.

After some cajoling, tribe member Clumpy III managed to wrangle a Tootsie back to the pen behind the Tribal Hut. Delicious Tootsie eggs should be served shortly!

Meanwhile, the rest of the tribe decide to pay the Brown Gremlo Chieftain a visit, bringing a gift. As they arrive, the village is being terrorized by an Epic Phatburd!

In what could have been the most foolish decision ever, Chieftain Clumpy summons his five troops, and begins a long and vicious attack on the Epic Phatburd...

...and emerges victorious! This helps break the ice, and after some tense (and multiple) negotiations, Chieftain Clumpy and the Gremlos become firm friends! Alas, Clumpy is an herbivore, so the Epic can't be harvested for meat.

Level 2: Pulverizing Pink

Clumpytown: Level 2.0. Torches and a hut holding Gathering Canes are now added.

Thanks to the Gremlos, fruit production can continue to rise, as a Gathering Canes Tool Hut is immediately constructed. Clumpy would fish, but the fruit forest is closer.

While most of the tribe collects fruit, and three additional babies are born as quickly as possible, one member grabs a Flaming Torch, and heads straight for the multitude of Busters nested on the nearby plains. He tackles the first...

Chieftain Clumpy reveals the most awesome power of the Refreshing Storm. One member reckons ghosts are responsible. The truth is that the leader is incompetent; he summoned the storm in the village, not the fruit forest!

...and is eventually beaten down after rampaging through almost a dozen Busters! As the meat can't be harvested by herbivores, the rest of the tribe becomes interested in this newfangled implement of destruction. "Team Torcher" is formed!

Three tribes have appeared on the mini-map, and a quick look at the nearest village reveals a tribe of Yoyos. In the grassy plains to the east trot a herd of Texs, strange wide-legged beasts that would be great to eat if Clumpy were carnivorous.

Feeling that tackling a newcomer tribe early is better than leaving them to grow more powerful, Chieftain Clumpy decides to quickly end the Pink Tribe. Checking stats, Clumpy equips accessories give his tribe higher Health. The assault begins!

Although Flaming Torches are better suited to burning buildings down, they still deal better damage than Clumpy's claws. The attack is frantic, and complete mayhem ensues! Notice the hut on the left? It houses Wooden Horns; Clumpy's got his eyes on them!

Chieftain Clumpy uses a firebomb to deal with any Yoyo stragglers, then "Team Torcher" descends on the main hut, using the torch's special attack to quickly burn down the entire village in record time. The Pink Tribe is no more.

Level 3: Sing-Along with Cyan

Clumpytown: Level 3.0. Bring on the Horns! Pink team's hut takes up space on the west side of town.

Word must have gotten out at the sheer impressiveness of Clumpy's crew, because a gift-giving party of two Crikiits from the Cyan Tribe buzz along to drop off a parcel.

Grabbing the delicious gift from the Crikiit advance party, Clumpy sends five of his best gatherers over to the Cyan village to give some gifts back. Actually, this is a sneaky reconoiter; there are Healing Rod and Stone Axe Tool Huts over at this village!

Clumpy makes an executive decision: he builds a Wooden Horn Hut and sends a single tribe member over to examine the new tool. The results are interesting, and the noise is an acquired taste. Clumpy sends the member over to the Crikiit village.

Tribe member Clumpy IX finishes a quick romp across the grass to the Cyan village, clicks on one of them, and begins to play. The response? Crickets... not Crikiits, but a complete lack of interest from the rival tribe. What an insult!

Clumpy IX waddles over to the Green village for a sneaky look at these newcomers, and brings a fellow horn blower. Their attempts at a concerto receive a chilly response from the Liesperluffs; which is a shame, because they've got Stone Axe Tool Huts!

The two tribe members head dejectedly back to Clumpytown, cheering themselves up a little by inspecting a crash site of a strange, saucer-shaped object. When they get back to the village, Clumpy has remembered a very important point....

The Chieftain himself needs to be there to conduct his tribe! Everyone grabs a Wooden Horn, and the entire tribe wanders over to the Crikiit village, determined to put on a show. The music begins, and the Crikiits ask for a Horn solo!

Of course, in the excitement, Clumpy forgets to order his Horn section to play a solo, and the Crikiits award the concert with a merger score of two. Although tempted to come back and burn the entire village down, Clumpy perseveres...

...and on his second attempt, he brings in a solo player, rocking the Crikiits with exceptional Horn control, while a couple of other tribe members bring additional gifts. The generosity and showmanship don't go unnoticed. The Cyan alliance is formed!

Level 4: Lobbing Projectiles at the Lavenders

Clumpytown: Level 4.0. After a hut, fire pit, and totem pole upgrade, all building sites are filled.

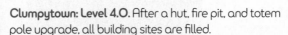

Just before dawn, Clumpy checks out the Purple Tribe to the east, and realizes he can quickly seize the opportunity to strike these Murgawgli down.

Running low on supplies, Clumpy kits out a couple of his tribe with Gathering Canes and sends them foraging for fruit. He puts up a Healing Rod Tool Hut, giving a shamanic Healing Rod to a trusted associate. Then he accepts some gifts from the Brown Tribe.

He sends a tribe member back to the Brown village to return with a gift, so they stay friends. The Cyan Tribe also offers goodies, which are gladly accepted. With all this spare currency, Clumpy builds a Fishing and Spear Hut. Those spears look interesting....

Assembling a strike team of nine, he leads the charge across the grassy hills.

Stopping just outside of the Murgawgli perimeter, Clumpy orders a volley of spears to be thrown, and they whiz through the dawn skies, sticking into a couple of hapless enemies. As the rest of the foes charge in, Clumpy lets loose a firebomb!

This brings down the Murgawgli Chieftain with a death-gurgle. Let the razing begin! Although spears aren't the best weapon for destroying a Tribal Hut, or a cheeky wild animal nibbling at Clumpy's village food supply, the hut falls quickly.

Level 5: Seeing Red and Going for Green

Clumpytown: Level 5.0. A Fishing Hut is demolished, and a building producing Stone Axes is erected instead.

Crossing the windswept plains, Clumpy's crew are an imposing force, but the way to the Green village is blocked by a herd of grazing Mages. A couple of Dainty Corns come over to watch, but quickly flee the scene.

Excitement reaches a fever pitch as the Fishing Hut, built at lavish expense but never used, is torn down in favor of a brand-new Stone Axe Tool Hut! The entire tribe, feeling a bloodlust coming on, trots over to try out these nasty weapons!

A couple of wild animals won't be stealing Clumpy's food any more, and the domesticated animal is fed again, producing a delicious egg! The entire tribe gathers at the totem to eat before going on their ultimate hunting expedition!

The Mages don't stand a chance as Clumpy's elite force of berserkers test out their Stone Axes to great effect. Almost a dozen Mages get sliced and diced. Clumpy orders his tribe not to get too carried away though; the important fight is yet to come!

Clumpy stops his army just outside the village limits, and watches the Liespurluffs for a sign of weakness. When the leader steps away from the pack, the entire tribe charges and frantic hand-to-axe fighting takes place!

The battle is hard-fought, as the Liespurluffs are a hardy bunch. However, their pack mentality is just what Clumpy needs; he unleashes hot fury and rains firebombs down on the battle. The tide turns, and Clumpy claims the camp! Victory is assured!

With the final village in smoldering ruins, Clan Clumpy returns to the village, chows down on some fruit because mayhem is hungry work, and celebrates with a quick tribal dance around the newly revamped fire pit.

Finally, at the end of this stage, Clumpy reveals an architectural tendency to his word bubbles, and the tribe enthusiastically agrees. This village could be so much more...it could be the seat of a great civilization! Let the next stage begin!

TIP At the end of this stage, the "Evolve to Civilization" button becomes available. Press this to enter the Civilization Stage, and begin to build your City Hall. If you want to explore more, do this before you enter the Civilization Stage. Additional "Civilization" accessories are now available.

primagames.com

civilization stage

the fourth rung of your evolutionary ladder

After making peace with (or pieces out of) your rival tribes in the Tribal Stage, it's time to progress to the **Civilization Stage** of *Spore*. In the Civilization Stage, the race of creatures you commanded in the Tribal Stage has emerged as the dominant life form on your world. When you first reach this new level of cultural sophistication, you must also design a City Hall, the seat of government in each city your civilization establishes. You also have to create a land vehicle to explore the world outside of your city limits, and you are encouraged to create a unique outfit for your race to set it apart from their formal tribal attire.

During the course of the Civilization Stage, you also need to design buildings for your citizens to live, work, and relax in. The land, sea, and air vehicles that you design reflect your nation's method of dealing with rivals. A military nation seeks to expand its borders by conquering all other cities, while a religious society wins control of other cities by winning the hearts of its citizens. An economic culture creates vast wealth and uses it to expand its sphere of influence.

This book contains comprehensive guides to building City Halls, Houses, Factories, and Entertainment buildings; designing military, economic, and religious vehicles for land, sea, and air; and outfitting your citizenry in the latest fashions. Finally, it also provides a detailed walkthrough of the Civilization Stage and the many ways you can progress through it.

> **NOTE** You'll spend a lot of time creating and customizing vehicles and buildings during the course of the Civilization Stage, much more than you spend in any other stage of the game. Fortunately, every part you can use in the various Creators is available from the very beginning of the stage, so there's nothing to unlock.

Titan of Clumpton

Clumpton Villa

Clumpnaught

Robo Clumpy

Clumpton Industries

Clump Towers

MechaClumpy

building creation

▶ City Hall

Every city in your nation revolves around its City Hall, the central structure where important decisions are made and important scandals are hushed up. As you journey through the Civilization Stage, you use the City Hall to design and build other structures and vehicles, to outfit your citizenry, to compose a national anthem, and much more.

Titan of Clumpton

A Monumental Accomplishment: From the Sphinx to the Statue of Liberty to the secret base inside of George Washington's head in Mount Rushmore, cultures have created buildings that resemble living or mythical creatures. Clumpton is no different. As a reflection of cultural pride—or narcissism running wild—Clumpton's City Hall is the world-renowned Titan of Clumpton, a massive structure that resembles the Clumpys who built it.

 Acicularis (x2)
These serve as the pupils in the Titan's "eyes."

 Esphereal (x2)
Two of these are used for the sky-blue irises in the Titan's peepers.

 Donut (x2)
Donuts compose the whites of the Titan's eyes.

 Antu Receiver
No other device receives more antus, guaranteed.

 Loggia (x5)
This versatile part serves as the Titan's eyestalks, arms, and tail.

 Ponte Vexio
Rotated upside-down, this makes a perfect beak for the Titan.

 Raw Demagogue
When extended, it's the Titan's lower jaw.

 Dollop Habitat (2)
Shrink it down, and it's the Titan's head. Bloat it a bit, and it's the Titan's torso!

 Carousel (x3)
When placed between (and mostly inside) the two Tube Cabins, it makes a dandy bit of decoration.

 Hanging Fang (x6)
The Titan's claws are made up of six Hanging Fangs.

 Egress
It's on the Titan's butt! (Hee hee!)

 Chincook Sensor
We're not sure if this actually works, because there's no record of it ever sensing a single chincook.

 Pedoep (x6)
These form the Titan's six toes.

 Promenada
The Promenada forms the Titan's midriff balcony.

 Archway
This nearly invisible arch buttresses the Titan's torso. (Hee hee! We said "butt" again!)

 Futuro (x2)
Here's the solid foundation on which the Titan stands.

 Pod Bay Doors
These provide access to the balcony on the Titan's tummy, if you can convince HAL to open them.

 Tube Cabin (x6)
The Titan's neck and legs are each made from two of these.

 Vacuum Porthole (x7)
These round portals let in a little natural light and keep the Titan's inhabitants from feeling like a digesting meal.

 Berry Roof (x3)
This tasty top forms the Titan's shoulders and hips.

 Yepun Seeker
This would probably find more yepuns if it wasn't placed on the end of the Titan's tail and pointed straight at the ground.

Constructing the Titan

Building parts don't have any stats, so the only things we had to worry about were our budget and the complexity of our City Hall. We started with a budget of 50,000 (shown in the screen's lower left corner), and an empty Complexity Meter (in the upper right corner). As we added parts, the budget went down and the complexity went up.

1. We started with the Titan's feet, each of which was composed of a Futuro and three Pedoeps.

2. Next, we placed a Tube Cabin and a Carousel on top of each foot to form the Titan's lower legs.

3. We stuck another Tube Cabin on top of each Carousel to complete the legs and dropped an Archway inside them to create a base for the torso.

4. A Berry Roof on each leg formed the hips, and an enlarged Dollop Habitat formed the Titan's ample midsection.

5. To form the Titan's tail, we stuck an Egress on its backside and stretched a Loggia out from it, topping it off with a Yepun Seeker.

6. A Promenada formed the Titan's midriff balcony, and some Pod Bay Doors gave the Clumpys access to it.

7. We stuck on seven Vacuum Portholes and another Berry Roof to finish off the lower half of the Titan.

8. Another Tube Cabin formed the upper torso of the Titan, with a Chincook Sensor for a bit of flair.

9. Two more enlarged and elongated Loggias made great arms...

10. ...and a half dozen Hanging Fangs made for some impressive claws.

11. As we did with the legs, we placed a Carousel on the upper Tube Cabin and surrounded it with another Tube Cabin to make a neck.

12. A Dollop Habitat did the trick for the Titan's head, and the Raw Demagogue made a great lower jaw.

13. An inverted and enlarged Ponte Vexio served nicely as the Titan's beak.

14. Yet another pair of Loggias worked perfectly as the Titan's eyestalks, and an Antu Receiver topped it off nicely.

15. With a shrinking budget and nearly maxed-out Complexity Meter, we added a pair of Donuts to create eyes for the Titan.

16. We had just enough wiggle room left to pop a pair of blue Esphereals and black Acicularises in to complete the Titan's eyes.

NOTE The more complex your City Hall, the more careful you need to be about watching your budget and Complexity Meter. Some examples of other City Halls appear at the end of this section on buildings.

🏠 Houses

The more Houses you have in your cities, the more vehicles your civilization can support. When placed next to Factories and Entertainment buildings, they multiply the productivity and happiness of the city, respectively. They are the bedrock of your communities, and the more you have, the greater your potential for global dominance!

Clumpton Villa

Home Is Where the Head Extends From: Like everything else in Clumpton, its Houses have been designed to evoke the likeness of the Clumpys that live in them. Clumpton Villas are rounded like the Clumpys themselves, and their chimneys resemble a Clumpy head peering over the hedgerow to see what the neighbors are up to.

Acicularis (x2)

Once again, these make excellent pupils for the Villa's eyes.

Esphereal (x2)

A pair of blue irises for the Villa.

Donut (x2)

The whites of the Villa's "eyes."

Smokey Fungi

This mushroom-capped smokestack lets you know that the home fires are still burning.

Loggia (x2)

A pair of these make perfect eyestalks.

Ponte Vexio

Upside-down, it's not much of a balcony, but it makes a great beak.

Up Periscope

We stretched this out to form the Villa's neck.

Vacuum Porthole (x4)

These windows give Clumpys a well-rounded view of the world.

Berry Roof (x3)

There's no more delicious way to top off the Villa.

Industry Light (x5)

These provide plenty of illumination and discourage prowlers.

Hanging Fang (x3)

These evoke the three-toed hands of the Clumpys.

Building Block

It's a block. And you can build with it.

Raw Demagogue

This balcony is the lower jaw of the Villa's head.

Party Favors (x7)

Who doesn't love a weird little curly thing or seven?

Stonewall (x3)

This serves as a reminder to young Clumpys to STAY OFF MY LAWN!

Pod Bay Doors

Only the most modern entrance will do for a Clumpton Villa.

Dollop Habitat (x3)

The whole Villa is built on this trio of spherical structures.

Lawn Art (x3)
A bit of landscaping really brightens the place up.

Raising the Roof

Many of the Villa's unique characteristics, like the Clumpy head jutting up from it, were built using the same parts and methods used for the similar structures in the City Hall. In fact, six of the seven categories of building parts are exactly the same as the City Hall's. The only new one is the Housing category, which replaces the City Hall category.

1. Construction began with a trio of Dollop Habitats of different sizes, for a bit of variety.

2. Next, we did a bit of landscaping with the addition of three Lawn Arts and three Stonewalls.

3. Our Pod Bay Door didn't sit flush against the Dollop Habitat the way we wanted, so we placed a Building Block behind it, partly inside of the Dollop Habitat.

4. Next, we added four Vacuum Portholes for Clumpys to look out of, and three Hanging Fangs to discourage anyone from peeping in through them.

5. Seven Party Favors (extended and curled) and five Industry Lights completed the decoration on the main body of the house.

6. We topped off the Dollop Habitats with three yummy Berry Roofs.

7. Similar to the City Hall, we used an Up Periscope, a Raw Demagogue, and an upside-down Ponte Vexio to start the Clumpy head.

8. Two Loggias and a Smokey Fungi were added to flesh out the eyes and make it clear that the "head" is also a chimney.

9. Finally, we finished off each "eye" with a Donut, an Esphereal, and an Acicularis, just as we did with the City Hall.

NOTE Duplicating design motifs from one building to the next is a great way to create the sense of a unified architectural design in your cities. However, you also should make each building unique, so that you can tell at a glance how many of each you have in your city.

 # Factories

Factories are the beating heart of industry in every city you own. The more Houses you place next to Factories, the more productive your citizens are, and the more Sporebucks they deliver to your civilization's coffers. However, Factories also increase the unhappiness of the citizenry, and all work and no play leads to riots and a huge decline in revenues.

Clumpton Industries

Power from the People: In keeping with the rest of Clumpton's architecture, Clumpton Industries uses similar motifs: Berry Roofs, Pod Bay Doors, and, of course, the distinctive Clumpy head rising into the heavens. As with the other building types, the parts used in its construction have no stats that affect gameplay, and the only things we had to concern ourselves with were the Complexity Meter and our budget.

Acicularis (x2)

As before, these work perfectly for the pupils of the Factory's "eyes."

Esphereal (x2)

These make the blue irises of the Factory's eyes.

Donut (x2)

Donuts are perfect, as always, for the whites of the eyes.

Loggia (x5)

These provide the Factory's eyestalks, neck, and arms.

Fancy Fan

This was installed as a result of some generous contributions by some fancy types.

Hanging Fang (x8)

The claws of the Factory's paws and some additional sharp decor.

Pod Bay Doors

Employees enter through these. Sometimes they're even allowed to leave!

Berry Roof (x5)

Roofs keep the rain off of the workers' heads (a concession to the unions).

Dollop Habitat (x5)

These make up the main body of Clumpton Industries.

Beamed

A bright and not-at-all menacing source of illumination.

Kuba Steamer

This is also great for making mammoth cappuccinos.

Steampunk Mill

Clumpton Industries gets a quarter of its power from wind.

Carbon Vent (x2)

What's a little carbon emission in the name of progress?

Party Favor (x5)

These were used in an unsuccessful attempt at making work fun.

Spotty Light

Now employees have no excuse to stay past sundown!

Criket Pump

What's it pumping, exactly? Better you don't know.

Twirl Gear

This makes a toothy symbol of industry.

Ponte Vexio

This serves as the beak of the Factory head.

Stoking the Fires of Industry

As with the House, our Factory uses many of the same parts and motifs as the City Hall, providing a unified feel to our city's architecture. This was made easier by the number of parts available to all three structures: the Bodies, Roofs, Connectors, Doors, Windows, and Details parts categories contain the same parts as the same categories for the other buildings. Only the 20 parts in the Factory category are unique to Factory construction.

1. We started with a quintet of Dollop Habitats, elongated and squished in the middle. A Pod Bay Door fit nicely on one to provide an entrance.

2. We jazzed things up a bit with five Party Favors, two Hanging Fangs, a Spotty Light, and a Beamed.

3. Each Dollop Habitat is topped with a delicious-looking Berry Roof (which we had to remind the employees not to eat, to avoid bankrupting the company dental plan).

4. More gizmos and gadgetry! A Steampunk Mill, a Fancy Fan, a Twirl Gear, and a Criket Pump all indicate that *something's* going on in there.

5. A pair of Loggias with three Hanging Fangs apiece make up the Factory's "arms."

6. Another Loggia and an overturned Ponte Vexio form the neck and beak of the Clumpy head.

7. Two Carbon Vents and a Kuba Steamer belch out the byproducts of progress.

8. One final pair of Loggias serve as the Factory's eyestalks...

9. ...and a pair of eyes were quickly crafted with the old Acicularis-Esphereal-Donut combo.

NOTE This Factory didn't turn out to be all that complex, but because we used so many Factory parts, we almost blew the budget before we were done. Generally speaking, the generic building parts common to all types of buildings are much cheaper and less complex than the "function parts" unique to that specific building type.

Entertainment

There's more to life than working and sleeping, and that's where Entertainment buildings come in. Each Entertainment building increases the happiness of a city's citizens, and the more Houses placed near it, the greater the happiness-boosting effect. Extremely happy cities will hold celebrations, during which their revenue stream is boosted dramatically. Happy cities are also more difficult for religious rivals to take over. On the other hand, citizens in unhappy cities have frequent protests which stops the production for that city for a period of time.

Clump Towers

Kick Back and Relax: Clump Towers rises high above the Clumpton skyline, emphasizing the high value that the Clumpys place on their leisure time. Instantly recognizable as a Clumpton building, it also maintains a distinctly different look from the city's Houses, Factories, and City Hall. And just like every other building, there are no stats associated with this Entertainment structure's parts, so as long as we didn't make it too complex or blow our budget, we had free rein to design whatever we wanted.

Fire Fly Beams (x3)
These eye-catching lights emphasize the height of the Towers.

Loggia (x2)
As usual, the eyestalks are made of these parts.

Lamski Sign
Your message here! Only 50 Sporebucks!

Vacuum Porthole (x5)
Clumpys who suffer from vertigo are advised to avoid these.

Archway (x3)
Three Archways hidden inside the Dollop Habitats unite the two towers into a single structure.

Cubilous Sign
Some Clumpys will stare transfixed at this for hours without ever entering the building.

Dollop Habitat (x9)
The bodies of both towers are constructed of stretched and pinched Dollop Habitats.

Raw Demagogue (x2)
One of these forms the Towers' lower jaw, and the other sits atop the higher tower.

Ginog Sign
This keeps Clumpys informed of breaking news stories and upcoming events.

Little Beam (x2)
These Entertainment-specific parts serve as the pupils and irises for the Towers' "eyes."

Bubble Tops (x4)
Clumpys young and old love the sight of these bubble-spewing structures.

Berry Roof (x3)
Two of these sit at the foot of the Towers, and the third rests atop the lower tower.

Pod Bay Doors (x3)
These are the only entrances a true Clumpton building needs.

Ponte Vexio
The ever-present beak common to all Clumptown structures.

Donut (x2)
A couple of these serve as the whites of the Towers' eyes.

Building Excitement

Clump Towers uses many of the same parts as Clumpton Villa, Clumpton Industries, and the Titan of Clumpton. We made good use of the part handles on each to give Clump Towers its own unique look, while preserving its visual link to the other Clumpton buildings. We also went a little nuts with the visually appealing Entertainment parts, which are unique to Entertainment buildings.

1. We started with two Dollop Habitats, expanding the bottoms of each, and placed a narrow Archway on top of them.

2. Another pair of Dollop Habitats surrounded the legs of the Archway. The second Archway we placed was off-center, but that wouldn't matter in the finished design.

3. Another pair of Dollop Habitats and another Archway further extended the Towers upward.

4. Three more Dollop Habitats finished off the main body of the Towers.

5. We added a Berry Roof to the top of the lower tower and a pair of them at the towers' feet, with a Pod Bay Door in each.

6. A balcony on the upper tower was made from a Raw Demagogue and a Pod Bay Door. Another Raw Demagogue and a Ponte Vexio made for the beginnings of the Clumpy head.

7. In a modest break from tradition, we used Loggia and Donuts to create the eyestalks, but placed Little Beams in the middle of them to finish off the eyes.

8. And now, a bit of flair! Five Vacuum Portholes, three Fire Fly Lights, and three different sign types jazzed up Clump Towers nicely.

9. Finally, a quartet of Bubble Tops finished off Clump Towers, just barely within budget!

NOTE The four Bubble Tops and multiple flashing lights and signs make it immediately obvious that this is an Entertainment building. This helps to identify at a glance which cities have them, and which cities need them (or risk rioting and religious upheavals).

building creator

The first time you encounter the Building Creator in the Civilization Stage is at the very beginning, when you design your City Hall. Once the stage begins, you can revisit the Building Creator to design Houses, Factories, and Entertainment buildings by pointing to any City Hall you control and clicking on the City Planner.

Each building type appears in a thumbnail image on the left side of the screen. If you have already designed a building of that type, three icons appear below the thumbnail:

Select allows you to replace the building with one in your Sporepedia, or to choose a pre-created building if you haven't already designed one.

Modify takes you back to the Building Creator and lets you edit your existing building.

Create Your Own enables you to start from scratch and design a new building from the ground up.

NOTE If you haven't created or chosen a building for one of the building types, clicking on the icon in the thumbnail image takes you to the Building Creator, where you can design a new building from scratch. You can also click the Select icon below the thumbnail to choose a pre-created building instead.

As mentioned previously, there are no statistics associated with any building parts. The parts you choose have absolutely no effect on gameplay in the Civilization Stage. Your citizens will be just as productive in a Factory made of dozens of complex parts as they would be in a Factory made from a single Building Block. Other than how awesome your building looks, the only things you have to consider are the budget for the building and its complexity.

You start with a budget of 50,000 for your building. (50,000 what? We're not sure.) Every building part has a cost associated with it. All of the parts that are common to each building type cost 500 each. The function parts that are unique to a specific building type cost considerably more. If you break the bank, you're not allowed to purchase any more parts unless you remove some of the parts you've already added.

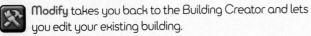
The more parts you add to a building, the more complex it becomes. The size of a building has very little to do with its complexity. Parts with a lot of detail (ridges, spikes, curves, etc.) are more complex than parts with smooth sides and simpler shapes. For instance, the Bristly Abode in the Bodies category of parts is significantly more complex than the Dollop Habitat in the same category. When the Complexity Meter is red and nearly full, you are limited to adding simple parts to your building, unless you remove some of the more complex parts from it first.

NOTE Nothing that you do to a part will make it any more or less complex. Use the part handles to stretch, enlarge, and rotate the part to your heart's content. Slap all sorts of wacky color schemes on it in Paint mode. It won't matter. The part's complexity will not change.

Common Build Parts

Each building has seven categories of parts. Six of them are common to all four building types (Bodies, Roofs, Connectors, Doors, Windows, and Details) and contain the exact same parts. All common build parts cost 500 each.

Bodies

 Cubicle
 Columnar
 Octo-cottage
 Candominium
 Buttresshead
 Castle Ramparts
 Archway
 Octo-Tower

 Bachelor Vat
 Bubble Fab
 Thinkin' Logs
 Octo-Lashings
 Scare-itecture
 Bristly Abode
 Bungle-oh!
 The Haunt

 Futuro
 Deco-Toaster
Maxx Ramparts
Concentricle
Building Block
Tube Cabin
Octa-Roost
Dollop Habitat

Design Hints: Parts in the Bodies category should make up the main part of your structure. Most of them tend to be less complex than other parts, and creative use of the part handles can produce nearly infinite variations, each with its own distinct look. These parts can also overlap with each other and with other parts.

Roofs

 Barn Roof
Civic Roof
Tower Roof
Dome Roof
Narva Roof
Ivangorod Roof
 Merlon Roof
Drum Roof

 Leather Roof
 Stretched Tarp
 Cream Topping
 Berry Roof
 Yagura Roof
 Mempo Roof
 Kabuto Roof
 Himeji Roof

Cake Top Roof
Balboa Roof
Van Alen Roof
Gehry Roof
 Pyramid
 Bivouac
Top Cap
Buckyhome

Design Hints: Roofs don't have to be placed on top of other parts. They can also be laid right down on the ground and built upon. So if you really want to make the A-frame house of your dreams, consider using a Himeji Roof as a base. The Cake Top Roof can be expanded into a ziggurat, and the Pyramid is great for making...well, pyramids.

Connectors

 Colaba Causeway
 Kesher
 Attache
 Connexion
 Overpassed
 Fastenate
 Marry Way
 Weaver

 Correlation Station
 Walkthrough
 Hitch
Promenada
Piazza Della Spora
Portico
Stoa Way
 Ponte Vexio

 Passage
 Veranda
 Jetway
Skywalked
 Rejoinder
 Up Periscope
 Colonanade
Loggia

Design Hints: Connectors can only be attached to other parts. They cannot be placed on the ground or left floating in space. Also, only one end of a connector is the "connecting end." If you're having trouble getting the connector to behave the way you want it to, stick it anywhere it will stay, and then hold down Tab to bring up the advanced part handle options. Try rotating and manipulating the connector until you achieve the desired effect.

Doors

Double Doors	Civics Lesson	Double-Deco	Lancet Columns	Sci-Fi Slider	Cobbled Gate	Drawbridge	Portcullis	Arched Hut Door	Lashed Entrance
Bio Window	Tree Fort	Terror Nook	Horned Portal	Aperture	Egress	Escape Hatch	Pressure Hatch	Irising Opening	Pod Bay Doors

Design Hints: Like Connectors, Doors must be placed against or on top of other parts. Also, be sure to play with the part handles on all of the doors. Almost every door has at least one part handle that changes its shape dramatically. For example, the Tree Fort can sprout leaves or retract its branches into nubby stumps, while the Egress can bare its fangs or retract its horns.

Windows

Glazier Box	Beveled Bay	Porthole	New Colonial	Muntin	Spoorish Lancet	Machicolation	Cobbled Portal	Wishbone Pane	Hearth Hole
Domed Ledge	Amoebic Outlook	Fang Porthole	Trophy Porthole	Gaping Maw	Portal Nostrils	Vacuum Porthole	Bolted Porthole	Window Flaps	Polygon Window

Design Hints: Even the simplest window is more complex than it looks. If you want a building with a lot of windows, stick with simpler ones such as Vacuum Porthole, Machicolation, and Polygon Window (the official window of Aphex Twin Manufacturing). Start placing the windows early in the design process so that you can see how much of a complexity hit you're going to take on them. Also, try stretching them out and seeing if you can achieve the desired effect with fewer windows.

Details

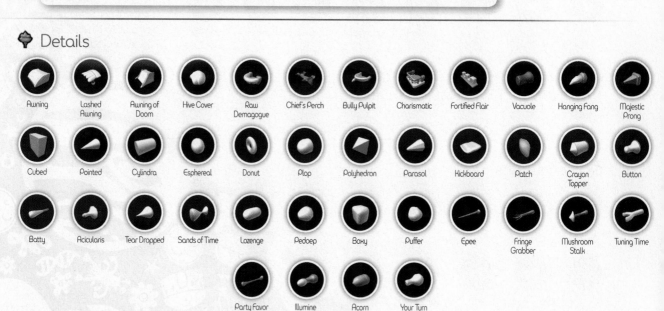

Awning	Lashed Awning	Awning of Doom	Hive Cover	Raw Demagogue	Chief's Perch	Bully Pulpit	Charismatic	Fortified Flair	Vacuole	Hanging Fang	Majestic Prong
Cubed	Pointed	Cylindra	Esphereal	Donut	Plop	Polyhedron	Parasol	Kickboard	Patch	Crayon Topper	Button
Batty	Acicularis	Tear Dropped	Sands of Time	Lozenge	Pedoep	Boxy	Puffer	Epee	Fringe Grabber	Mushroom Stalk	Tuning Time
		Party Favor	Illumine	Acorn	Your Turn						

Design Hints: Use details to finish off your building. By the time you get to adding them, you should have the general structure built, and the details should just be the parsley garnish on the side. You can also use multiple placements of the same details to create a design motif common to all of your buildings. Details usually aren't very complex, so add as many as you want. Finally, be sure to experiment with their part handles, because most details have at least one that dramatically changes the look of the part.

Function Build Parts

Each building type has a seventh category of parts that is unique to that particular building type. The parts in this "function" category are more expensive and complex than the common parts, but they also tend to be the flashiest parts and the ones that can give the building its unique character.

City Hall

 Little Johnny (2,000)
 Friar Tucker (1,500)
 Mad Maid Marian (2,000)
 Sherwood Fawks (2,000)
 Yepun Seeker (3,500)
 Antu Receiver (3,500)
 Qua-Yen Sighter (3,500)
Me-Li-Pal Finder (4,500)

 Levanter Finder (3,500)
 Sciroco Vane (3,500)
 Huba Seeker (3,500)
Chincook Sensor (3,500)
Teepee (500)
Fiercesom (500)
Jefferson (500)
Carousel (500)

Design Hints: City Hall parts, like all function parts, are basically additional details that you can add to make your City Hall more distinctive. The top three rows of parts in the Building Creator all function as Details and must be attached to existing structures. The bottom row of parts, however, behave like Roofs and can be placed on the ground, independent of other parts.

Housing

 Street Lamp (2,500)
 Torchiere (2,500)
 Light Sphere (2,500)
 Industry Light (2,500)
 Black Smoker (2,500)
 Smokey Fungi (2,500)
 Light Cane (2,500)
Picnic Time (500)

 Lawn Art (500)
 Window Boxing (500)
 Wishing Well (500)
 Pajaro Paradiso (2,500)
 Overlook (500)
 Stonewall (500)
Portal (500)
 Entree (500)

Design Hints: Most Housing build parts do not need to be attached to an existing structure. That means that you can use parts like Wishing Well, Stonewall, and Light Cane to do a bit of landscaping. However, keep in mind that Housing parts can be placed on the ground only if they're on the raised circular dais in the middle of the Building Creator, so leave some room there if you want to do this.

Entertainment

 Little Beam (2,500)
 Orbit Shiner (3,500)
 Spot Light (3,500)
 Fire Fly Beams (2,500)
 Daisy May (2,000)
 Viking Horn (2,000)
 Segrada Uva (2,000)
 Anemone Planta (2,000)

 Cublious Sign (2,500)
 Mosko Sign (2,500)
 Lamski Sign (2,500)
 Ginog Sign (2,500)
 Bubble Tops (2,500)
 Old Spewie (2,500)
 Confetti Blower (2,500)
Little Puffer (2,500)

Design Hints: All function build parts are complex and expensive, but this is especially true of the Entertainment parts. If your Complexity Meter is almost maxed out and your coffers are nearly depleted, try enlarging a couple of these parts and see if you can make do with fewer. Place at least a couple these flashy items in prominent places on your Entertainment building so that you can instantly recognize the building type when skimming over your cities.

Factory

 Soot Belcher (2,500)
 Carbon Vent (2,500)
 Beamed (2,500)
Spotty Light (2,500)
Twirl Gear (3,500)
 Fancy Fan (3,500)
Metal Twister (7,500)

 Aqua Swisher (3,500)
 Gear Boxen (4,500)
 Power Converter (4,500)
 Plasma Still (4,500)
 Fission Station (6,000)
Piston Pusher (5,000)
Kuba Steamer (4,500)

 Tire Pouse (5,000)
 Criket Pump (5,000)
 El Quixote (3,500)
 Steampunk Mill (3,500)
 Artisan Mill (3,500)
 Air Powered (3,500)

Design Hints: Factory parts are among the most expensive parts in the Civilization Stage. All of them contain moving or glowing parts, which dramatically increase their complexity cost. If you're planning to use a lot of Factory parts, keep your structure cheap and simple. You might also want to see if one large Factory part can replace several small ones. If you want to design a wind-powered factory, for instance, try placing a couple of huge Artisan Mills on it instead of half a dozen smaller versions of the same part.

Building Examples

On the following pages, you'll find a dozen examples of the four different building types, along with the parts used to create them. Use them for inspiration (or as a warning of what not to do!) as you plan your own structures.

City Halls

The Off-White House

Based on one of the most recognizable seats of power in the world, the Off-White House uses a simple, geometric design that even a novice should be able to duplicate. The main body is a Building Block set atop a squashed Cubicle, lined with Fortified Flair. A Barn Roof overlooks the four Candominium columns, and a Little Johnny flagpole perches on another Cubicle on the roof. Glazier Box and New Colonial windows complete the structure.

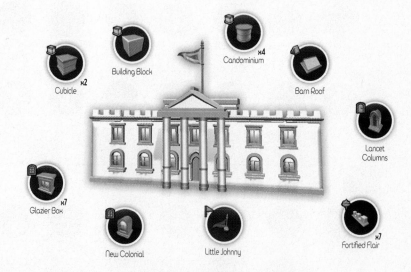

Cubicle x2

Building Block

Candominium x4

Barn Roof

Lancet Columns

Glazier Box x7

New Colonial

Little Johnny

Fortified Flair x7

Eight Flags

Pulled straight from the pages of a fairy tale or the middle of an amusement park, Eight Flags is named for the eight Little Johnnys that flap above each of its Tower Roofs. The main body is composed of Candominiums, Cubicles, and an Octo-cottage, with Spoorish Lancet windows and Fortified Flair attached to them. An Archway surrounds the Drawbridge door, and a Raw Demagogue balcony perches atop it. Note that many of these parts were used in the Off-White House as well, despite the fact that the two City Halls could not be more different.

Octo-cottage

Cubicle x2

Drawbridge

Spoorish Lancet x2

Candominium x6

Little Johnny x8

Archway

Raw Demagogue

Tower Roof x8

Fortified Flair x2

Der Schwarzepalast

This tower was designed for maximum brutality, starting with the four Scare-itectures that make up the main body of it, which is topped off with a Fiercesom. A pair of Stoa ways extend diabolically from it, and a Terror Nook and a Bully Pulpit provide an elevated balcony to look down upon the masses from. Spoorish Lancets, Trophy Portholes, and Portal Nostrils allow light into the bottom half of this dark structure, and an Egress yawns wide at its base for anyone brave—or foolish—enough to enter.

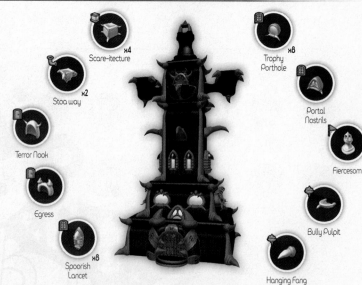

Scare-itecture x4

Trophy Porthole x8

Stoa way x2

Portal Nostrils

Terror Nook

Fiercesom

Egress

Bully Pulpit

Spoorish Lancet x8

Hanging Fang

Houses

Sporf Village

This fungal bungalow is the perfect getaway for little blue folks on the run from alchemic sorcerers and their cats. The base is constructed from a Dollop Habitat, with a Berry Roof on top of it. Four Window Flaps and some Double Doors provide excellent airflow on the first floor. The Smokey Fungi means that there's a fire burning in the hearth. And the charming little attic (made of a Barn Roof and a Glazier Box) is ideal for quiet reflection.

Dollop Habitat

Glazier Box

Window Flaps ×4

Barn Roof

Smokey Fungi

Berry Roof

Double Doors

Boiler Rooms

Judging from the steel plating, the Bolted Portholes, and the four Black Smokers, the Boiler Rooms are probably the preferred residence of a race of *extremely* warm-blooded creatures. The main body is made of a Bachelor Vat and a Bubble Fab, topped with a Balboa Roof. Verandas extend out from it, ending in Bubble Fabs and a Concentricle with a Charismatic balcony and Hive Roof awning attached. Inhabitants enter and exit through Pod Bay Doors inside of an Archway, with an extended Light Sphere overlooking them.

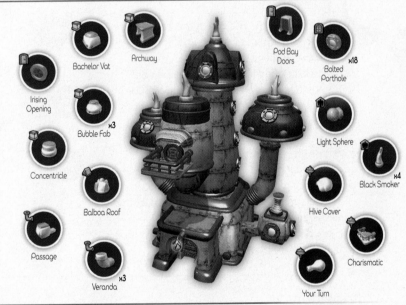

Bachelor Vat

Archway

Pod Bay Doors

Bolted Porthole ×18

Irising Opening

Bubble Fab ×3

Light Sphere

Concentricle

Black Smoker ×4

Balboa Roof

Hive Cover

Charismatic

Passage

Veranda ×3

Your Turn

Twee House

This elevated jungle abode is an example of how an elaborate design need not be all that complex or costly. When we finished this structure, we still had two-fifths of our budget left, and the Complexity Meter was only half-full. The key is the reliance on basic parts, like the nine Thinkin' Logs that make up the ascending pillars and the support pillar in the middle. The hut itself is just an Octo-Lashings with a Stretched Tarp for a roof, and its balcony is made of a Chief's Perch and a Wishbone Pane. Bio Windows and Hitches form the two nests jutting out from the side of the hut. To put things into perspective, the eight multicolored Light Spheres cost twice as much as the rest of the structure and accounted for over half of its complexity!

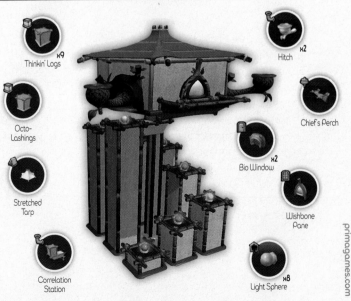

Thinkin' Logs ×9

Hitch ×2

Octo-Lashings

Chief's Perch

Bio Window ×2

Stretched Tarp

Wishbone Pane

Correlation Station

Light Sphere ×8

Factories

Koffwerks

This brick behemoth belches clouds of smoke out into the sky at such a rate that it's no wonder why it lowers the happiness level of any citizens unlucky enough to live near it. Four massive Carbon Vents and 10 Soot Belchers make Koffwerks an asthmatic's nightmare. The main structure is composed of three Columnars and an Octo-cottage, lined with grimy Muntin windows. A Cobbled Portal hangs above the Double Doors entrance, casting its milky glaze upon the workers as they trudge to and from the Factory.

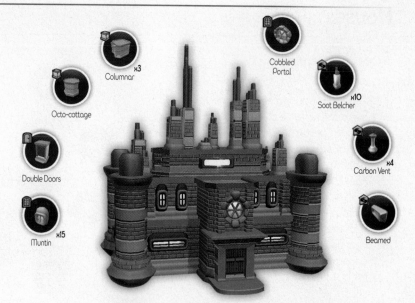

Columnar x3

Octo-cottage

Double Doors

Muntin x15

Cobbled Portal

Soot Belcher x10

Carbon Vent x4

Beamed

Futuro Industries

Futuro Industries, the Factory of the future! (Or, at least, the past's view of what the future would look like.) This space age structure is dominated by the multicolored Skywalkeds that extend from its Dollop Habitats and Tube Cabins. A Twirl Gear and three Fission Stations sit on the balconies, and the Kuba Steamer and pair of Plasma Stills attached to the main structure lets you know that some serious science is going down in there. A single stretched Spotty Light attached to one of the two Van Alen Roofs shines an illuminating beam over the citizens—who don't give a hoot about science and just grumble about that @#$?! light shining through their windows, day and night.

Dollop Habitat x6

Tube Cabin x2

Spotty Light

Twirl Gear

Van Alen Roof x2

Skywalked x9

Pod Bay Doors

Plasma Still x2

Fission Station x3

Kuba Steamer

Millapalooza

Who says that Factories have to trash the environment? Millapalooza's enormous Steampunk Mill harvests all of the wind power this jolly green machine needs to power its four floors of fun, frolic, and frivolity. Three oversized Piston Pushers and a tiny Tire Pouse on the roof keep everything puffing along, and rows of Vacuum Portholes give the lucky working stiffs plenty of natural light. Castle Ramparts and a Buttresshead comprise the main body, with a Cobbled Gate for an entrance.

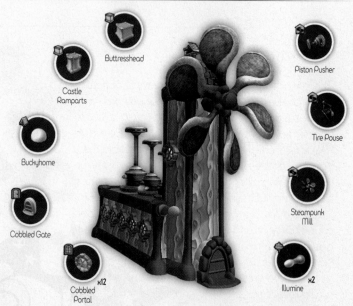

Buttresshead

Castle Ramparts

Buckyhome

Cobbled Gate

Cobbled Portal x12

Piston Pusher

Tire Pouse

Steampunk Mill

Illumine x2

Entertainment

Laff Kastle

Laff Kastle is designed to put a smile on the faces of its guests almost as large as the one it wears on its own facade. Architectural genius or garish disaster? That's for the critics to decide. But with two Ginog Signs, two Confetti Blowers, a big Little Puffer, a pair of Spot Lights, four Little Beams, and six—count 'em, six—Bubble Tops, you can't accuse it of not trying hard enough. The body of the building itself is extremely simple: an extended Octo-cottage with a stretched Tube Cabin in front of it and a Double-Deco door on each side for the patrons. The "eyes" are a pair of Connexions, and the "nose" is a Kesher.

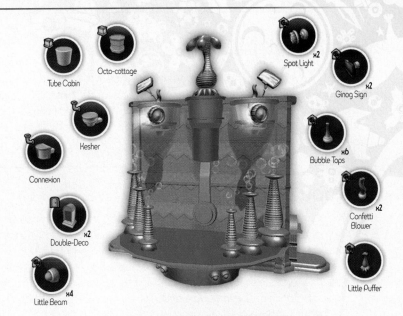

Tube Cabin

Octo-cottage

Spot Light x2

Ginog Sign x2

Kesher

Connexion

Bubble Tops x6

Double-Deco x2

Confetti Blower x2

Little Beam x4

Little Puffer

Funderdome

We're not really sure why this structure is called "Funderdome," when it's clearly not a dome. Regardless, there's no doubt that this simple Entertainment facility has been designed for industrial-strength amusements. The four Cublious Signs that surround its massive Tube Cabin body list the names of the winners and victims of the combat sports inside. The Tube Cabin is topped with The Haunt and a Drum Roof, and four Horned Portals admit new warriors and spectators alike.

The Haunt

Tube Cabin

Drum Roof

Horned Portal

Cublious Sign x4

Hut o' Yucks

Here's an example of how to blow your entire budget on a very simple structure. We're not sure what the appeal of the tiny Hut o' Yucks holds for the limited number of patrons that can fit inside, but it might have something to do with the hypnotic powers of the 16 pricey Fire Fly Beams that line the walls and the Orbit Shiner perched atop the roof. The designers overspent so badly on the glitz that the only other parts in the modest little structure are an Octo-cottage, a Tower Roof, and Lancet Columns.

Octo-cottage

Tower Roof

Lancet Columns

Orbit Shiner

Fire Fly Beams

vehicle creation

🛸 Land Vehicles

One of your very first tasks in the Civilization Stage is to create a prototype land vehicle for your nation. Once this vehicle is designed, you can purchase additional, identical land vehicles from the City Planner (assuming that you have enough Sporebucks and haven't yet reached your vehicle cap). Land vehicles can be used to capture spice geysers and tribal huts, attack wild animals or rival units, or lay siege to an enemy city. They can't cross bodies of water, so their usefulness is limited to the continent that they're first created on.

Robo Clumpy

Part Clumpy, Part Machine, All Business: After getting a glimpse of Clumpton's architecture, it should come as no surprise that their vehicles resemble Clumpys as well. Robo Clumpy is a prime example. This mecha-Clumpy is armed to the eyestalks and ready to obliterate any opposing forces in the name of expanding the glorious Clumpton empire. A good balance of speed, health, and military power ensures that it has no obvious weaknesses.

TIP Speedy vehicles are great early in the game to capture goodie huts and spice nodes.

Plasma Lathe

The bright and shiny "eyes" of the Robo Clumpy.

Celestial Orb

The orbs at the end of Robo Clumpy's eyestalks.

Snow Cone

Part of Robo Clumpy's eyestalks.

Slow and Low

The head of Robo Clumpy.

The Horns

Combined with Snow Cone to complete the eyestalks.

Roadstah

When turned upside-down, this creates the base of the Robo Clumpy.

Wyrm Rider (x2)

These make up Robo Clumpy's craning neck.

Duo Blaster
A further boost to Robo Clumpy's firepower.

War Crime

The guns at the end of Robo Clumpy's arms.

Leggsy

The mechanized legs of the Robo Clumpy.

Duck Bill (x2)

Each arm is made of a pair of Duck Bills.

Split Cabin

Robo Clumpy's operators ride in style in this cockpit.

Ultra Wide-Band

This antenna doubles as a tail.

Building Robo Clumpy

Just like buildings, vehicles have budget and complexity limits. Additionally, most vehicle parts have statistics for health, speed, and/or power (military, religious, or economic) associated with them. These three stats determine how the vehicle performs in combat. We'll get into the nitty gritty details in a bit, but basically, bumping up one stat usually means sacrificing a bit from the other two. For example, if you add several parts that come with health bonuses, your vehicle's health does increase, but its power and speed also drop slightly as a result. For now, however, all you need to know is that we set out to create a well-rounded Clumpy military mech, and here's how we did it:

1. We started with a Roadstah, turned upside-down to provide a flat base to build off of.

2. A Split Cabin with slightly elongated rear made for an excellent cockpit, and a pair of Leggsys served nicely as our mech's means of locomotion.

3. The Duo Blaster we added above the cockpit bumped up our military power considerably, and a narrowed Duck Bill served as the start of each arm.

4. We finished off the arms with another narrowed Duck Bill and a War Crime for each and added an Ultra Wide-Band for a tail. Our military power represented 50 percent of the vehicle's ability at this point.

5. Two tweaked and rotated Wyrm Riders served as the Robo Clumpy's neck, and we used a Slow and Low for the head. These parts' health and speed bonuses evened out the three statistics nicely.

6. To the head, we added The Horns, the start of the Robo Clumpy's eyestalks.

7. We elongated The Horns and stuck an inverted Snow Cone at the end of each one to further develop the eyestalks.

8. Celestial Orbs topped off the eyestalks nicely. Because Detail and Effect parts don't have stats associated with them, nothing that we used for the eyestalks affected the vehicle's stats.

9. We finished off the Robo Clumpy with a Plasma Lathe for each "eyeball," and our beady-eyed wonder was complete!

NOTE As you work with vehicle creation, you'll learn that many parts are bilaterally symmetrical, meaning that placing the part on one side of the vehicle creates a duplicate of it on the other side at no additional cost or complexity. In that sense, creating vehicles is much more similar to creature creation than building construction. The parts we used for the legs, arms, and eyes of the Robo Clumpy all fit this definition, allowing us to stretch our budget further.

⛵ Sea Vehicles

Sea vehicles can be created only in the City Planner of coastal cities. If you don't control any cities on the water, you can't create any sea vehicles. As you can probably guess, they can only travel on water, which prevents them from moving against inland cities and spice geysers. However, they're invaluable for seizing control of and guarding spice geysers in the middle of the ocean, and they can also be used against coastal cities.

Clumpnaught

Scourge of the Seas: Because we decided that Clumpton would be a military civilization, we created the Clumpnaught to be a military sea vehicle. As always, it prominently features a Clumpy head as part of the design, and we used a number of the same design parts as we used for the Robo Clumpy, to preserve a unified design for Clumpton's vehicles. We also decided to focus a little bit more on military power and cut back on speed.

Plasma Lathe

Reprising their role as the Clumpnaught's eyes.

The Horns

Mess with the Clumpnaught, and this is what you get.

Bubble Rider

The head of the Clumpnaught.

Wyrm Rider (x2)

Two of these form the Clumpnaught's neck.

Ultra Wide-Band (x2)

This flashy antenna adds a bit of flair to the Clumpnaught.

Klaxxon

Another bit of bling for the sea vessel.

Plasma Vent

An essential part of the Clumpnaught's cooling system.

Shaft of Light

Good for illuminating the Clumpnaught's path and blinding enemies.

The Nebulizer (x2)

These missile launchers give the Clumpnaught the edge in combat.

Rivahboat

The Clumpnaught's main source of propulsion.

Water Wings

Another source of speed for the Clumpnaught.

Glow Slats (x4)

Placed over the cockpit windows to create a glow effect.

Paddleshot

Another high-powered weapon to bolster the Clumpnaught's firepower.

The Sightseer

The crew quarters of the Clumpnaught.

Cargo Hold

One half of the main body of the Clumpnaught.

The Hotdogger

And here's the other half.

Building Clumpnaught

Not only did we use a lot of the same parts for the Clumpnaught that we used for Robo Clumpy, we also swiped Robo Clumpy's paint scheme by going into Paint mode and selecting one of the "Paint Like..." options at the bottom of the paint palette. This brought up the Sporepedia, and we simply chose the Robo Clumpy to ensure that the Clumpnaught would have the same paint job.

1. We formed the base of the Clumpnaught from The Hotdogger, a Cargo Hold, and The Sightseer.

2. Some carefully resized Glow Slats placed over the cockpit windows created a dramatic glow effect.

3. For propulsion, we added Water Wings and a Rivahboat. At this point, health made up 2/3 of the vehicle's attributes, and speed made up the other 1/3.

4. To beef up our military power, we added a pair of The Nebulizers and a Paddleshot. This gave us 57 percent military power and cut the speed and health by half.

5. We jazzed up the hull with two Ultra Wide-Bands, a Shaft of Light, a Klaxxon, and a Plasma Vent. None of these affected the vehicle's stats.

6. Two Wyrm Riders and a Bubble Rider formed the head and neck of the Clumpnaught. This also boosted its health to 37 percent, mostly at the expense of military power.

7. We stuck The Horns on the Bubble Rider to form eyestalks for the Clumpnaught. This didn't change the stats either.

8. Finally, we placed a Plasma Lathe on The Horns to complete the Clumpnaught—and just in time, since our Complexity Meter was completely maxed out!

NOTE In the Sea Vehicle Creator, you construct your craft on a virtual ocean. To make sure that the vehicle looks right in the game, it's important to place the base of the vehicle on the water line. But if you get halfway through the construction and realize that it's actually hovering above the water, don't panic. Just hold down SHIFT to be able to click and drag the entire vehicle down where it belongs.

✖ Air Vehicles

Air vehicles become available only once you control four cities. Until that point, you can only build land vehicles (and sea vehicles, if you control a coastal city). If you lose control of a few cities and have fewer than four to your name, you also lose the ability to build air vehicles. Once you can build air vehicles, you can build them in every city you control. Because air vehicles can reach any target on land or sea, they're the most valuable vehicles in the game. They're also the most expensive.

MechaClumpy

Clump from Above: Because the Robo Clumpy was so well-rounded and the Clumpnaught emphasized military power, we decided to design an air vehicle that specialized in speed, so that it could quickly reach any target on the planet. Behold: the MechaClumpy, a fairly durable military air vehicle that's light on firepower but has more wings and turbines than an airport runway. We're not sure exactly how this less-than-aerodynamic vehicle actually keeps itself in the air, but we're not about to jinx anything by asking too many questions.

Military Air ✖

The Horns

These continue to serve nicely as Mecha-Clumpy's eyestalks.

Slow and Low

MechaClumpy's head.

Plasma Lathe

Once again, this forms Mecha-Clumpy's eyes.

Wyrm Rider (x2)

Two of these form MechaClumpy's neck.

Commercial Jet

Another speed-boosting bit for MechaClumpy.

Trident Ray
MechaClumpy's only weapon system is a good one.

Thermojet (x2)

Two of these give MechaClumpy its tremendous speed.

Armored Flight

Another set of wings for Mecha-Clumpy.

Quantum Jet (x3)

MechaClumpy's arms are built from these.

Mech-Wing

The giant pair of wings on Mecha-Clumpy's back.

Sporeman Grill

A vehicle as complex as this needs some serious cooling.

Tapered Brick

This forms MechaClumpy's shoulders.

Buoy o Buoy

MechaClumpy's lower thrusters are attached to these.

Cargo Hold

One of the three parts that make up Mecha-Clumpy's main body.

The Stapeler

The second of MechaClumpy's main body parts.

Inscrutable Eye

This cockpit is the third of MechaClumpy's three main body parts.

Building MechaClumpy

MechaClumpy was by far the most complex of the three Clumpton vehicles we constructed. Part placement required a great deal of fine-tuning, and toward the end, we kept running up against the complexity limit. For instance, our original plan called for full legs for MechaClumpy instead of thrusters, but we just didn't have room for them. Most of MechaClumpy's parts were shrunken, enlarged, stretched, compressed, or rotated in one or more directions, and the advanced part handle options (accessed by holding down TAB) proved to be invaluable.

1. We started by forming Mecha-Clumpy's main body from an Inscrutable Eye and a Cargo Hold placed almost completely inside of The Stapeler so that only the corners protruded.

2. A Tapered Brick across Mecha-Clumpy's back formed its shoulders, and we fit a Buoy o Buoy on either side of the cockpit.

3. We attached Mech-Wings to the Tapered Brick shoulders, boosting Mecha-Clumpy's speed to 43 percent. We also added a Sporeman Grill for looks, which had no effect on the stats.

4. Each of Mecha-Clumpy's arms was constructed from three Quantum Jets and carefully rotated into position.

5. We then added a speed-boosting Armored Flight wing to each forearm and a Trident Ray to the end of each arm.

6. A Wyrm Rider formed the start of Mecha-Clumpy's neck. We also added Turbojets to the top and bottom of the vehicle, as well as a pair of Commercial Jets, raising the speed to 55 percent.

7. Another Wyrm Rider and a Slow and Low finished off the neck and head of Mecha-Clumpy.

8. We created Mecha-Clumpy's eyestalks from The Horns, and rotated them so that they faced forward.

9. Finally, we added Plasma Lathes to the ends of The Horns, completing the eyestalks and the vehicle as a whole.

NOTE Bodies and Cockpit parts automatically snap to the center line of the vehicle that you're creating. That means that you can't use them to create parts that jut out from the main body of the vehicle, like MechaClumpy's arms do. Use parts from the other four categories to achieve this effect, keeping in mind that anything placed off of the center line will be echoed symmetrically on both sides of the vehicle.

vehicle creator

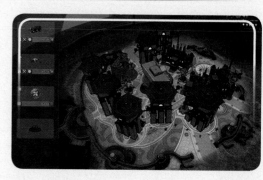

You must create your land vehicle at the start of the Civilization Stage. Air and sea vehicles are created at the City Hall in any of your cities. To create a vehicle, click the City Planner icon that appears when you point at the City Hall. Click the **Vehicles** tab in the upper left corner to bring up a column of vehicle thumbnail images similar to the building thumbnails you saw earlier in the Building Creator.

If you've already created a vehicle type, click the "Buy" button (the + icon below its thumbnail) to order another one to be built instantaneously. The vehicle cost, in Sporebucks, appears to the left of the "Buy" button. "Select," "Modify," and "Create Your Own" buttons also appear below the thumbnail and have the same functions as the same buttons in the Building Creator.

If you haven't created a certain type of vehicle yet, but you have fulfilled the conditions for being able to do so (see table), a blue icon appears in the thumbnail box. Click it to enter the Vehicle Creator and design the vehicle. You can also click the "Select" button below it to pick a pre-created vehicle from the Sporepedia.

If you have not fulfilled the conditions for being able to build a vehicle type (see table), you get a gray icon instead of a thumbnail. This changes to blue icon if you satisfy the conditions for being able to build this vehicle type. Click the blue icon to design or select your vehicle.

NOTE You can also buy additional vehicles without entering the City Planner. Point to any City Hall and click the vehicle icons below the City Planner icon to instantly buy a vehicle of that type. If a vehicle icon is grayed out, that vehicle cannot be bought because it's not available or you haven't designed it yet.

Vehicle Creation Conditions

Vehicle Type	Cost	Conditions
Land	1,000	Must control at least one city
Sea	1,500	Can only be built in coastal cities
Air	2,000	Must control four cities

NOTE You've probably also noticed that there's a grayed-out spaceship icon in the City Planner as well. You need to gain control of all 12 cities on the planet to be able to design and build a spaceship. Doing so ends the Civilization Stage of Spore and starts the Space Stage.

Like buildings, vehicles have budget and complexity limits, represented by the same meters as in the Building Creator. If the part icons in the Vehicle Creator start turning red, it's because you're coming dangerously close to maxing out your budget or the complexity of the vehicle.

Each vehicle also has three statistics: speed, health, and power (religious, economic, or military). Most vehicle parts also have one or more of these statistics, and adding a part bumps up the stat(s) associated with it. However, your vehicle's rating in each of the stats isn't determined by how many parts you add that have that stat. It's determined by each stat's percentage of the total number of stat points.

For example, a vehicle built from parts that have a total of 10 speed points, 5 health points, and 5 power points would have the same stats as a vehicle whose parts total 2 speed points, 1 health point, and 1 power point. That's because, in both cases, 50 percent of the stat points are speed points, 25 percent are health points, and 25 percent are power points. Therefore, both vehicles would have 50 percent speed, 25 percent power, and 25 percent power and would perform identically in the game.

NOTE A perfectly well-rounded vehicle would have 33 percent in each statistic. Any stat above 33 percent is therefore above average, and any stat below 33 percent is below average.

Because the stat percentages always have to add up to 100, it's impossible to raise one stat without lowering at least one of the other two. That means that you have to decide what your vehicle's strengths and weaknesses are going to be before you finish building it.

TIP If you find that the vehicle you created doesn't mesh well with your play style, you can always return to the City Planner and click the "Modify" button under the vehicle's thumbnail to edit it and adjust its stats.

Speed Strategies

Vehicles with high speed can reach their targets more quickly. They can also cut and run from battles that aren't going their way and stand a much better chance of outrunning any pursuers. And that's a good thing, because speedy vehicles have to sacrifice health and/or power, which puts them at a disadvantage when the shooting starts. Still, individually fast but weak vehicles can swarm over their rivals, overwhelming them with numbers before they can react.

TIP Speed is a great characteristic for economic vehicles to have. One of the major goals in an economic strategy is to develop trade routes, and the faster your vehicles move, the more frequently they'll be able to run the trade route.

Health Strategies

The higher a vehicle's health, the longer it can withstand enemy fire. High health is a good way to protect your investments in vehicles; repairing damaged vehicles is free, but replacing destroyed ones can get expensive. If you're a military or religious culture, your vehicles will come under fire more often than those of economic cultures, so you should have at least average health.

CAUTION Don't compromise too much on your power for the sake of boosting health, especially if you're a military civilization. The advantage of having more durable vehicles is erased if a low military power stat increases the amount of time it takes for your vehicles to destroy your enemies'.

Power Strategies

Power is a generic term that describes your vehicles' ability to carry out the strategy you've chosen. For military vehicles, power is firepower that destroys enemy units and brings city walls crashing down. For religious units, it's a measure of how quickly they can convert rival cities and shatter enemy vehicles. And for economic vehicles, power determines the amount of Sporebucks earned on each stop in a trade route.

NOTE We'll go into detail on the three strategies in the walkthrough. For now, just think of power as a measure of how good the vehicle is at getting the upper hand on rival cities and units.

Common Build Parts

Each vehicle has six categories of parts. Four of them are common to all four building types (Bodies, Cockpit, Effect, and Detail) and contain the exact same parts.

Bodies

Slow and Low	Trailfin	Roadstah	Battle Ready	Tear Drop-ship	Catchamaran	Skiffy Skiff	YoHoHoBoat	Stubbybubble	Aft Bluster	Hulldragger	Airbreather
(200)	(200)	(200)	(200)	(100)	(200)	(200)	(200)	(200)	(200)	(200)	(200)

Light Venom	Vetted	Ghost Rocket	Girded Saucer	Smooth Lozenge	Tipped Plug	Astro Kernel	Pointed Node	Void Chaser	Crying Onion	Cosmic Flare	Comet Wasp
(200)	(200)	(200)	(200)	(100)	(100)	(100)	(100)	(100)	(100)	(100)	(100)

Tapered Bulge	Shellbeak	Bird of Prey	Ridged Cabin	Cubby	Tubed	Dunce Cap	Orbed	Breadboxen	The Cowbell	More Cowbell	Sapphire Body
(100)	(100)	(100)	(100)	(100)	(100)	(100)	(100)	(100)	(100)	(100)	(100)

Flying Toaster (100) · Event Horizon (100) · Wimp (100) · Macho (100) · The Sleekstream (200) · Bubble Rider (200) · Flying Anvil (200) · The Hotdogger (200) · Tippy Canoe (100) · The Hawt Tub (200) · Roe Boat (200) · Caviar Cruiser (200)

Strutter (100) · The Stapeler (200) · Jet Stream (200) · Wyrm Rider (200) · Astro-Rocket (200) · The Lozengator (200) · Horseshoe Flyer (200) · Star Deployer (200) · Cargo Hold (100) · Tapered Brick (100) · Beveled Lozenge (100) · Kessel Runner (100)

NOTE Parts in the Bodies category always snap to the center line in the Vehicle Creator. Some are a bit on the pricey side, but they tend not to be too complex. Bodies provide a base to build the rest of the vehicle off of. You can overlap Bodies with other parts to create new shapes. You can also rotate them so that they face forward or backward, or you can create symmetrical intertwined pairs of parts by rotating them away from the center line. All Bodies have health and/or speed stats associated with them.

Cockpit

Exsporatorium (100) · Lander Capsule (100) · Chill Bubble (100) · Fly Cuspid (200) · Moon Men (100) · Inscrutable Eye (100) · Bubblecraft (200) · Glass Elevator (200) · Recessed Bay (100) · Clipped Cone (200) · Gondola (200) · Conning Tower (200)

Viewing Pod (100) · Advance Scout (200) · Sleek Fighter (200) · Executive Suite (200) · Utility Cockpit (200) · Split Cabin (200) · The Sightseer (200) · Blue Thunder (200) · Colonial Camper (100) · Flarestream (100) · Flying Car (200) · Mid-Life Crisis (200)

The Viewfinder (100) · The Sar (200) · Speed Eraser (200) · Bubblerider (200) · The Viewkeeper (100) · Starseed (200) · Star Whisp (200) · Viewmaster (200)

NOTE Like Bodies, Cockpits always snap to the center line in the Vehicle Creator. They are similarly priced, but they're also slightly more complex than Bodies. You can use Cockpit parts as building bases and attach other parts to them, or overlap other parts with them. You can also rotate them forward and backward, or create intertwined pairs by rotating them away from the center line. All Cockpits have speed and/or health stats associated with them.

Effect

All Effect parts cost 25 each.

| Singularitron | Premium Service | Wide-band | Plasma Vent | Port Hole | The Looktangle | Side View | Nemo Peeper | Shaft of Light | Holding Pattern | Authority | Roving Spot |

| Glow Slats | Smog Light | Ring of Light | Anthropomorph | Tri-Beams | Crystal Ball | Plasma Lathe | Photo Deco | The Glowcone | The Glowport | Portal of Light | Klaxxon |

| Night Light | Glowing Nose | Camping Torch | Halcyon Days | Photon Cover | Glowbubble | Shine Lozenge | Old 57 |

> **NOTE** Unlike Bodies and Cockpits, Effects have no stats associated with them, and they must be attached to an existing structure. Effects are also bilaterally symmetrical, so placing an Effect on one side of the vehicle duplicates it on the other side. Many Effects glow, which makes them more complex than parts that don't. However, they're also dirt cheap, so if your vehicle isn't very complex, you can add quite a few of them, even if your budget is running low.

Detail

All Effect parts cost 25 each.

| Bendy Band | Classin' It Up | Brood Ornament | The Coat Hook | Hermes | Mercurial | Bat-Borne | Zoomerang | Ice Cubed | Sillynder | Snow Cone | Celestial Orb |

| Flower Power | Spazzberry | Deedly-Bopper | Wunderstar | Trellis | Die-Cut Plate | Sturdy Strut | Coaster Harness | Gas Sublimator | Plasma Duct | Quantum Jet | NOS Combustor |

| Sporeman Grill | Steampunk'd | Roadsterama | Spacetime Grill | Spore Spoiler | Spoiled Rotten | Space-burner | Whale Tailed | Bicycle Seat | Back Tooth | Duck Bill | Tear Drop |

| The Horns | Ultra Wide-Band | Space Whiskers | Craft Beanie | Storm Chaser | Eraser | Buoy o Buoy | Chapeau | Clam Shell | Space of Ades | Crescent Phase | Hedge-Row |

> **NOTE** Details are very similar to Effects: they have no stats, they only cost 25 apiece, they must be placed on existing structures, and they're bilaterally symmetric. They're also generally less complex than Effects, which is good for your Complexity Meter. If you want to build parts that jut out from the vehicle (like MechaClumpy's arms), these are the parts to go with.

Vehicle Type Build Parts

Each vehicle is designed to operate on land, in water, or in the air. Depending on the vehicle, you get one category of parts that corresponds to its type. Land vehicles get Land parts, air vehicles get Air parts, and sea vehicles get Water parts.

Land

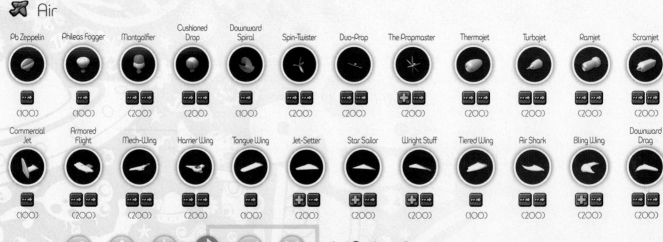

Spinmill	Rocket Keg	Carbon Belcher	Swamp Heater	Weft Coil	Tread Smartly	Making Tracks	Batterpillar	Bespoked	Wagon Wheel
(100)	(200)	(200)	(300)	(100)	(200)	(200)	(200)	(200)	(200)

Cart Wheel	Fly Wheel	Dune Buggy	Track Marker	Red Rover	Sunday X3	Slip Gripper	Drag Eraser	Dust Eater	Burn Rubber
(200)	(200)	(100)	(200)	(200)	(200)	(100)	(100)	(200)	(200)

Formula Won	The Go-Ped	Wheel Well	The Chariot	Locomoleg	Mechpedal	Leggsy	Crawler
(200)	(300)	(300)	(300)	(200)	(200)	(200)	(200)

Water

Craft Propeller	Hooded Turbine	Jet Propulsion	Propeller Box	Aquatic Fan	Bilateral Oars	Rivahboat	Fluid Turbine	Grobby Paddle	Voidstroker
(100)	(200)	(200)	(200)	(100)	(200)	(200)	(200)	(100)	(100)

Hydraulic Oar	Antimatter Fan	Mainsail Ahoy	Scurvy Canine	Spinnaker	Fine Junk	Water Skis	Aqua Sled	Water Wings	Hydroplane
(200)	(200)	(100)	(200)	(200)	(200)	(200)	(200)	(200)	(200)

Air

Pb Zeppelin	Phileas Fogger	Montgolfier	Cushioned Drop	Downward Spiral	Spin-Twister	Duo-Prop	The Propmaster	Thermojet	Turbojet	Ramjet	Scramjet
(100)	(100)	(200)	(200)	(100)	(200)	(200)	(200)	(200)	(200)	(200)	(200)

Commercial Jet	Armored Flight	Mech-Wing	Harrier Wing	Tongue Wing	Jet-Setter	Star Sailor	Wright Stuff	Tiered Wing	Air Shark	Bling Wing	Downward Drag
(100)	(200)	(200)	(200)	(100)	(200)	(200)	(200)	(100)	(200)	(200)	(200)

Helix Wing	Spoar	Ornithopteryx.	Air Cutter	Bat Flapper	Archaeoptery	Dorsal Crest	Urvogel

(100)	(200)	(200)	(200)	(100)	(200)	(200)	(200)

Power Parts

Each city is designated as either a military city, an economic city, or a religious city. This determines the strategy that the city's forces use to take over other cities. We'll talk more about the three strategies in the walkthrough section of this chapter, but for now, all you need to know is that each vehicle has a set of power parts that reflects the strategy of the city it's built in. The only way to increase a vehicle's economic, military, or religious power is to add parts to it from this power category.

> **NOTE** Power parts behave like Details and Effects. They're bilaterally symmetrical, and they have to be attached to existing parts. They also tend to be fairly complex and expensive. Power parts are arranged into four columns in the Vehicle Creator. The leftmost column contains the cheapest and least powerful parts, and the right column features the most expensive and powerful ones.

⚔ Military

Some of these weapons are unique to *sea, **land, and/or ***air vehicles.

*Comet Duster	*Meteor Mister	*Asteroid Belter	*The Nebulizer	**Bombardier	**Ye Olde Cannon	**Boom Rocket	**Undue Force	***Astro-Ray	***Space Modulator

✗✗✗✗	✗✗✗✗	✗✗✗✗	✗✗✗✗	✗✗✗✗	✗✗✗✗	✗✗✗✗	✗✗✗✗	✗✗✗✗	✗✗✗✗
(100)	(200)	(300)	(400)	(100)	(200)	(300)	(400)	(100)	(200)

***The Cauterizer	***Trident Ray	Uranium Gun	Fortune Hunter	Planet Sniper	War Crime	Tuber Gun	Duo Blaster	Spinfire	Paddleshot
✗✗✗✗	✗✗✗✗	✗✗✗✗	✗✗✗✗	✗✗✗✗	✗✗✗✗	✗✗✗✗	✗✗✗✗	✗✗✗✗	✗✗✗✗
(300)	(400)	(100)	(200)	(300)	(400)	(100)	(200)	(300)	(400)

💰 Economic

Stacked	Grab Bag	Bully Bullion	Overcompensator	Coin-siderate	Merit Badge	High Roller	Charmed Quark

💰💰💰💰	💰💰💰💰	💰💰💰💰	💰💰💰💰	💰💰💰💰	💰💰💰💰	💰💰💰💰	💰💰💰💰
(100)	(200)	(300)	(400)	(100)	(200)	(300)	(400)

Ho Hum Heraldry	Banner Day	Standard Bearer	Vexillum Verus	Apogee	Binary Suns	Wings of Flame	Hanging Crests
💰💰💰💰	💰💰💰💰	💰💰💰💰	💰💰💰💰	💰💰💰💰	💰💰💰💰	💰💰💰💰	💰💰💰💰
(100)	(200)	(300)	(400)	(100)	(200)	(300)	(400)

✳ Religious

Squawk Box	Charisma Nest	Sousaphone	Goes to 11	Shofar Victrola	Gammaphone	Crazaphone	Pi Piper
✳✳✳✳	✳✳✳✳	✳✳✳✳	✳✳✳✳	✳✳✳✳	✳✳✳✳	✳✳✳✳	✳✳✳✳
(100)	(200)	(300)	(400)	(100)	(200)	(300)	(400)

Note of Accord	The Harmonium	Sensual Harp	Harp's Accord	Kick-Thumper	Cymbal Crasher	Clarion Bell	Bombastic Gong

✳✳✳✳	✳✳✳✳	✳✳✳✳	✳✳✳✳	✳✳✳✳	✳✳✳✳	✳✳✳✳	✳✳✳✳
(100)	(200)	(300)	(400)	(100)	(200)	(300)	(400)

Vehicle Examples

On the next several pages, you'll find a dozen and a half examples of vehicles we created: two religious, military, and economic styles of land, air, and sea vehicles. As you'll see, there's practically no limit to the versatility of the Vehicle Creator, and we didn't even scratch the surface.

Land Vehicles

FRED-209

FRED-209 is an experiment in fully automated law enforcement. Nearly half of its stats are devoted to military power, which makes it a formidable force on the battlefield (and, in one regrettable instance, the boardroom). FRED is armed to the teeth with War Crimes and Spinfires and is propelled by Carbon Belchers and a pair of Locomolegs. Smog Lights, Shaft of Lights, and an Authority make sure that everyone sees FRED coming, which dramatically reduces civilian injuries. And despite all of the Effects and Details that enhance FRED's menacing appearance, the whole vehicle is based around a simple combination of a Bubble Rider and The Stapeler.

Bubblerider · The Stapeler · Smog Light x2 · Celestial Orb · Locomoleg · Carbon Belcher · War Crime · Plasma Duct x2 · Plasma Vent · Spinfire · Spacetime Grill · NOS Combustor · The Looktangle · Shaft of Light · Authority · Back Tooth · Eraser · Quantum Jet

Combined SPC

The Combined **S**hielded **P**ersonnel **C**arrier is a heavily armored all-terrain vehicle capable of dominating any field of battle. Its greatest strength is its high health, which makes up over 50 percent of the vehicle's stats. It owes its defensive prowess to health-boosting armored parts like Utility Cockpit, multiple Cubbys, and The Cowbell, while its Spinfire and Paddleshot make sure that its targets don't escape with even half a life.

Battle Ready · Hulldragger · Shellbeak · Cubby x5 · Roving Spot · Tri-Beams · Coaster Harness · Breadboxen · The Cowbell · Glow Slats · Gas Sublimator x2 · Trellis · NOS Combustor · Beveled Lozenge · Quantum Jet · Utility Cockpit · Red Rover x2 · Spinfire · Paddleshot · Singularitron x3 · Premium Service · Plasma Duct · Wimp

Pretty Freight Machine

The Pretty Freight Machine is designed to drive the hard bargain along trade routes and maximize profits. It's not heavily armored, and its speed is average at best, but if it can avoid hostiles, nothing brings in the Sporebucks at a faster clip. Its Overcompensator, High Roller, and Hanging Crests are responsible for its high economic power stat. The rest of this surprisingly affordable vehicle isn't much more than a Breadboxen and a Flare-stream on two pairs of Wheel Wells.

Breadboxen · Hanging Crests · High Roller · Flarestream · Spore Spoiler x2 · Burn Rubber · Wheel Well x2 · Steampunk'd · Overcompensator · The Glowport · Portal of Light

Money Spider

This affluent arachnid is a juggernaut of commerce, propelled along by four pairs of Crawlers. A Bully Bullion, a Grab Bag, and two Banner Days boost the Money Spider's economic power over the 50 percent mark. The main body of the vehicle is just a Crying Onion and a Comet Wasp overlapping each other, and its top hat is just a pair of manipulated Sillynders. A handful of Details rounds out the Money Spider's classy appearance.

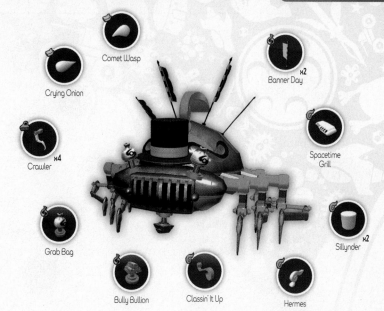

Comet Wasp · Crying Onion · Banner Day x2 · Crawler x4 · Spacetime Grill · Grab Bag · Sillynder x2 · Bully Bullion · Classin' It Up · Hermes

Marshal Law

The Marshal Law roars around on two pairs of Drag Erasers, passing judgment on everyone within earshot. And thanks to its Pi Piper and Goes to 11, that's just about everyone. Its multiple light Effects draw even more attention to itself and discourage unbelievers from looking directly at it. The body is composed of a Roadstah, a Ridged Cabin, a Tubed, a Flying Car, and three Beveled Lozenges, but we'll leave you to puzzle out how they all fit together. Extra credit: Can you figure out how we made that grill out of one Steampunk'd?

Goes to 11 · Ridged Cabin · Roadstah · Steampunk'd · Roadsterama · Drag Eraser · Tubed · Quantum Jet · Wunderstar · Flying Toaster · Camping Torch · The Glowport · Beveled Lozenge · Authority · Flying Car · Pi Piper · Wide-band · Shaft of Light · Klaxxon · Portal of Light

God Head

The name of this exotic religious vehicle literally translates as "God Head," but much of the beauty of the name is lost in translation from the musical language of the monks who constructed it. The God Head's unusual design captivates onlookers. It's based around an Astro Kernel (forehead), two Orbeds (head), a Tapered Bulge and Beveled Lozenge (nose), a Celestial Orb and Duck Bill (ears), a Flying Toaster (base), and a stretched Ghost Rocket (hat). The holy music played on its Pi Piper, Kick-Thumper, Cymbal Crasher, and Clarion Bell transports listeners into a transcendent state, mesmerized by the Crystal Ball on the God Head's forehead, symbolizing enlightenment and the truth and beauty in all things.

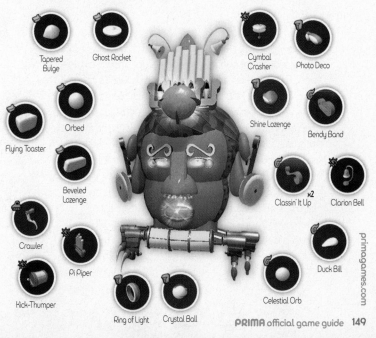

Tapered Bulge · Ghost Rocket · Cymbal Crasher · Photo Deco · Orbed · Shine Lozenge · Bendy Band · Flying Toaster · Beveled Lozenge · Classin' It Up x2 · Clarion Bell · Crawler · Pi Piper · Duck Bill · Kick-Thumper · Celestial Orb · Ring of Light · Crystal Ball

Sea Vehicles

Waveclumper

The Waveclumper was our first attempt at creating a fast, light military sea vessel for the inhabitants of Clumpton. Its two sources of speed are a Rivahboat on the back of the vessel and three pairs of Hydraulic Oars. The trademark Clumpy head is just a Slow and Low with Plasma Lathes encircled by Rings of Light for eyes, and the arms are a Horseshoe Flyer with Tuber Guns at each end. A Spinfire and a Comet Duster round out the Waveclumper's offensive capabilities.

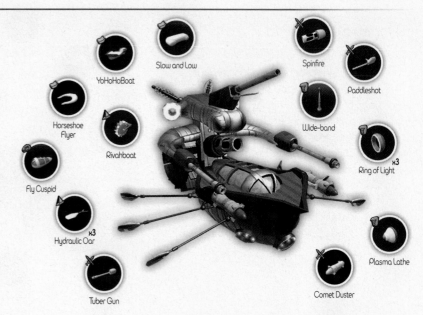

YoHoHoBoat

Slow and Low

Spinfire

Horseshoe Flyer

Paddleshot

Rivahboat

Wide-band

Fly Cuspid

Ring of Light x3

Hydraulic Oar x3

Plasma Lathe

Tuber Gun

Comet Duster

Water Sporepion

This scaly, speedy military sea vehicle's War Crime and Duo Blasters give it a nasty sting, and its Hydraulic Oars and Bilateral Oars ensure that it can escape from any fight that isn't going its way. Its massive tail is a Horseshoe Flyer embedded in a Wyrm Rider, which (along with a Roadstah) makes up the main body of the vehicle. If any of these parts sound familiar, it's because this is what the Waveclumper turned into after we decided to take a different approach for Clumpyton's naval armada!

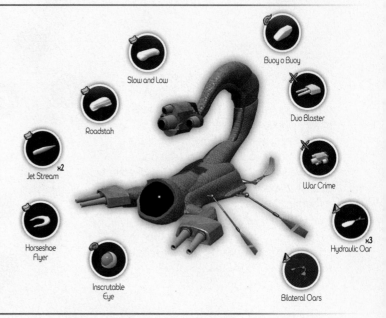

Slow and Low

Buoy o Buoy

Roadstah

Duo Blaster

Jet Stream x2

War Crime

Horseshoe Flyer

Hydraulic Oar x3

Inscrutable Eye

Bilateral Oars

Miss Sip

Ah, the life of the riverboat gambler! Wine, women, and celebrations when your luck is up, and a voyage spent washing pots in the mess hall when it's down. Miss Sip is a luxury gaming yacht that runs along trade routes, picking up vacationers, newlyweds, and folks who just plain get the itch to play some cards. Its Rivahboat is its sole means of propulsion, which accounts for its lethargic speed. But its durable hull and quarters (made from a Catchamaran, a Conning Tower, two Glass Elevators, and three Flarestreams) give it average health, and its Charmed Quark, Stacked, and multiple Vexillum Veruses boost its economic percentage so high that it's a sure bet that the house will always win.

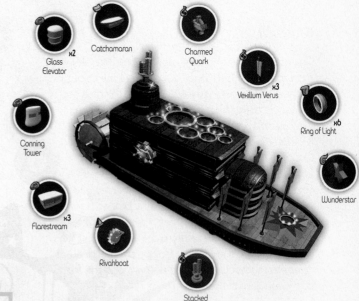

Glass Elevator x2

Catchamaran

Charmed Quark

Vexillum Verus x3

Conning Tower

Ring of Light x6

Flarestream x3

Wunderstar

Rivahboat

Stacked

Goldbug

Ladies and gentlemen, may we present what is possibly the least seaworthy craft ever built. Goldbug has a meager 5 percent health stat, almost 12 times less than its economic power. The multiple placements of Coin-siderates across its back (made of a Comet Wasp) might look pretty, but they'll be on the bottom of the ocean if the Goldbug doesn't steer very clear of trouble with its Antimatter Fans.

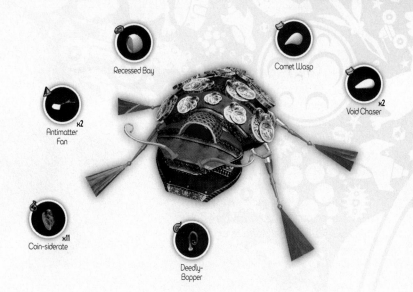

Recessed Bay

Comet Wasp

Void Chaser ×2

Antimatter Fan ×2

Coin-siderate ×11

Deedly-Bopper

King Red

According to legend, the prototype for King Red was a talking boat that steered into port one day looking for its master: a young boy dressed in green, who was supposed to be the legendary hero of a distant land. When asked where this land was, the boat only replied, "I rule!" Eventually, it left to continue its search, but not before inspiring a cult of followers who sail out to sea and play brassy melodies on their Crazaphones, Squawk Boxes, and Bombastic Gongs in an attempt to wake the wind itself.

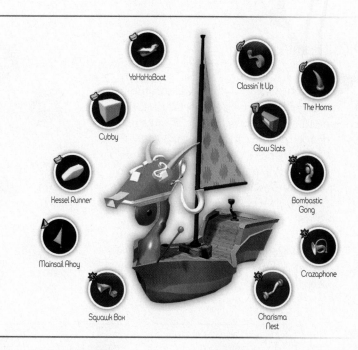

YoHoHoBoat

Classin' It Up

The Horns

Cubby

Glow Slats

Kessel Runner

Bombastic Gong

Mainsail Ahoy

Crazaphone

Squawk Box

Charisma Nest

Hopemobile

This well-rounded religious sea vehicle features an enlarged Utility Cockpit surrounded by sheets of revolutionary translucent polymers guaranteed to protect even the least popular self-proclaimed demigod from the reprisals of an angry mob. Its multiple horns (Squawk Box, Crazaphone, Goes to 11) broadcast your spiritual messages loud and clear across the waves, and its slightly above-average speed comes in handy if the locals take a dislike to what you're preaching.

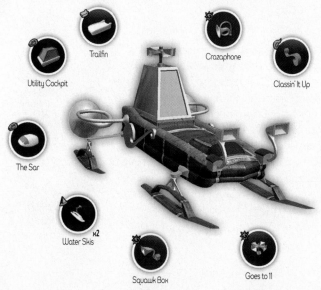

Trailfin

Crazaphone

Utility Cockpit

Classin' It Up

The Sar

Water Skis ×2

Squawk Box

Goes to 11

Air Vehicles

Sporelon Raider

Sporelon Raiders have slightly above-average speed and military power and slightly below average health. There are unconfirmed rumors that the reason they aren't more heavily armored is that they are unmanned drones. Silent and lethal, the Raider's inverted Horseshoe Flyer wings are instantly recognizable from a distance, giving the sharp-eyed a chance to protect themselves against the Raider's Fortune Hunters and Planet Snipers.

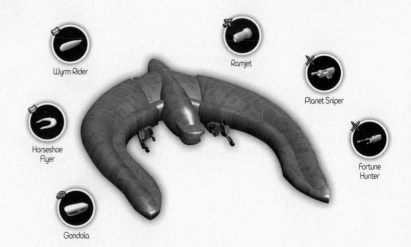

Wyrm Rider

Ramjet

Planet Sniper

Horseshoe Flyer

Fortune Hunter

Gondola

Clumpwing

This early Clumpton air vehicle attempt showed some promise, especially in its high military power rating, but we ultimately decided it just wasn't...mecha enough. Still, the Clumpy head—a Roadstah and a Gondola perched atop a Whale Tailed, with Plasma Lathes on Roving Spots for eyes, and a Glowing Nose and Zoomerang for flair—looks almost aerodynamic. And the quad-wing design (two pairs of Bling Wings stuck onto another Roadstah) helped to maintain the Clumpwing's speed rating, despite the plethora of high-powered weapons at its command.

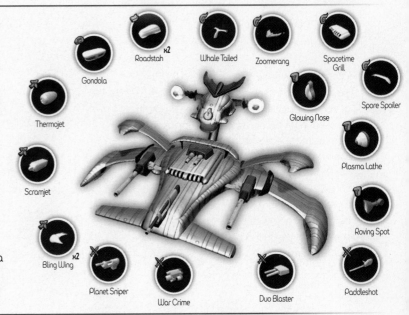

Roadstah ×2

Whale Tailed

Zoomerang

Spacetime Grill

Gondola

Spore Spoiler

Thermojet

Glowing Nose

Plasma Lathe

Scramjet

Roving Spot

Bling Wing ×2

Planet Sniper

War Crime

Duo Blaster

Paddleshot

Dastardly

The Dastardly is an almost perfectly balanced economic air vehicle held aloft by flapping Urvogels and The Propmaster. A Bat-Borne and Zoomerang stabilize the back half of the plane, and the Wings of Flame and Merit Badges on its sides let everyone know that you're flying in style. The hull itself is just an upside-down Event Horizon mashed together with an upside-down Bird of Prey, with an Exsporatorium sunk into them for a cockpit.

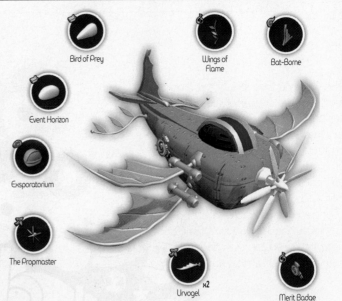

Bird of Prey

Wings of Flame

Bat-Borne

Event Horizon

Zoomerang

Exsporatorium

The Propmaster

Urvogel ×2

Merit Badge

Piggy Bank

If you've ever had a rival civilization say that they'll open a trade route with you "when pigs fly," here's your response. The Piggy Bank looks like its health should be higher than 12 percent, but the "steel" walls of its hull (composed of a Clipped Cone, a Conning Tower, and a Ridged Cabin) are actually paper-thin. However, that just makes it easier for its Commercial Jet, Armored Flight, and Mech-Wing parts to bump up the vehicle's speed to 50 percent, virtually guaranteeing a safe escape from any conflicts. The Roving Spots we stuck on the bottom of the airship? They just look neat.

Ridged Cabin

Bully Bullion

High Roller

Shaft of Light

Clipped Cone

Roving Spot x2

Conning Tower

Armored Flight

Mech-Wing

Deedly-Bopper

Commercial Jet

Holy Floater

The fact that the Holy Floater can fly at all is a testament to the faith of the earnest believers who created it. Held aloft by a Phileas Fogger and propelled by a Duo-Prop, this meager aircraft is simply a Strutter, a Kessel Runner, and a Sleek Fighter cockpit that's just big enough to support an array of joyful noise-makers.

Strutter

Duo-Prop

Kessel Runner

Commercial Jet

Sleek Fighter

Sousaphone

Phileas Fogger

Cymbal Crasher

Peace Bee With You

This extremely simple insectoid air vehicle was built by a religious sect in search of the land of milk and honey, and at least they achieved the delicious half of their goal. Peace Bee With You is 50 percent religious power, thanks to the Craza-phones on the underbelly that double as emergency landing gear if needed. Three sets of Ornithopteryx propel it through the skies, and the main hull itself is just a Comet Wasp, an Astro Kernel, an Inscrutable Eye, and a bad mamma-jammin' paint job.

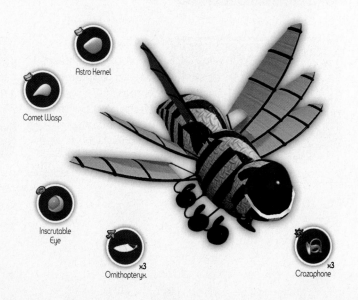

Astro Kernel

Comet Wasp

Inscrutable Eye

Ornithopteryx x3

Crazaphone x3

civilization stage walkthrough

In the Tribal Stage, your race of creatures became the dominant life form on your world. Now, in the Civilization Stage, you must guide a nation of those same creatures to global dominance, uniting the world under your faith, economic system, or military might. You begin with a single city. There are 9 others dotted across the globe. Your objective is to seize control of all 10 cities by conquering them in battle, converting them to your faith, or buying them outright.

NOTE You must always control at least one city. If you lose control of all of your cities, the stage ends, and you must restart it from the beginning.

As in every other stage, the Progression Bar at the bottom of the screen (divided into 10 segments) charts your progression through the Civilization Stage. Each time you capture a city, another segment of the bar is filled in. Click the "History" button to the right of the Progression Bar to see a detailed view of your civilization's evolution, including when new civilizations spring up, when you conquer or lose control of a city, and when you purchase vehicles to aid you in your quest.

When you capture all 10 cities, the Progression Bar fills completely, and the "History" button changes to an "Advance" button. When you are ready, click this button to finish the Civilization Stage and progress to the Space Stage.

city planner

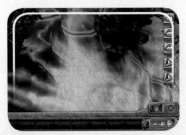

Every city that you control has your City Hall in the center of it. Mouse over the City Hall to bring up the "City Planner" button, and click on it to enter the City Planner. Here, you can design, buy, and arrange the city's buildings. You can also create and purchase vehicles for your fleet, as seen in the previous sections of this guide.

You need to spend Sporebucks, the official currency of **Spore**, to purchase buildings and vehicles. Your Sporebuck balance is always displayed in the screen's lower left. For more information on how to raise funds, see "Earning Sporebucks."

The Building and Vehicle Creators, as seen in the previous sections of this guide, are accessible through the City Planner. You can create new buildings and vehicles whenever you have enough Sporebucks to purchase them and have fulfilled any other requirements. You can also edit your buildings and vehicles at any time, and the changes are retroactive to all of your existing buildings and vehicles.

TIP Tweaking vehicles is a great way to adjust your Civilization Stage strategy. If you're a military culture, for example, and you find that your vehicles don't have enough health to survive protracted firefights, go into the Vehicle Creator and rework the vehicles so that their health rating increases.

Buildings and vehicles designed in one city's City Planner can be purchased in any of your cities (assuming that you have the funds and have fulfilled any conditions). You can have only one type of each building and vehicle in your civilization. That means all of your cities will produce the same Factories, the same military land vehicles, the same religious air vehicles, and so on.

Finally, you can also use the City Planner to decorate the current city, compose a national anthem for your entire civilization, or outfit all of your citizens with the official attire of your civilization. All of these are discussed in detail in the following pages.

City Information

When you're in the City Planner, look in the screen's upper right corner to view the city info, which includes the following information:

1. The name of the city.
2. The city's population, determined by the number of Houses in the city.
3. The happiness (or unhappiness) rating of the city's populace, determined by the number and arrangement of Entertainment buildings, Houses, and Factories.
4. The city's income per minute in Sporebucks, determined by the number and placement of Factories and Houses.
5. The defense rating of the city, determined by the number of Turrets installed along its walls.

Assembling a Fleet

To interact with the world outside your city walls, you need land, air, sea vehicles, collectively referred to as a Fleet. The specialty you've chosen for the city (religious, economic, or military) determines the type of vehicle that can be created in the city. Each city can only create one type of vehicle, because each city can have only one specialization.

Any city can create a land vehicle at any time, provided you've got the Sporebucks to spend. However, only coastal cities can produce sea vehicles, and you cannot build air vehicles until you control at least four cities. Once you control four cities, you can build air vehicles in any city you control. You cannot build a spaceship until you have completed the Civilization Stage and have progressed to the Space Stage.

Once you've designed a type of vehicle, you can buy it from the City Planner by clicking the "Buy" button under its portrait. You can also click the vehicle's icon when mousing over the City Hall to instantly purchase the vehicle without having to enter the City Planner.

Fleet Limits

Even if you have unlimited funds, you can't build as many vehicles as you like. The number of vehicles that your civilization can support is called the Fleet Limit, and this Fleet Limit applies to your entire civilization, not just individual cities. The Fleet Limit is determined by the number of Houses and cities your civilization owns. You can have a maximum of 36 units. Large cities provide up to 8 units (2 for the city and 6 for houses) while small cities can only provide up to 4 units. (1 for the city and 3 for houses).

Fleet Limit Factors

Condition	Fleet Limit
Initial Fleet Limit	6
Each House (all cities total)	+1
Each Large City (beyond the first)	+2
Each Small City (beyond the first)	+1

Additionally, the total number of military, economic, and religious vehicles you can build is determined by the number of cities you control that are of that specialty, as well as the number of Houses in each of those cities. If three-fourths of your Houses are in military cities, then approximately three-fourths of your Fleet Limit will be reserved for military vehicles only. If you reach the Fleet Limit for a certain type of vehicle, you must conquer a city with that type of specialty in order to build more of them.

The vehicles in your Fleet are represented by icons in the Fleet List on the right side of the screen, just like your Tribal Stage creatures were. Select vehicles by clicking their icons or dragging a box around the vehicles themselves.

Setting Your Stance

In the screen's lower right, you'll find two buttons that set the stance of the selected vehicles:

Stand Ground: The vehicles will remain in place. They will react to hostile challenges, but they will not engage or pursue enemies.

Aggressive: Any enemy unit that approaches the vehicles will be attacked on sight and pursued until one side is destroyed.

Repairing Vehicles

If your vehicles are damaged in combat, just move them close to any walls of any friendly city, and they will automatically start to repair.

TIP If you conquer a city with military vehicles, leave your vehicles outside the city until they are fully recovered from battle.

Building Placement

Once you have designed a building, mouse over its thumbnail icon in the City Planner to see the spots where you can place them. All buildings must be placed adjacent to existing buildings, and the links between the buildings determine the effects that the buildings will have on the city's populace.

Building placement is extremely important to maximizing the benefits of each building. Essentially, you need to strike a balance between the happiness and income levels of the city, but if you're clever, the two aren't necessarily mutually exclusive.

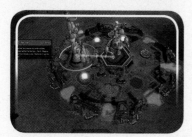

Purchasing Entertainment buildings increases the happiness of the citizenry, but placing an Entertainment building near your City Hall increases it even more. Putting Houses around the Entertainment building (or vice-versa) further increases the happiness benefit.

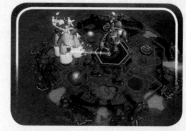

Factories increase the city's income, but each one you place makes the populace more unhappy. The worst thing you can do is place a Factory next to an Entertainment building, as that doubles the unhappiness created by the Factory, effectively negating the Entertainment building's positive effect.

However, you can place Houses near Factories and increase the Factory's income-boosting properties without suffering any additional unhappiness. So to boost your city's income level, first try to arrange Houses around a single Factory before resorting to adding another Factory and suffering additional unhappiness penalties. You get the same income boost as you'd get from adding another Factory, and your citizens stay happier.

TIP As a general rule of thumb, start by placing a Factory and an Entertainment building on opposite sides of the City Hall, and then build Houses around each of them to multiply their positive effects while minimizing the Factory's negative effect.

NOTE The higher your city's happiness, the more often your citizens will celebrate, which brings in more income to the city. It also makes it much more difficult for religious rivals to convert your city and take it over.

Happiness Bonuses and Penalties

Action	Effect
Placing a Factory anywhere in the city	☹
Placing a Factory near an Entertainment building	☹ x2
Placing an Entertainment building anywhere in the city	☺
Placing an Entertainment building near City Hall	☺ x2
Placing a House near an Entertainment building	☺ x2

Unhappy citizens are prone to rioting, which temporarily disrupts productivity and impacts the city's income. An unhappy populace is also ripe for religious conversion by your rivals.

The colored links drawn between each structure in the City Planner tell you how the buildings' placement is affecting the city's happiness and income.

Happiness vs. Income

Link Color	Seen When	Effect
Blue	A Factory is placed near City Hall	Increases income
Blue	A House is placed near a Factory	Increases income
Green	An Entertainment building is placed near City Hall	Increases happiness
Green	A House is placed near an Entertainment building	Increases happiness
Red	A Factory is placed near an Entertainment building	Decreases happiness

TIP As long as there's an open building spot in the City Planner, you can move existing buildings around without paying any Sporebuck penalty. If there isn't, you need to sell at least one building to create one. On Easy difficulty, you can sell a building back for its full purchase price. On higher difficulties, you suffer a sellback penalty.

Damaged and Destroyed Buildings

Buildings damaged in combat automatically regenerate their health after combat is over. You can also drag damaged buildings off the City Planner to sell them. Damaged buildings actually sell back for the regular sell-back price. Destroyed buildings eventually fade from the City Planner; you can also choose to build a new one on top of the rubble to clean it up quickly.

Turrets

The best way to defend your city is by purchasing Turrets and placing them at predefined spots along the city wall. There are a limited number of Turret spots, and you can only purchase as many Turrets as there are spots. Unlike other structures on the Building tab of the City Planner, you don't need to design Turrets before you can buy them.

Turrets automatically fire upon any land, sea, or air vehicle belonging to an attacking civilization. And while it's true that vehicles placed around your city for defense will do the same thing, Turrets aren't counted in your Fleet Cap, so they free up your Fleet for offensive maneuvers. A city with all of its Turret spots filled is almost certain to repel any enemy attack, which justifies the somewhat steep cost of the Turrets.

City Decorations

Click on the Decorations tab in the City Planner to purchase decorations, which you can place in your city at predefined points. They don't take up building or Turret spots, and they're not very expensive, so feel free to drop a few spare Sporebucks on jazzing the place up a little. Decorations have no in-game effect whatsoever; they're purely for looks. All City Decoration parts cost 25 each.

Available Decorations

Giggles n Greens	Bouncy Botany	Sim Flora	Green Tentacle	Foliage Folly	Blooms of Euphoria	Pleather Shrub	Bac-Slapping Bush

Snappy Sprout	Festivity Fountain	Slapstick Spring	Gushing Smiles	Irrepressible Illumination	Light-Hearted	Lamp of Delight

National Anthem

Click the Anthem tab in the City Planner to create a national anthem, broadcast from the City Halls of every city you control. You can adjust the beat, anthem, and ambience of the music manually, or you can simply hit the "Random" button to generate new anthems until you find one you like.

Beat

Click each of the "Beat" buttons to hear different rhythms, and use the volume slider to adjust the relative volume of the beat.

Anthem

Each of the "Anthem" buttons is a different instrument, which plays the anthem notes. You can adjust the volume of the anthem with the slider.

Click the "Note" buttons to add or remove notes from the anthem, from a minimum of 0 notes (no anthem) to a maximum of 16. Drag the notes themselves up or down to change their pitches, and use the mouse wheel or arrow keys to adjust the length of time that the note is held for. The larger the square around the note, the longer it is held.

Ambience

Ambience is the ambient sound of the entire planet, which is heard everywhere at all times, whether you're viewing a city or not. Click the "Ambience" buttons to hear different sounds. You can select up to four different ones, so try out different combinations and see what you like. As with the other two sections, you can use the volume slider to raise or lower the ambience volume.

City Outfitter

Finally, click the City Outfitter tab to create an outfit worn by all of your citizens. This garb lets you show how your race has evolved fashionably since they rose up from their tribal culture and embraced civilization. It functions exactly like the Tribal Outfitter, except that no stats are associated with the City Outfitter parts. The outfit you design is purely aesthetic and has no in-game effect.

The City Outfitter contains all of the same parts as the Tribal Outfitter and more; refer to the Tribal Stage section of this guide for the Tribal Outfitter parts.

New City Outfitter Parts

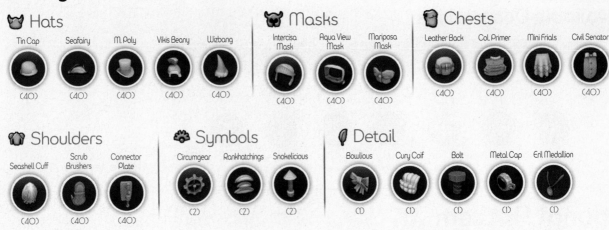

🐾 Hats

Tin Cap	Seafairy	M. Poly	Vikis Beany	Wizbang
(40)	(40)	(40)	(40)	(40)

😈 Masks

Intercisa Mask	Aqua View Mask	Mariposa Mask
(40)	(40)	(40)

🦷 Chests

Leather Back	Col. Primer	Mini Frials	Civil Senator
(40)	(40)	(40)	(40)

🐚 Shoulders

Seashell Cuff	Scrub Brushers	Connector Plate
(40)	(40)	(40)

⚙ Symbols

Circumgear	Rankhatchings	Snokelicious
(2)	(2)	(2)

🍃 Detail

Bowlious	Cury Coif	Bolt	Metal Cap	Eril Medallion
(1)	(1)	(1)	(1)	(1)

Earning Sporebucks

Sporebucks are the universal currency in the Civilization Stage. You need them to buy buildings, vehicles, and city decorations. You can also spend Sporebucks to bribe other civilizations to fight on your behalf against an enemy, preserve alliances with nations that are growing restless, or give gifts to cultures that you want to impress.

NOTE Economic civilizations also use Sporebucks to buy out other civilizations' cities, and they need some serious cash to do so.

City Income

As mentioned previously, Factories create income in the cities that have them. Strategic placement of Factories and Houses increases the number of Sporebucks earned per minute in the city. And a citizenry that's kept happy will celebrate more often, which temporarily boosts the city's income level.

Spice Nodes

Seizing control of spice nodes around the planetary surface is another way to earn Sporebucks. To take control of a spice node, select a vehicle and right-click on the spice node. The vehicle will go to the node and use its offensive power to take over the node and set up a derrick.

NOTE The vehicle must be able to reach the spice node to claim it. For example, a land vehicle cannot seize a spice node that's out in the ocean. Air vehicles cannot capture spice derricks.

Make sure to guard spice derricks once you control them by leaving a vehicle there and setting its stance to Stand Ground. Unattended spice derricks won't remain under your control for long. You can also attack and seize spice derricks belonging to other cultures (with military or religious vehicles) or bribe the derrick operators to switch control to you (with economic vehicles), but doing so will worsen your relationship with the nation that previously owned them.

TIP Speedy vehicles are great early in the game to capture goodie huts and spice nodes.

Trade Routes

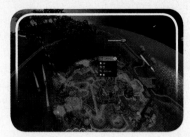

Economic cultures can also establish trade routes with friendly or allied nations, which creates income for both sides. See "Economic Strategy" for more information on trade routes.

Other Sources of Income

In a pinch, you can sell vehicles by highlighting their icons in the Fleet List on right side of screen, and then clicking the red X on the icon to disband the vehicle and recover some of its value. You can also sell a city's buildings by dragging them off the City Planner and make a few Sporebucks that way.

TIP If your city is about to fall to enemy forces, this can be a bit of a silver lining. Sell off every remaining building for whatever you can get for them. You get a few Sporebucks in your pocket, and the enemy takes control of a completely empty city.

Sometimes you'll also receive tribute from nations that want to improve relations or band together against a common enemy. If you accept the offer (and the money), be sure to follow through on your end of the deal, or you will tarnish your relationship with them.

other civilizations

During the course of the Civilization Stage, other civilizations will spring up from their tribal villages, just as yours did. Seek out these tribal villages before they become cities and explore them to get bonus vehicles or Sporebucks.

EPIC CREATURES

Another familiar sight from the Tribal Stage is the presence of huge Epic creatures that roam the land. However, now that your technology has advanced significantly, you'll find that they're much easier to take down! A religious vehicle or two attacking an epic can cause the epic to become charmed for a while. The epic will then follow the vehicle around and even attack its enemies.

As cities are founded, colored borders on the mini-map and the planet's surface represent national boundaries.

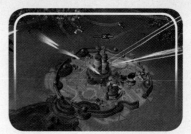
Seize control of other cities to increase your income and population, raise your Fleet Limit, take control of their remaining buildings (which change to your buildings), and move one step closer to space travel. For more information about taking over cities, refer to "One Nation Over All," which follows.

Mini-Map and Comm Screen

Find the mini-map and Comm Screen in the screen's lower left corner. They provide valuable information about every civilization on the planet.

Mini-Map

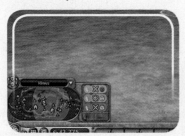

The icons on the mini-map represent cities, vehicles, and spice nodes. The colors of each icon match the colors of the civilizations that they belong to. Gray icons mean that the object does not belong to any civilization and can be seized without fear of reprisal. The colored borders around each city indicate the extent of each civilization's territory.

TIP Keep a close eye on the mini-map to anticipate enemy vehicles massing for an attack, to see where battles are taking place, and to find unclaimed geysers and get there first.

NOTE You can send vehicles to points on the map by selecting units and double clicking the mini-map.

Comm Screen

Once a culture has control of more than one city, its tab appears on the Comm Screen, next to an icon that indicates how the culture feels about you. You can click their tabs to conduct diplomacy, which works just like viewing the city and clicking the Contact icon above it (see following). Through the Comm Screen, you can also receive messages, declarations of war, and offers from other civilizations.

Relationship Icons

Icon	Description
☹	You are at war with this city. They will attack your cities and vehicles on sight, cancel any existing trade routes, and demand tributes from you.
☹	You're in a "cold war" with the city. If you don't improve things, they will attack. Suffice it to say, they're also not interested in trading with you.
☐	You have a neutral relationship with the city. They usually won't approve trade routes unless you improve the relationship, but they won't attack you either.
☺	You have a friendly relationship with the city. They will not attack you, and they'd be happy to establish trade routes.
☺	You are allied with the city. They will assist you if you ask for help fighting off an enemy, but prepare to reciprocate as well. They will always accept a trade route proposition.

Cultural Relationships

The decisions that you make over the course of the Civilization Stage determine how other cultures feel about your nation. Successfully navigating the Civilization Stage requires you to be proactive, not just reactive to other cultures' decisions.

Contacting Civilizations

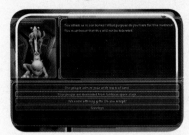

Contact other nations by clicking the Contact icon over one of their cities, or by clicking their tab in the Comm Screen. You can compliment or insult them, ask them to fight on your behalf, or give them a gift to attempt to improve relations.

NOTE You can also give gifts by clicking the Gift icon over a city. This is a slightly more efficient but otherwise identical method to choosing Contact and selecting the Gift option from the menu.

Relationship Events

Event	Effect
Compliment them	Slightly improves the relationship
Establish a trade route	Each route slightly improves the relationship until it maxes out
Give a gift of Sporebucks	Each gift improves the relationship according to how much you give until it maxes out
Purchase their city for more than they hoped	Slightly the improves relationship
Accept an offer to join an alliance with them	Slightly improves the relationship
Use an economic vehicle to buy one of their spice nodes	Slightly worsens the relationship
Insult them	Slightly worsens the relationship; multiple insults worsen it further
Attack them or their spice derricks with a military vehicle	Significantly worsens the relationship; each attack worsens it further
Attack them or their spice derricks with a religious vehicle	Moderately worsens the relationship, each attack worsens it further
Try to buy their city for less than they think it's worth	Slightly worsens the relationship; multiple failed attempts worsen it further
Reject one of their demands	Slightly worsens the relationship; multiple rejected demands worsen it further
A declaration of war	Significantly worsens the relationship
Renege on a deal	Slightly worsens the relationship the first time it happens; significantly worsens it each additional time you renege
Use a nuclear weapon	Severely worsens the relationship
Fight their enemy	Slightly improves the relationship
Your borders are too close	Slightly worsens the relationship
Your nation is too large	Slightly worsens the relationship
Cultural incompatibility (military vs. economic, for example)	Slightly worsens the relationship

TIP If you're not actively trying to conquer a civilization, it pays to maintain at least a neutral relationship with it to avoid having to deal with its attacks while you focus on other goals.

NOTE There is actually a very slight chance that NPCs will accept trade routes with you if your relationship is neutral.

one nation over all

There are three types of cultural specialties for conquering other cities: military, economic, and religious. If you've started your game at the Civilization Stage, you choose the specialty for your first city. If you're continuing from the Tribal Stage, your decisions in the Tribal Stage determine your cultural specialty.

Effects of Tribal Style

Tribal Play Style	Civ. Specialty
Aggressively attacked other tribes and crushed them	Military
Interacted socially with other tribes and played music for them	Religious
Attacked or converted other tribes	Economic

Consequence Abilities

If you played through the Creature and/or Tribal Stages to get to the Civilization Stage, you also earn Consequence Abilities that give you a leg up on other civilizations. There are also a few high-powered Consequence Abilities that you earn toward the end of the Civilization Stage, whether or not you played the Creature or Tribal Stages.

Consequence Abilities

Ability	Description	How to Get It
Invulnerability	All of your vehicles within radius are temporarily invincible.	Carnivore in Creature Stage
Healing Aura	Repair all of your buildings and vehicles within radius.	Herbivore in Creature Stage
Static Bomb	temporarily immobilizes vehicles, turrets, and buildings	Omnivore in Creature Stage
Diplo Dervish	Temporarily ally with an enemy nation.	Social in Creature Stage; capture two cities
Bribe Bomb	Enemy vehicles attack each other and any buildings nearby.	Adaptable in Creature Stage; capture two cities
Mighty Bomb	Small bomb good for destroying vehicles or buildings.	Predator in Creature Stage; capture two cities
Black Cloud	Cause a plague of diseased creatures to rain down on a city, temporarily disabling Turrets and Entertainment buildings.	Social in Tribe Stage; capture three cities
Ad Blitz	A marketing offensive makes the city immediately available for purchase.	Adaptable in Tribe Stage; capture three cities
Gadget Bomb	A nuclear bomb capable of destroying an entire city.	Predator in Tribe Stage; capture three cities
ICBM	Launch nuclear weapons at all cities not under your control. Instantly destroys them and puts what's left of them under your control.	Start with a military strategy; capture six cities
Fanatical Uprising	Instantly convert all other cities to your religion, putting them under your control.	Start with a religious strategy; capture six cities
Global Merger	Take over every remaining city with a worldwide advertising campaign.	Start with an economic strategy; capture six cities

General Strategies

The basic city maintenance and defense strategies are the same for military, economic, and religious cities, but each have vastly different ways of conquering other cities and require different play styles. When you conquer a city, you can choose to convert it to your cultural strategy type, or you can have it remain the type of city that it was. For instance, if you're an economic culture and you buy out a military city, you can change it to an economic city that produces economic vehicles or leave it as a military city and build military vehicles there.

NOTE If the city's cultural strategy is the same as your own, you don't have a choice to change it to any other type.

Specializing in a single cultural strategy strengthens it considerably, because all of your vehicles will be of the same type and will all work together toward the same goals. If all of your cities are religious cities, for instance, you can focus solely on churning out religious vehicles and converting the unhappy masses with an undiluted focus.

However, you can also choose to diversify your forces a bit, to balance out the strengths and weaknesses of each cultural strategy type. For instance, economic vehicles have no offensive power and cannot defend themselves against military or religious vehicles, so it might make sense to have one military city to provide spice derrick guards. Religious vehicles can also benefit a military strategy since they do area of effect damage, making them great for attacking groups of enemy vehicles.

There's no right or wrong answer when it comes to cultural strategies. This is your civilization to shape, and each of the three strategies are equally viable.

Military Strategy

What is best in life? To crush your enemies, to drive them before you, and to hear the lamentations of their lifemates.

Goal

To achieve a military victory, you must conquer every other city on the planet by sending powerful assault vehicles out to lay waste to their buildings and defenses.

Live By the Sword

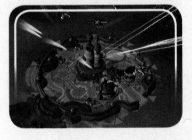

The military cultural strategy is by far the most direct strategy. Start by building a bunch of military vehicles, selecting them, right-clicking on an enemy city, and choosing "Attack." Your military vehicles automatically target threats like enemy military and religious vehicles and Turrets first; you can also direct them to attack specific targets by right-clicking on the target with vehicles selected.

TIP Before attacking a city, check its Defense Rating to get an estimate of how large a force you'll need to conquer it. To do this, simply mouse over the city's City Hall and bring up its info box.

As your vehicles begin attacking the enemy's City Hall, the Conquer Bar over the city starts to fill. When the Conquer Bar fills completely, City Hall is completely destroyed the and city is yours!

TIP Superior numbers are the key to a military victory. Fill each of your cities with a Factory and lots of Houses to keep the Sporebucks rolling in and raise your Fleet Limit, which allows you to purchase a huge Fleet of vehicles and send them out to conquer your rivals.

Stiff Resistance

Expect to be disliked if you're pursuing a military strategy. As it turns out, running around the world and blowing things up isn't the best way to earn trust. Who knew? Other cultures tend not to like military cultures, and the more aggressive you are, the less they like you.

Obviously, any nations you attack will not be happy with you, and they may fall back on alliances with other nations and get them to attack you on their behalf. This is especially true of economic cultures, which thrive on cultivating positive relationships with their neighbors.

The cities that you conquer will be extremely unhappy at first—apparently it has something to do with you blowing up their homes? So before you set out to conquer a city, make sure you have enough Sporebucks to immediately place an Entertainment building in the city when you seize it, and add some Houses around it as well. Remember, the more Houses you have, the higher your Fleet Limit.

Cultural Combos

Military and economic cultures are like oil and water. One needs good relationships and peace for trade routes, while the other incites fear and hatred through wanton destruction. If you're careful not to attack nations that you want to establish trade routes with, you can manage it, but the very fact that you are an aggressive military power will not sit well with many civilizations, which makes it harder to trade with them. The additional income from trade routes definitely comes in handy for building more military vehicles, but you might wind up spending a lot of it on bribes to keep those trade routes going.

Religious cultures are similar to military cultures in tactics, but their vehicles don't have nearly as much attack power (although they don't damage relationships with other cultures as badly as military ones do, either). Religious vehicles can help military attacks by stunning turrets. You can use military power to destroy Entertainment buildings and Turrets while your religious vehicles convert the city, but generally speaking, a military culture's best bet is to go it alone and stick to its simple, straightforward strategy of crushing everything in its path.

Religious Strategy

Hi there. Can you spare a few moments to take a look at some of our literature. No, seriously. *Look at it.*

Goal

The goal of a religious culture is to convert every other city on the planet to their faith by sending religious vehicles out to sway them.

Spreading the Word

The process of converting a city with religious vehicles is almost identical to conquering it with military vehicles. Start by selecting one or more religious vehicles, right-clicking on the target city's City Hall, and clicking the Convert icon to send them over and start spreading the word. Like military vehicles, they stand outside the city walls and "attack" the city with religious music. A Conversion Bar appears over the City Hall, measuring your progress. When the bar is full, the city has been converted!

Religious vehicles can also attack spice geyser derricks owned by other civilizations, just as military vehicles can. It just takes them a little longer to conquer the derricks than military vehicles.

Why Won't They Listen?

The happier a city's populace is, the harder it is for you to convert them. Happy citizens will hurl rocks and firebombs at your religious vehicles if you try to convert them. If you don't stop, Turrets and vehicles will open fire on you. So start off by choosing cities that are already unhappy (mouse over their City Halls and look at the city info to see their happiness level).

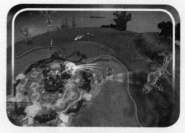

You can also select your religious vehicles and right-click on the city's Entertainment buildings to temporarily disable them, lowering the city's happiness. You can temporarily knock out their Turrets using the same method. The big advantage that religious cultures have over military cultures is that, when you eventually convert the city, you gain the use of these structures and don't have to rebuild them.

Cultural Combos

If you're a religious culture, having a few military vehicles to back you up is a natural fit. They can quickly destroy cities' Turrets and Entertainment buildings to lower the defenses and happiness of the city. Of course, once they're destroyed, you need to rebuild them when you take control of the city. Military vehicles also provide good cover fire for religious vehicles and are much better at defending spice derricks.

The income that economic vehicles can provide to a religious culture is certainly an advantage, and religious cultures tend not to degrade relationships between different cultures as badly as military vehicles do. But you still have to be careful if you're going to combine the two, because religious conversion does worsen relationships, and economic vehicles need strong relationships with other cultures to establish lucrative trade routes.

Economic Strategy

I'd buy that for a Sporebuck...or 64,000!

Goal

Economic cultures focus on peacefully purchasing the allegiance of every other city on the planet by establishing trade routes with them and ultimately buying the cities outright.

Trading Up

To start the process of buying a city, first buy a number of economic vehicles, and then contact the city and give it compliments and gifts of Sporebucks to establish a friendly or allied relationship (a blue or green smiley face). As long as your relationship with them is better than neutral, you can proceed.

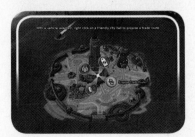

Next, select your vehicles, right-click on the city, and choose Propose Trade Route. Your vehicles head for the city, and when they arrive, a communication from the city tells you if they've accepted your trade proposal. If they do, your vehicles travel back and forth between the cities. Each stop they make adds Sporebucks to your coffers and improves your relationship with the city.

Work on maintaining your relationship with your trading partner, and don't do anything to jeopardize it, like seizing one of their spice derricks or refusing an alliance. You might need to refuse to fight on their behalf if they ask, because you won't have any offensive capabilities if you don't have any military or religious cities.

The more vehicles you send to trade with a city, the more Sporebucks you earn per minute, and the faster the Purchase Bar fills up. When the bar is full, you get an offer to buy the city. You can either make an offer right away, or you can come back later using the Comm Screen or the Contact icon over the City Hall to make your offer. If they accept, the city and all of its structures are yours!

Free Trade Isn't Free

The better your relationship with the city's civilization, the cheaper you can buy them out for. However, you need to be careful—there's no telling what they think their city is worth exactly, and if you low-ball them, they'll be insulted and cut off your trade route, which means you have to start over.

TIP It's always better to bid high for a city, within your budgetary constraints, of course. Not only is it a better guarantee of success, overbidding for the city also improves your relationship with the civilization that formerly owned it (if that civilization still exists once you add the city to your nation). This makes it even easier to maintain good relations with them and buy out their remaining cities.

Economic vehicles can't directly attack other vehicles or buildings (although they can use their economic power to bribe spice derricks), so you need to ask allies to come to your defense and let your Turrets deal with invaders, or establish a military or religious city to provide some offensive vehicles.

Cultural Combos

The best fit for an economic culture looking to diversify its portfolio is a military city, but you have to be careful how you use it. Don't send military vehicles to attack other cities or vehicles unless you've already got a bad relationship with them and intend to conquer them with military force. Instead, limit military vehicle use to defensive purposes, like guarding spice derricks and trade routes.

Religious vehicles can be used in the same way, but they're not as tough as military vehicles. They don't worsen relationships as severely as military vehicles can, but you probably don't want to do anything with a military vehicle that would jeopardize your chances at establishing trade routes anyway.

civilization levels: clumpys of the world, unite!

One Down, Nine to Go

What follows is a day (or several years, in Clumpy-time) of our beloved band of Clumpys, which have risen from their Tribal village to form a military city. This is just one of the infinite number of ways that the Clumpys' story could have played out.

mayor clumpy

Mayor Clumpy is Clumpton's beloved leader—so beloved, in fact, that every one of his citizens dresses exactly like him. His attire reflects his noble station among Clumpys and was chosen for the gravitas that it conveys.

Eril Medallion
This oversized medallion tells the whole world that this Clumpy is a winner.

M. Poly
This top hat makes Mayor Clumpy look even taller, an essential psychological tactic to use in negotiations.

Civil Senator
A classy button-down shirt gives the good mayor something to worry about spilling soup on.

Mustache
A carefully cultivated beak warmer is the ultimate status symbol in Clumpy culture.

Snokelicious (x2)
A two pairs of these smokin' accessories show that Hizzoner's got plenty of steam.

Mini Frials
Normally placed on the chest, these decorative bits of fabric are also good for keeping Clumpy thighs warm.

Cury Coif
Are those curls real, or are they just a powdered wig? Only his barber knows for sure!

Dressing the Mayor

Unlike the Tribal Stage, there are no statistics associated with the outfitter parts in the Civilization Stage (other than the cost of the part). Our sartorial choices were based strictly on how the parts looked on our Clumpy model. We could have sent the Clumpy into the Civilization Stage as bare as the day he was hatched, and it wouldn't have had any effect on gameplay. But we weren't sure if the world was ready for a nation of nudists bent on world domination!

1. We started with the same Clumpy model used in the Tribal Stage and stripped off all of his tribal accoutrements. Anybody feel a draft in here?

2. Next, we gave him a Mustache, always a true sign of dignity and good breeding.

3. A Cury Coif was next, framing our Clumpy's face nicely and keeping his (nonexistent) ears warm.

4. The M. Poly top hat required our Clumpy to cut some holes in the brim for his eyestalks to poke through, but it's a small price to pay for fashion.

5. Maybe it had something to do with how good he looked in a stovepipe hat, but we couldn't resist putting two pairs of Snokeliciouses on the Clumpy's ankle and hip joints.

6. After that, we added a Civil Senator shirt front and didn't tell Clumpy that those are customarily worn with suit jackets.

7. We had such high hopes for our new race of Clumpys that we added an Eril Medallion, in recognition of all of the great accomplishments we anticipated achieving.

8. Finally, a pair of Mini Frials completed the outfit. We permitted ourselves a quick ogle before continuing.

civilization: clumpton's rise to power

The type of strategy you use to take control of all the cities in the Civilization Stage depends on how you completed the Tribal Stage. Therefore, there are three possible courses Clumpton can employ to take over the world. Each has a unique method of taking control of other cities one by one.

Blitzkrieg Clumpy

As the militant Clumpys create their own city, they now control their first vehicle—the Robo Clumpy. This vehicle can take control of spice geysers and attack the units of other cities, as well as the cities themselves. Mayor Clumpy City is the first city on the planet, so it has an advantage.

Robo Clumpy

+383   ✗23   ➡16

The first order of business is to get some income coming in for Mayor Clumpy City. It begins with only 3,000 Sporebucks and has no income. The easiest way to earn Sporebucks right away is to gain control of spice geysers. The Robo Clumpy is sent out on the mission. Because there are no other cities, all of the spice geysers are unclaimed. Once Mayor Clumpy City begins mining the spice, it earns 1,000 Sporebucks per minute.

Once the first spice geyser is claimed, the Robo Clumpy is sent out to another spice geyser to claim it. Mayor Clumpy City tries to gain control of as many spice geysers as possible before other cities appear and begin claiming the geysers for themselves.

While the Robo Clumpy is claiming spice geysers, Mayor Clumpy sets about building up his city to make it profitable. The way a city is laid out is very important. The mayor builds a House near the center so he can create more vehicles. To increase income, he also builds a Factory so that it connects to the City Hall and the House. Finally, because the Factory makes the citizens unhappy, he provides an Entertainment building next to the House. The net result is a happy city that produces 800 Sporebucks per minute.

Clumpnaught

➕ 496　⚔ 41　➡ 12

Mayor Clumpy notices some spice geysers in the ocean. Because his Robo Clumpy cannot reach them, he designs and builds a ship. He then sends the Clumpnaught to claim these geysers to add even more income to his city.

As cities on the same continent begin appearing, Mayor Clumpy knows that as the leader of a military city, he eventually needs to conquer them. The earlier he starts, the less prepared they will be. With the income from his Factory and spice geysers, Mayor Clumpy builds up four additional Robo Clumpys and sends them to the nearby city of Pasian. Once they all arrive just outside the city, he orders the attack.

Because the city is new, it has only a couple vehicles, and they are out looking for spice geysers. The Robo Clumpys bombard the city, destroying its buildings and finally its City Hall. Once City Hall falls, the mayor of Pasian surrenders the city.

Pasian is a military city, so it has to remain such. That's no problem, because Mayor Clumpy has further conquest in mind. To make the captured city beneficial, he constructs a Factory for income and a couple Houses to increase the size of his fleet so he can build more vehicles. Not wanting unhappy citizens in his new city, the mayor also builds an Entertainment center.

The Lavender Nation, centered on an economic city, offers Mayor Clumpy a trade route. Because this city is on the same continent, Mayor Clumpy knows it will not become hostile if he trades with it. Plus, they will pay taxes for each shipment of cargo. This is definitely a win-win situation, so Mayor Clumpy agrees to the deal.

There is one more city on the continent—Ottabriln. Mayor Clumpy builds some more Robo Clumpys at his new city of Pasian and then sends his entire fleet of Robo Clumpys to attack and capture this town. While it has a few more vehicles for defense, the Robo Clumpys outnumber them and easily take control of the city.

Because Mayor Clumpy controls or trades with all of the cities on the continent, and the remaining cities are across the oceans, he decides to build up a fleet of Clumpnaughts. These seagoing vehicles can attack coastal cities.

After capturing three cities, the Clumpys invent the aero funnel and vortex tube. Now they can produce air vehicles.

The coastal city of Rouldia is the first target. The Clumpnaught fleet sails to a point offshore and begins bombarding the city. Not expecting a naval attack, Rouldia is virtually defenseless, and surrenders. Because it's a religious city, Mayor Clumpy can choose to keep it religious or make it a military city. Because he wants to continue a strictly military strategy, he turns it into a military city and builds new structures for both income and to increase the size of his fleet.

Clumpwing

After building several Clumpwings, Mayor Clumpy sends them to attack the city of Varester. Because it is on the coast, he also sends his Clumpnaughts to help attack. The city doesn't stand a chance against the combined air and sea attack, and one more city falls.

🔲 261   ⚔ 29   ➟ 36

As each city is captured, Mayor Clumpy builds them up to create more income and build an even bigger fleet. Because there are no hostile cities on the main continent, he sells off some of his Robo Clumpys to make more room for Clumpwings. Caramura, the next target, falls without much of a fight. Mayor Clumpy is on a roll, and sends his fleet from one city to the next. No one can stop him!

ICBMs

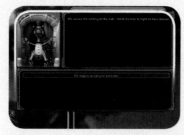

After he captures a sixth city, Mayor Clumpy gains the option of using ICBMs. This ability, though very expensive at 24,000 Sporebucks, can launch missiles at the remaining cities, destroying their City Halls and forcing them to surrender. However, Mayor Clumpy is having too much fun attacking, so he decides to continue using his fleet to capture cities one at a time.

Finally, only one city remains. The mayor of the Lavendar Nation, who has been trading with Mayor Clumpy's cities, sees the writing on the wall and surrenders his city without a fight. Mayor Clumpy has conquered the entire planet and is ready to begin the Space Stage.

🚀 spaceship creation

At the end of the Civilization Stage, click on the "Advance" button to take the next great leap into the heavens and begin the **Space Stage**. But before you can do that, you must design a spaceship. Spaceship creation is identical to land, air, and sea vehicle creation. In fact, all of the parts for those vehicles are available to you when designing your spaceship. There's also an additional category of Space parts at your disposal.

> **NOTE** Although all of the spaceship parts have the same budget cost as their land, air, and sea vehicle counterparts, there are no statistics associated with any of them, so your spaceship design choices should be purely aesthetic ones.

Clumping Around the Universe

star clumper

As with every other vehicle ever designed by Clumpy hands, the Star Clumper bears a resemblance to its makers. How will other races react upon meeting its crew? Will they be impressed at the level of technical sophistication, or horrified at the obvious level of cultural self-absorption?

Roadstah
There's a lot of complex technology in here. We could tell you about it, but it would make your head explode.

Gondola
The crew quarters for the Star Clumper.

Astro Kernel
A vital component of the Star Clumper's solid hull.

Fusion Coil
The Star Clumper's sole means of propulsion. Let's hope it doesn't break down!

Glow Slats
A bit of artificial light keeps the dark void from seeming quite so empty.

Asteroid Belter
A bit of friendly persuasion in case first contact goes badly.

The Glowport (x5)
There's actually not much to see in space most of the time.

Plasma Lathe
The "eyes" on the Star Clumper's nacelles.

Vacuum Cups
These little suckers absolutely suck, in exactly the way that they're meant to.

Sonic Reducer
These are the two nacelles that jut out from the Star Clumper's hull.

Vacuum Spatula
A subspace receiver that ensures the Clumpy crew never misses an episode of their favorite shows.

primagames.com

Constructing the Star Clumper

There are no stats associated with the parts that spaceships are constructed from, so we just had to stay within our budget of 10,000 (shown in the screen's lower left corner) and not go too crazy with the complexity; as always, the Complexity Meter is in the screen's upper right corner. As we added parts, the budget went down and the complexity went up.

1. First, we used a Roadstah to form the main hull of the Star Clumper and stretched it a bit to get a pair of wings.

2. We added a Gondola below it to give the crew somewhere to sleep.

3. An Astro Kernel and a Fusion Coil on the back end gave the ship its engine.

4. We jazzed the Star Clumper up with Glow Slats and five of The Glowports.

5. Astro Belters on either wing made us feel a little safer about heading off into the great unknown.

6. A pair of Vacuum Cups seemed like a good idea, especially if we wanted to grab any souvenirs.

7. The Vacuum Spatula looked appropriately space-y, so we stuck it on there as well.

8. A pair of Sonic Reducers...uh, helped reduce the sonics a bit?

9. And finally, Plasma Lathes evoked the eyes of the narcissistic Clumpys who pilot the Star Clumper.

the spaceship creator

You must create your spaceship at the start of the Space Stage, because once the stage begins, the spaceship is how you travel around the galaxy and interact with the various alien races you encounter. Spaceship creation is exactly like land, air, and sea vehicle creation, so refer to those sections of the guide if you need a refresher course.

Spaceship Parts

Every single land, air, and sea vehicle part is available to you in the Spaceship Creator. In addition, there's a new category of 20 Space parts for you to play with.

🛸 Spaceship Parts

 Astrograbber (400)

 Exo-Arm (400)

 Vacuum Cups (400)

 Utility Clasper (400)

 Guided Thrust (1,000)

Plasma Jet (1,000)

Particle Drive (1,000)

 Fusion Coil (1,000)

 Vacuum Spatula (25)

 SETI Jammer (25)

 Function Plate (25)

 Rabbit Ears (25)

 Rocket Facade (1,000)

 Crustaceanaut (1,000)

 Sonic Reducer (1,000)

 Blast Wings (1,000)

 Landing Gear (1,000)

Landing Cushion (1,000)

Tread Lightly (1,000)

Hard Landing (1,000)

> **Design Hints:** Space parts behave like Details and Effects. They tend to be a bit spendy, and they must be placed on existing structures. They're also bilaterally symmetrical, like most vehicle parts, so adding a Space part to one side of the spaceship duplicates it on the other. Space parts tend to be fairly complex, so pick and choose carefully!

Sample Spaceships

Here are examples of three very different spaceships. Like the Vehicle Creator, the Spaceship Creator allows for almost infinite customization of your spacecraft, so let your imagination run wild!

The Trekenberry

Designed by an inspirational genius who turned generations of eyes to the skies, the Trekenberry is powered by a pair of Sonic Reducers with Klaxxons on the ends. The main hull is a Ghost Rocket connected to an Aft Bluster with a Tapered Brick, and a Plasma Lathe and an Ultra Wide-Band finish off the vessel for its enterprising crew to go boldly into the unknown.

Aft Bluster

Ghost Rocket

Tapered Bulge

Sonic Reducer

Plasma Lathe

Klaxxon

Ultra Wide-Band

Spacestacean

Hailing from Crab Nebula, this clawed craft is composed of a Fly Cuspid and a Bird of Prey perched atop a Skiffy Skiff. A Spinnaker harnesses the power of the solar wind and channels it into the Guided Thrusts on the Rocket Facades. A pair of Landing Cushions assist the ship in touching down on plantetary surfaces, while a pair of Crusta-ceanauts reach out and crush anyone foolish enough to get too close.

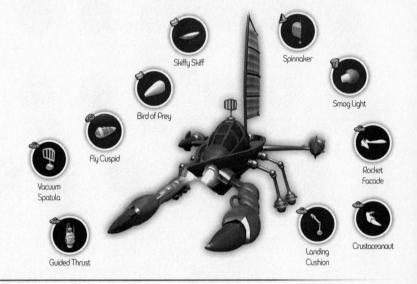

Skiffy Skiff

Spinnaker

Smog Light

Bird of Prey

Fly Cuspid

Vacuum Spatula

Rocket Facade

Guided Thrust

Landing Cushion

Crustaceanaut

Whoodoo

What is this supposed to be? A salt shaker? A roll-on deodorant? Something best hidden in the very back of a dresser drawer? It has a reputation as being one of the most fearsome devices in the galaxy, but frankly, it just looks a bit cheap, doesn't it? Sure, the dozen Glowports look nice, but at only 25 budget points a pop, they're hardly a bank buster. Nor are the pair of Tubeds that make up its main body, the doubled Exsporatorium cockpit, or the shrunken Plasma Ducts on top of it. It does have a Charisma Nest that sits front and center, however, so maybe that's why we find the thing so strangely appealing.

Tubed x2

Charisma Nest

Exporatorium

The Glowport x12

Plasma Duct x12

space stage walkthrough

The Fifth and Final Frontier

Once you've conquered the world, there's nowhere else to go—except to another one! In the Space Stage of *Spore*, you create a space-worthy vessel and set about exploring the known and unknown universe. Seek out new life and new civilizations, and ally yourself with them or reduce them to cosmic dust. Your goal is up to you—conquer all other spacefaring races, form a galactic alliance, become a collector of rare artifacts, or journey to the mysterious center of the galaxy—but your adventure doesn't stop there. The Space Stage is open-ended, which means that your journey is never truly over!

space stage basics

A Sense of Scale

The difference in scale between the Civilization Stage and the Space Stage is as huge as the scale difference between Cell Stage and Creature Stage. You're about to discover that the planet you've spent your entire life on so far is just one tiny speck in a vast cosmos!

NOTE To zoom out from a planetary view to a star system view to a starmap view, use the mouse scroll wheel or the + and – keys.

Planetary

At the planetary level, the Space Stage looks a lot like the Civilization Stage, and your spaceship feels like a souped-up air vehicle. Cities and colonies dot the surface of settled planets, and the mini-map in the screen's lower left displays the same types of information.

The mini-map shares space with terraforming information about the planet's surface. Click the toggle button in the upper right corner of the mini-map to switch between the two views. For more information on the terraforming information, see "Terraforming and Colonization."

While you're on the planetary surface, you can scan plants and animals to add them to the Sporepedia, abduct flora and fauna with the Abduction Beam, terraform and colonize the planet, recover valuable tools and items, and attack rival cities and spaceships.

Star System

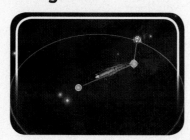

While in the star system view, you can jump from planetary orbit to planetary orbit by clicking on the planets. If you want to initiate communication with a planet, you must be in orbit around that planet.

To initiate communication, click the blue "Open Communication" button in the screen's lower left. This gives you the following options:

Trade: Engage in a bit of interstellar commerce with the planet. Sell objects in your cargo hold, and buy new items. Shop around for good deals and highly motivated buyers!

Repair: Replenish your ship's health, usually at a price.

Recharge: Refill your Energy Meter; this usually costs you some Sporebucks as well.

Missions: See if the planet's leader offers you any missions.

Diplomacy: Much like the Contact option in the Civilization Stage, you can offer gifts, establish trade routes, form an alliance, ask for help fighting an enemy, dissolve a partnership, and more. The options available depend upon your relationship with the planet's empire.

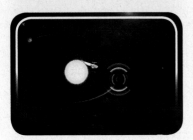

Mousing over a planet lets you know if there's something valuable on its surface to be discovered. If you see yellow rings radiate from the planet when you mouse over it, it's worth flying down to the planet's surface to take a look.

CAUTION Each star system can be controlled by a single race. If you're not on good terms with them, they might not like you entering their system, and may attack.

NOTE For information about which spice types are found on which planets, refer to the Planetary Spice Guide in the Space Stage Appendix section of this guide.

The colors of the planets' orbit trails and the color of the sun in the star system indicate the relative ease of terraforming the planet and the type of spice that you can expect to mine there.

Starmap

The starmap shows a constellation of star systems. Star systems are to the starmap what cities are to the planet in the Civilization Stage. Mouse over a star system to see who controls it, which planets are in the system, and if it has any bearing on any currently open missions.

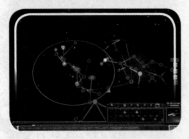

To travel to another star system, click the star. Traveling costs energy, represented by a blue bar in the screen's lower right. You can recharge your energy for free at your homeworld, for a nominal cost at your colonies and allies' colonies, and for some serious Sporebucks at neutral colonized worlds. Systems whose owners have a dim view of your civilization will not recharge your energy.

Traveling without energy is like being completely hungry in the Creature and Tribal Stages. If you don't recharge your batteries immediately, your spaceship's health will start to decline.

NOTE When you first start exploring the galaxy, you can make only short hops between nearby star systems in the starmap. As you upgrade your ship's capabilities, you can travel farther between systems. See the list of Tools in the Space Stage Appendix for more information.

The galaxy is a big place, and the starmap can quickly become confusing. Fortunately, six filters in the starmap's lower left corner allow you to toggle certain types of information on and off, which is a tremendous help when it comes to figuring out where you're going, where you've been, and who's where:

My Empire: Highlights systems where you have established colonies.

Allies and Enemies: Indicates which systems are controlled by races you are allied with or at war with.

Empires: Toggles linking lines between systems that are controlled by a single race.

Missions: Indicates which systems are important to the missions that you've accepted. (To remove a mission's systems from this filter, uncheck the "Track this mission" box in the mission description in My Collections.)

Travel Trail: Shows the path you've traveled between systems since your last visit to your homeworld.

Visited: Highlights the systems that you have traveled to.

Missions, Badges, and Titles

Because the Space Stage is so open-ended, it's up to you to decide what to do. Visit your homeworld, colonies, and friendly planets to see the missions that are available from each, and accept the ones that seem most interesting to you. Remember, this is your story. The goal isn't to see and do everything, but to tell your own story. The assignments that you accept and refuse are a big part of that.

NOTE For a list of the various types of missions available, as well as the types of missions that different races are likely to offer you, refer to the Space Stage Appendix.

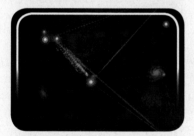

Completing missions earns you tidy sums of Sporebucks and helps you progress toward earning different badges. It also improves your relationship with other empires, which makes it easier to establish trade routes and cheaper to replenish your health and energy at their worlds.

As you complete missions, you earn different badges that correspond to the missions that you have completed. For instance, conquering two planets earns you the first Conqueror badge (Conqueror 1). Conquer three more planets, and you earn the Conqueror 2 badge.

NOTE For a complete list of available badges and the conditions needed to earn them, see the Space Stage Appendix.

Earning badges unlocks new spaceship tools for purchase at any planet that you can trade with. For example, you can't purchase the Anti-Matter Missile weapon tool until you have earned the Conqueror 3 and Colonist 3 badges. Your homeworld will always have all unlocked tools available for purchase. Other friendly empires' planets will also have some, but they won't have the full list, and they may charge a lot more—or, if you're lucky, a lot less!

NOTE All badges and the conditions for earning them appear in the Space Stage Appendix.

Finally, earning badges gives you badge points toward a new title. There are 10 titles in all, which correspond to the 10 chapters of the Space Stage, measured on the progress bar at the bottom of the screen. Your ultimate goal is to achieve the Title of Omnipotent, but there's no single path to get there. As long as you keep completing missions and earning badges, you'll rack up the badge points that will grant you the title!

Tools

As mentioned previously, earning badges unlocks tools for purchase at your homeworld or other friendly worlds. There are several categories of tools:

Socialization: These tools allow you to interact with a planet's inhabitants and are required by certain missions.

Weapons: There are a lot of hostile races out there. Maybe you're going to be one of them. Either way, you should be familiar with these.

Main: These are tools that you'll use frequently in a variety of missions.

Colonization: Intended for use on terraformed planets, these tools help ensure the safety and success of your colonists.

Planetary Atmospheric: Use these tools to terraform a planet and transform it into one capable of supporting life.

Planet Sculpting and Planet Coloring: These two tool sets change the look of a planet.

Cargo: Although this is listed as a tool set, it's actually a list of the plants, animals, and items that you have stored in your ship's cargo bay.

Frequently Used Tools

You'll be using the following tools often, so get to know them!

Radar

The Radar is one of the most useful tools on your ship. You'll find it in the Main Tools section, and it can be toggled on or off. When it's on, the Radar points you toward mission-critical items or creatures when you're on a planet's surface. The more frequent the pings, the closer you are to the object of interest.

Scan

Use the Scan tool (in the Main Tools section) to upload information about any creature, vehicle, building, plant, or planet to your Sporepedia. Not only does this allow you to examine it in greater detail, it also makes it available for your own personal use in *Spore*. Many missions also require you to scan every plant and animal type on a planet, so the Scan tool will get quite a workout!

Abduction Beam

We've all heard the stories of spaceships swooping down and abducting hapless yokels. Now you can do the same! Select the Abduction Beam (found in the Cargo section), target a creature, plant, or object, and hold down the left mouse button. If there's enough room in your cargo hold, the item will be sucked onboard your spacecraft. To clear space in your cargo hold, mouse over a cargo hold icon and click the X in the upper left corner.

To return an item from your cargo hold to the surface, select it in the Cargo section and click and hold the target area until it has safely reached the ground. Release the mouse button too quickly, and it will fall from a great height, with generally messy results.

The Abduction Beam is essential for completing missions that involve bringing plants or animals from one world to another, for recovering valuable items, and for populating terraformed worlds with flora and fauna. Know it, use it, love it.

CAUTION This permanently destroys the creature, plant, or object, so be very sure that you don't need it for anything before you delete it.

NOTE The space in your cargo hold is limited, but you can expand it by purchasing the Cargo Hold Upgrade tool.

Trading

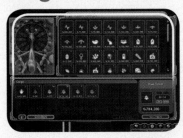

Every time you go into orbit around a planet that has one of your spice-harvesting colonies on it, the spice they've harvested since your last visit is automatically transferred into your cargo hold. You can then travel to other friendly worlds and attempt to trade it with them. You must have at least neutral relations with an empire to be able to trade items with them, and note that trading items is different than setting up a trading route.

TIP Different races have different needs, so shop around for the most eager buyers. Don't just unload your spice for a couple hundred Sporebucks. There are empires out there that will pay thousands!

terraforming and colonization

Your spacefaring empire starts out with a single homeworld, which is barely enough to call an empire. To increase your income and spread your influence throughout the galaxy, you need to do some colonization.

Choosing a Planet

Planet Atmospheric tools make it possible for you to engineer even the most inhospitable rock into a verdant paradise. However, those tools are expensive, and they can be used only once, so unless you're specifically trying to earn badges related to terraforming, you're better off locating a planet that's already capable of supporting life.

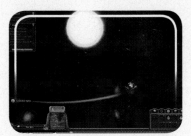

The best way to do that is to look at the color of the planet's orbit trail. A red trail indicates that the planet is too hot. A blue trail means it's too cold. A green trail is just right. When you find a planet that looks like it might do the trick, head down onto it to get a better look.

CAUTION Uninhabitable planets often have violent storms or lava eruptions raging across their surface. Steer clear of these, or your spaceship will suffer damage!

Understanding Habitability

To view a planet's terraform information, click the "Terraforming/ Minimap" button in the upper right corner of the mini-map to bring it up. There are three important sections:

1) Terraform Score

The circle on the left side of the terraform information indicates the atmospheric condition and temperature of the planet. Notice that there is a small dot inside the circle. On an ideal planet, that dot would be in the exact center of the circle, but no planet is perfect.

The vertical position (Y axis) of the dot indicates the atmospheric conditions on the planet. If the dot is above the center line, the atmosphere is too dense. If the dot is below the center line, there's not enough atmosphere.

The horizontal position (X axis) of the dot indicates the temperature of the planet's surface. If it's to the left of the center line, the planet is too cold, and if it's to the right, the planet is too hot.

Usually, the dot will be somewhere off-center on both axes, indicating that there's a problem with both the atmosphere and temperature. For example, if the dot is in the upper right quarter of the circle, the planet is too hot and its atmosphere is too dense.

The three concentric circles in the middle of the circle represent the planet's Terraform Score. If the dot is in the outer one, the planet is considered T1, barely capable of sustaining life. If it's in the inner one, it's a T3 planet and capable of supporting a diverse ecosystem.

The dot needs to be in one of these three circles before the planet can be colonized. If it's not, the planet has a Terraform Score of T0.

2) Food Web

The Food Web is a grid of 18 dots: three rows across six columns. At the top of each column is an icon representing a type of plant or animal. To the left of each row is a Terraform Score number. Rows that correspond to Terraform Scores higher than the planet's are grayed out and unavailable.

These dots represent the amount of biodiversity that the planet is capable of sustaining. A T1 planet can support only one species of each of the plant and animal types indicated by the column heads (small, medium, and large plants; two herbivores; and a carnivore or omnivore), because only the T1 row is available. A T2 planet could support two species of each type, and a T3 could support three of each.

3) Colony Limit

Finally, the right column is the Colony Limit. Like the Food Web, the planet's Terraforming Score determines how many open slots are available. A single colony can establish itself on pretty much any planet, but to have more than one colony working the planet, you need to improve the planet's Terraforming Score.

Terraforming

To make a planet more habitable, use Planetary Atmospheric tools to change the temperature and atmospheric conditions of the planet to something more favorable to organic life. These tools are unlocked and made available for purchase at your homeworld, colonies, and friendly worlds as you earn badges by completing missions.

The tools are all single-use items, so be sure that you've chosen the correct one before you use it. Planetary Atmospheric tools also consume a great deal of your spaceship's energy, so be prepared to recharge after using them.

Aesthetic Transformations

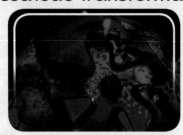

You can also change the look of a planet with Planet Sculpting and Planet Coloring tools. This doesn't have an effect of the Terraforming Score of the planet. They're just for looks. However, if you use them on another empire's colony worlds, they might not take too kindly to your prank!

Stabilizing the Environment

Once a planet has been terraformed to at least T1, you can populate it with species taken from other worlds to stabilize its environment. This fills in the dots on the Food Web and makes drastic atmospheric or temperature changes less likely.

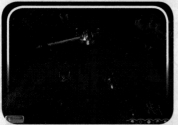

Use your Abduction Beam to snag plants and animals from other worlds, and gently place one of each species onto the planetary surface in the following order (left to right across the Food Web): small plant, medium plant, large plant, two herbivores, and a carnivore. An omnivore can be used in place of either a herbivore or carnivore.

If the planet's Terraforming Score is T2 or T3, put in two or three species of each type of plant or animal, but be sure to do it in the order of the Food Web. If you don't, you'll place species on the planet that have nothing to eat and cannot survive.

NOTE You only need to place one of each species on the planetary surface. You'll be shocked at how quickly they reproduce and spread across the entire planet!

Managing Colonies

Once a planet is habitable, you can drop a Colony Incredi-Pak tool on it to create a colony. Try to place it as close to a spice geyser as possible—yes, spice is still the most valuable commodity in the universe! The colony will spring to life in seconds, looking exactly like a city from the Civilization Stage, complete with a City Hall.

Colony Planner

The Colony Planner functions almost exactly like the City Planner from the Civilization Stage, so refer back to the Civilization Stage section of this guide if you need a refresher.

As in the City Planner, you can use the Colony Planner to design vehicles, although the colony itself purchases and maintains them, so you don't need to micromanage this. You can also create, purchase, and arrange buildings using the exact same strategies used in the Civilization Stage to keep income up without sacrificing the happiness of your colonists.

NOTE The only difference between Civilization Stage buildings and Space Stage buildings is that income is measured in spice instead of Sporebucks.

Each planet's colonies can have its own building and vehicle designs, and you can (and should) also purchase Turrets to defend the colony from enemy attacks. The higher the Terraform Score, the more buildings can be purchased and placed in the colony.

If a colony comes under attack, it sends out a distress call. As soon as you receive it, head straight for the colony and help them fend off the invaders. If you take too long, the colony will be destroyed, and your considerable investment in it will be lost. Even worse, if it was a rival empire that destroyed it, they might set up shop on the planet you worked so hard to establish!

Sometimes colonies will suffer natural disasters or other emergencies. When this happens, you'll also get a distress call. Travel to the colony immediately to learn the nature of the crisis and what needs to be done about it. As with colonies under attack, a colony facing disaster needs help quickly, or it will perish.

dealing with other empires

You'll quickly find that you're not alone in the universe—far from it, in fact! How you deal with other empires is up to you and the type of story you want to tell, but it's likely that you'll engage in a bit of diplomacy, some occasional combat, and a pinch of avoiding other empires to focus on your own goals.

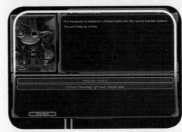

As in the Civilization Stage, you have a relationship with each empire you encounter. Some hate you on sight, while others are inclined toward friendship first. However, your actions will affect your relationships much more than the inherent cultural leanings of the empire.

Relationship Icons

Icon	Description
	You are at war with this empire. They will launch attacks on your colonies and attempt to erase your people from the galaxy. It's you or them, so make sure that it's them.
	You're in a "cold war" with the empire. Don't try crossing through their star systems, unless you're fond of the taste of laser blasts. They will not trade with you, nor will they approve trade routes. They may also offer missions that let you earn money and their trust.
	You have a neutral relationship with the empire. They won't approve trade routes unless you improve the relationship, but you can trade items with them.
	You have a friendly relationship with the empire. They're happy to trade and establish trade routes with you. They'll also usually have missions for you to take on.
	You can now ally with the empire. They will assist you if you ask for help fighting off an enemy, but prepare to reciprocate as well. They will also always accept a trade route proposition or offer you a mission, and you can ask them to add a spaceship to your fleet to accompany you wherever you go.

Diplomacy

Just as it was in the Civilization Stage, diplomacy is the key to creating and maintaining positive relationships with other empires in the Space Stage. The fastest way to get a neutral empire to look favorably upon you is to bribe them. Yes, it's a bit tacky, but it turns out that money can actually buy you love—or at least the benefit of the doubt.

NOTE A slightly more expensive way to go about improving relationships is to purchase Embassy tools and drop them on the surface of planets whose empires you want to impress. Over time, the Embassy will soften the rival empire's attitude toward you.

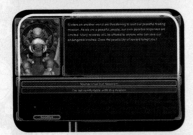

Once you have earned the empire's trust, start performing missions for them to further strengthen the relationship between your empires. Coming to their aid when they are attacked or suffering a disaster is also a great way to earn their gratitude and respect.

TIP And if all else fails, you can hit them with the Happy Ray tool and instantly befriend them!

Damaging Relationships

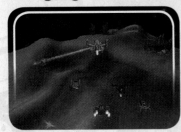

Establishing a solid relationship with an empire can be hard work. Sadly, it's much easier to ruin that relationship if you're not careful. Obviously, attacking a colony won't endear you to the empire who controls it, nor will using your Abduction Beam to steal spice from their colonies or terraforming their planet as a prank.

Trespassing on the territory of a neutral empire might cause them to take a dim view of you. So will breaking alliances or using powerful tools near their borders. Basically, anything that affected the relationship between your nation and another in the Civilization Stage will have the same effect between empires in the Space Stage.

Trade Routes

If you're on friendly terms with an empire, immediately propose trade routes between your empires. To do so, travel to any of the empire's colonies, choose the Diplomacy option from the Open Communication menu, and select the trade route proposal. If you have a strong enough relationship, they will accept, and the trade route will be established.

Trade routes are an excellent way to earn Sporebucks, and better yet, they also begin the process of buying the system that you're trading with. Just like the economic strategy in the Civilization Stage, a purchase bar appears over the system that you have the trade route with. When it's full, the empire contacts you about purchasing the system, just as in the Civilization Stage.

Purchasing a system adds all of its colonies to your empire, expanding your borders, and you immediately start mining spice from them. It's an expensive way to take over a system, but it pays for itself over time, especially considering that you're getting intact colonies with undamaged buildings, so there's nothing to replace or repair.

Forming a Fleet

When you have an alliance with an empire, you can visit their colonies, open a communication channel, and request that they donate a spaceship to your Fleet (if you've advanced far enough to be able to have a fleet). Having a Fleet to back you up makes a huge difference in the Space Stage and gives you an edge in combat that no single spaceship can match.

Combat

Combat is the opposite of diplomacy! In the Space Stage, combat takes place between two or more spaceships, or between spaceships and colonies. It's sort of a combination of the air-to-air combat in Civilization Stage and the tooth-and-nail scrapping of the Creature Stage. As in the Civilization Stage, it takes place on the surface of a planet, but as in the Creature Stage, you must select your weapons and use them to attack your targets.

The key to combat is to know your weapons, including how close you have to be to use them, what they work best against, and how much damage they inflict. Investing in a powerful arsenal does you no good if you don't know how to use it effectively.

NOTE A complete list of Weapon tools and how to unlock them for purchase appears in the Space Stage Appendix.

The second most important aspect to combat is to know when to flee from the fight, especially if you're far from home. If you're outnumbered or just outmatched, let discretion be the better part of valor and leave the planet's surface immediately. Zoom out to the starmap as quickly as possible, and jump back to friendly territory as fast as you can. Retreat to your homeworld if possible, where you can replenish your health and recharge your power for free.

Taking Damage

The green bar in the screen's lower right corner represents your spaceship's health. Similar green bars appear above the other spaceships you're engaged in combat with. When the green bar is completely empty, the spaceship is destroyed. If your ship is destroyed, a clone of your spaceship reappears at your homeworld, and you can retry whatever you were doing, or decide that it really wasn't that important after all.

NOTE If you had other ships in your Fleet when your spaceship was destroyed, they do not respawn with you. You must revisit allied star systems and request replacement Fleet ships.

Conquering Systems

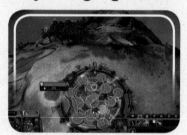

Conquering enemy colonies is a lot like laying siege to an enemy city in the Civilization Stage. Target the Turrets and other defenses first, and then bombard the rest of the colony.

As you inflict damage on their structures, the colony's surrender bar starts to fill, just as it did when you attacked an enemy city with military vehicles in the Civilization Stage. When they wave the white flag, accept their surrender, claim the colony, and move on to the next one.

NOTE Most colonies will surrender when they realize that their cause is lost. But some diehard zealots will fight to the bitter end and force you to completely destroy them.

THE GROX

As you explore the Space Stage, beware of the fearsome race known as the Grox. Initially, they cannot be negotiated with, which leaves you with only two options: fight or flee. It is a good idea to form alliances with other empires to help defend yourself against the Grox, especially if you are pursuing an economic or religious strategy and are not as concerned with building up your military strength. Also, build Turrets at your colonies so they can defend themselves against attack until you can come to their rescue.

rare item hunting

The vastness of the universe is truly a spectacle to behold. Exploration for its own sake can be very rewarding, but searching planet by planet for rare and valuable items can be even more so.

To hunt for rare items, explore every star system you come across, being careful not to inadvertently cross into unfriendly territory. Mouse over each planet in the star system to see if it contains anything of value. If your cursor radiates yellow rings, head down to the planet to check it out.

Switch on your Radar tool if it's not already engaged and follow its pulse to the item that you detected from orbit. You might find a new tool, or a rare item that's worth thousands of Sporebucks. Use the Abduction Beam to lift the item into your cargo bay and claim it for your own. Be ready to leave the planet quickly. Inhabitants don't take too kindly to aliens stealing their planet's items.

TIP Rare items are worth a great deal of Sporebucks to any empire who wants to trade for them. However, each item is also part of a set, and collecting the entire set of rare items multiplies their value substantially.

Beware of space pirates when exploring planets! Some of these scurvy dogs have figured out how to make it look as if there's an item on the surface, when in actuality there's only an ambush waiting for you. If you're not prepared for a fight, flee immediately!

space levels: to infinity and beyond

Ten Small Steps For Clumpy, Ten Giant Leaps for Clumpykind

Clumpy is about to leave the bounds of his homeworld where he has evolved from a single cell to a sentient life form. Just as there were different ways of achieving objectives during his evolutionary advancement, space offers even more ways to advance across the galaxy and create a Clumpy interstellar empire.

Dress for Success

With the new stage come new outfits. As during the Civilization Stage, these are only for looks. What you wear, or don't wear, has no effect on the game or your stats. Therefore, go clump wild!

🐨 Hats

Snogtib Cap	Beam Helmet	Jozz Illuminator	Cap. Cornhall	Smarnocker
(50)	(50)	(50)	(50)	(50)

🐨 Masks

Comet Sighter	Moon Gas Sensor	Oort Beam Mask
(50)	(50)	(50)

📦 Chests

Waspen Jet Pack	Cubewano Disk	Radio Way Plate	Iconel 625 Plate
(50)	(50)	(50)	(50)

🐨 Shoulders

Shoulder Cap	Air Propellar	Refractor Wing
(50)	(50)	(50)

✿ Symbols

Tinker Ticker	Crested Pear	Knexit
(2)	(2)	(2)

🍃 Details

Dishilious	Lock of Goldie	Twirlpellar	Eyebot	Coil Tron
(1)	(1)	(1)	(1)	(1)

astronaut clumpy

If Clumpy is going to represent his species as he travels through the galaxy, he's got to look the part. Therefore, he is changing from his stately mayoral outfit and going for something a bit more futuristic.

Beam Helmet

This aerodynamic helmet features dual antenna for communicating with the spaceship's crew.

Oort Beam Mask

While visiting planets with dangerous atmospheres, this mask will offer protection. Plus it adds an aura of mystery when dealing with alien species.

Coil Tron

This coil is the perfect accent to the helmet. Every spacefaring commander will be sporting one this year.

Waspen Jet Pack

Why walk across a planet's surface when you can fly. It also comes in handy for extravehicular space walks.

Inconel 625 Plate

Every space officer needs a chest plate like this. It just breathes authority.

Refractor Wing

If you are going to have a jet pack, then the wings just make the look so much more cool.

Dishilious (x2)

With these radar dishes on each knee, Captain Clumpy will know what is around him no matter how dark a planet or thick the atmosphere.

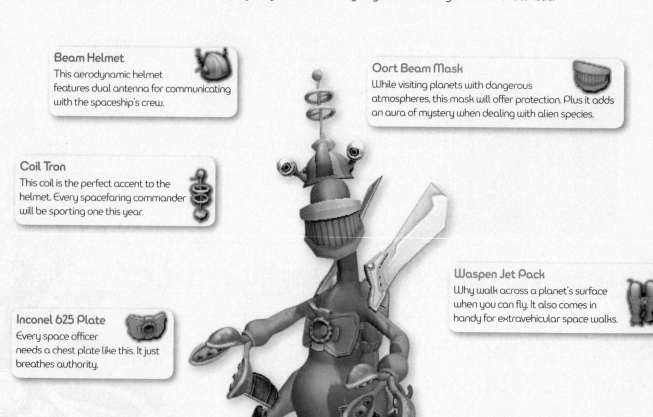

Dressing the Astronaut

As in the Civilization Stage, there are no statistics associated with the outfitter parts in the Space Stage. The following choices were made based on what looked best on Clumpy.

1. We started with the same Clumpy model used in the Civilization Stage and stripped off all of his mayoral vestments.

2. Next, we placed a Beam Helmet over his head, careful to provide holes for his eye stalks.

3. An Oort Beam Mask was next, making Clumpy look a lot tougher.

4. The Inconel 625 Plate provides some chest protection as well as warmth for the coldness of outer space.

5. The Waspen Jet Pack gives Clumpy a dash of supersonic flare.

6. After that, we added Refractor Wings to help complement the jet pack and add to the high-flying look.

7. The Dishilious was a must, so we finally settled on the kneecaps. Putting them on the wrists would have just looked silly.

8. Finally, the cherry on top of our space Clumpy. The Coil Tron added some techno bling to the rather plain Beam Helmet.

To Boldly Go Where No Clumpy Has Gone Before

Depending on how you go about conquering your world during the Civilization Stage, you will have some unique advantages for certain ways of playing through the Space Stage. During this narrative, Clumpy used an economic strategy.

Cadet Clumpy

Before setting off for space, Clumpy needs to learn how to operate his state-of-the art spaceship. To test his ability to maneuver, Clumpy flies through targets located above the cities of the planet. He also learns how to use the Radar to find objectives and scan those items, and then use the Abduction Beam to bring them onto the spaceship.

These skills will come in handy during Clumpy's exploration of space. After bringing specimens back to the city, Clumpy is informed that some creatures on the planet are sick and must be destroyed before they contaminate the ecosystem. To accomplish this, Clumpy gets some on-the-job training with the Mini Laser. He just aims at the infected creatures that are surrounded by a yellow aura and then fires.

As a result of completing the training on his home planet, Clumpy is promoted to Captain, earning his first badge. As Clumpy completes various objectives, he earns badges. Each badge is worth a number of badge points. The Captain's badge is worth one badge point. Clumpy is determined to earn four more badge points so he can receive the Title of Commodore. Eventually, after much work and space travel, his ultimate goal is to earn all 10 titles, culminating with the Title of Omnipotent.

Captain Clumpy

Captain Clumpy receives an interplanetary drive and installs it in his spaceship. This allows him to leave the planet and travel within a system. His first orders are to take his ship off of the planet and then set a course to the nearby planet of Colce to investigate a strange radio signal. After leaving his home planet, Captain Clumpy flies to Colce, and then enters the planet's atmosphere.

Flying over the surface of the planet, Clumpy locates a crashed spacecraft and scans it. The scan causes the crashed ship to send an interstellar drive and minor photon missiles directly onto Clumpy's spaceship as well as coordinates to another planet.

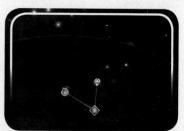

Captain Clumpy takes his ship up from the planet to the system, and then out of the system to the galaxy view. The coordinates indicate a nearby system around a red star. Clumpy orders his ship to fly to the system, and then takes his ship down to the surface of the planet Oreer.

Clumpy flies around until he finds a destroyed city on the planet. After Clumpy scans the city, a couple of drones begin to attack him. Quickly switching over to his weapon controls, Clumpy shoots down the drones with his Mini Laser. Before they attacked, the drones referred to Clumpy as the Grox. It must have been the Grox that destroyed this civilization. Exploring space could get dangerous. Clumpy decides to return home to report on what he had learned. While on his homeworld, Clumpy gathers some specimens to transplant to other worlds. Using his Abduction Beam, he picks up several small, medium, and large plants; at least two different types of herbivores; and some carnivores.

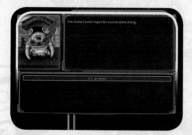

The leaders of his planet are excited about the news of other civilizations in the galaxy. They want to expand Clumpys off the planet by starting a colony on another planet. Clumpy flies his ship to the Rhaosa system, which is just in range of his interstellar drive, and then brings his spaceship down to the planet Marwis. After locating a suitable location near some spice geysers, Clumpy deploys the Colony Incredi-Pak to the surface to create an instant colony. He then returns home to report in.

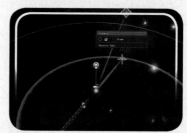

Clumpy needs to earn money to take care of his ship and to purchase the things he needs. Trading seems like a good way to go. When he visited his homeworld, some red spice was automatically loaded aboard his ship. He also received new orders to find another empire. A SETI device is installed in his system to help him find other races in the galaxy. As he exits his home system, he notices a signal coming from a not-too-distant system. Clumpy sets a course for the system to see what he can find.

When he arrives in the system, he opens communications and meets aliens of the Gooplet Empire. They seem nice, so he is kind to them. While exchanging pleasantries, the topic of trade comes up. Clumpy notices that red spice sells for nearly 17,000 Sporebucks a unit. He has five units from his last visit home, so he sells the spice for a nice profit. Seeing potential for more profit, Clumpy also requests a trade route. The Gooplet Empire agrees. Now Clumpy makes some money once he sells it. However, he will still directly trade because it is much more profitable. Also, the longer the trade route lasts, the more likely it is that the Gooplet Empire will offer to sell their system to him. Before leaving, he buys some purple spice—just one unit because it costs 14,000 Sporebucks.

Clumpy returns home to collect his rewards for finding another empire and trading with it. He also learns that purple spice is going for 29,000 Sporebucks per unit at home. So for a few trips, he carries red spice to the Gooplets, and then purple spice back home, and earns a handsome profit in the process.

Clumpy receives another mission. His homeworld wants him to go to the planet Oreer to pick up an animal. Clumpy travels to the planet, scans its inhabitants to find the correct animal, then uses the Abduction Beam to capture it.

Arriving at home, he is paid a reward in Sporebucks. Because this is his fifth completed mission, Clumpy gains the Missionista 1 badge.

After receiving this badge as well as some others, Clumpy now has enough badge points to be promoted. He receives the Title of Commander.

Trading is very lucrative for Clumpy. He also performs missions for the Gooplets as well as his own people. All the while he is exploring and improving his relationship with the Gooplets. Once they are very friendly, he offers them an alliance, and they accept.

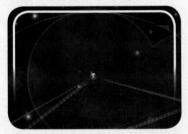

These actions earn Clumpy the Trader badge, the Merchant badge, and the Diplomat badge. Plus, because he has been holding on to his profits, he also earned the Golden Touch badge for his bank account reaching a certain number of Sporebucks.

The badge points are adding up and Clumpy receives the Title of Admiral. He is now three-tenths of the way to victory. However, each additional badge level requires more and more work. Of course, they're also worth more badge points.

Admiral Clumpy

Clumpy finally receives the Trader 4 badge, which lets him purchase a Large Cargo Hold for his spaceship. It's expensive, but worth it. Now he can carry a lot more while traveling from system to system.

The space lanes between systems are becoming very familiar to Clumpy. The Gooplets are great friends and he is becoming very wealthy. Because he is trading so much of the same spices, prices are beginning to drop. Therefore, he looks for some other types of spices.

During his exploration, he finds planets with other spices. He purchases Colony Incredi-Paks and places them on planets with at least a T1 Terraform Score. Any lower than that, and structures could not be built in those colonies. Without Factories, these colonies can't produce spice.

In addition to trading, Clumpy does missions for anyone and everyone. Not only do they provide income, they often provide actions leading toward badges, which in turn lead to promotions.

Some planets offer colors of spice that Clumpy wants. However, they don't have any terraforming. By now, Clumpy knows how to change planets to suit his needs. The planet Poleni is too hot. So he purchases an Ice Storm tool during trade at a planet. Returning to Poleni, Clumpy places the Ice Storm on the planet's surface and the temperature of the planet begins to cool down.

This temperature change is only temporary unless it is stabilized by introducing an ecosystem. So Clumpy opens up his cargo hold and beams down some of the things he has collected. It is important that he beam them down in the correct order, or they will not survive.

Clumpy begins by beaming down a small plant. He continues with a medium plant and a large plant. He only needs to place one of each because they will quickly propagate on their own. Next come a couple different herbivores and then a carnivore. Because he had already placed a colony on the planet, the ecosystem is complete and the terraforming changes are locked in at T1.

The terraforming changes not only the planet's environment, but even the color. Clumpy decides to bring the planet up another level to T2. Once again the planet is too hot for the next level, so he uses another Ice Storm to bring the temperature down. He then places three new species of plants and three more of animals just as he did before, and finishes it off with a second colony.

Now it's time for Clumpy to make the planet productive. By flying over one of the colonies, he uses the Colony Planner to add structures. Factories are the most important because they provide spice production. However, they must be balanced with Entertainment centers to keep the citizens happy.

Clumpy uses his terraforming tools on several other planets. He realizes that he does not have to carry around lots of each type of species. He only really needs a few of each because he can use the Abduction Beam to bring the plants and animals right back onto his ship a few second after placing them. Therefore, if he wants to terraform planets all the way to T3, he needs three varieties of each size of plant, six different herbivores, and three different species of carnivores.

The Grox

Clumpy has now been given a new mission. Reports of a hostile alien race known as the Grox have reached his homeworld. Therefore, he is being sent to locate the Grox to find out more about them. All that is known is that they are near the center of the galaxy. Because Clumpy is off in one of the arms, he has a long way to go. He purchases a Wormhole Key so he can use black holes as shortcuts across the galaxy.

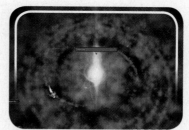

Along the way, Clumpy stops to make contact with various new species and empires as well as take in some of the galactic sites. Finding rare galactic formations helps him to earn his Sightseer badge.

Clumpy finally comes across a black hole. The only way to find out where it goes is to enter it.

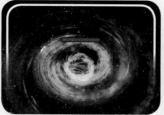

Clumpy enters the black hole the same way he would enter a system or the atmosphere of a planet. The wormhole then sends Clumpy's spaceship a great distance across the galaxy in a matter of seconds.

After several wormhole jumps, Clumpy finally finds some systems controlled by the Grox. With a lot of nervousness, he opens communications with this alien race known for its violence.

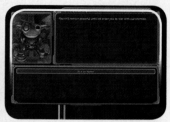

The Grox are not interested in trade and their initial attitude is hostile. However, Clumpy decides to see if he can improve relations. He starts by agreeing to do a mission for them.

Clumpy heads to a nearby planet and abducts one of its citizens and returns to the Grox so they can study it. As a result, the Grox become a bit more pleasant, but not yet friendly.

Because the Grox offer no more missions, Clumpy decides to head home to report on what he has found. Following his travel trails, he retraces his flights through wormholes back to his homeworld. Because the Grox are so far away, they may not be a threat just yet.

All-Powerful Clumpy

With all of his travels, Clumpy has earned many promotions and now has the Title of All-Powerful.

Clumpy is now more than 80 percent of the way to victory. What should he do now? Should he continue taking missions, trading spice, exploring more regions of space, purchasing more systems, or finding some other way to earn badge points?

Clumpy sets off once again into the unknown, rushing through wormholes as he discovers new and exciting planets and races.

For Clumpy, the galaxy is wide open.

space stage appendix

This section gives you all of the nitty-gritty Space Stage details you could hope for, from how to earn badges, to which planets have the different types of spice, to what determines your initial Space Stage personality and how to change it. Armed with this knowledge, you should have a clearer idea of how to chart your destiny, as well as how to earn every achievement in *Spore*.

> **NOTE** See the next section for a complete list of achievements and their conditions.

Badges

Complete missions to earn badges. Most badges have multiple levels, represented by the number after the badge name. Each badge also awards you a certain number of badge points toward your next title. Continue completing missions and earning badge points until you achieve the Title of Omnipotent.

Icon	Badge	Requirement
	Split Personality 1	Change personality 1 time to earn the Split Personality 1 badge.
	Split Personality 2	Change personality 2 times to earn the Split Personality 2 badge.
	Split Personality 3	Change personality 3 times to earn the Split Personality 3 badge.
	Split Personality 4	Change personality 4 times to earn the Split Personality 4 badge.
	Split Personality 5	Change personality 5 times to earn the Split Personality 5 badge.
	Body Guard 1	Defend 2 friends to earn the Body Guard 1 badge.
	Body Guard 2	Defend 5 friends to earn the Body Guard 2 badge.
	Body Guard 3	Defend 10 friends to earn the Body Guard 2 badge.
	Body Guard 4	Defend 20 friends to earn the Body Guard 4 badge.
	Body Guard 5	Defend 35 friends to earn the Body Guard 5 badge.
	Brain Surgeon 1	Promote 1 Creature to Tribe to earn the Brain Surgeon 1 badge.
	Brain Surgeon 2	Promote 5 Creatures to Tribe to earn the Brain Surgeon 2 badge.
	Brain Surgeon 3	Promote 10 Creatures to Tribe to earn the Brain Surgeon 3 badge.
	Brain Surgeon 4	Promote 20 Creatures to Tribe to earn the Brain Surgeon 4 badge.
	Brain Surgeon 5	Promote 40 Creatures to Tribe to earn the Brain Surgeon 5 badge.
	Captain's Badge	Prove your skills as a Captain of your spaceship to earn the Captain's badge.
	Cleaner 1	Complete 5 Eradication Missions to earn the Cleaner 1 badge.
	Cleaner 2	Complete 10 Eradication Missions to earn the Cleaner 2 badge.
	Cleaner 3	Complete 20 Eradication Missions to earn the Cleaner 3 badge.
	Cleaner 4	Complete 40 Eradication Missions to earn the Cleaner 4 badge.
	Cleaner 5	Complete 70 Eradication Missions to earn the Cleaner 5 badge.
	Collector 1	Collect 3 Artifacts to earn the Collector 1 badge.
	Collector 2	Collect 8 Artifacts to earn the Collector 2 badge.
	Collector 3	Collect 20 Artifacts to earn the Collector 3 badge.

Icon	Badge	Requirement
	Collector 4	Collect 50 Artifacts to earn the Collector 4 badge.
	Collector 5	Collect 100 Artifacts to earn the Collector 5 badge.
	Colonist 1	Place 5 Colony Buildings to earn the Colonist 1 badge.
	Colonist 2	Place 20 Colony Buildings to earn the Colonist 2 badge.
	Colonist 3	Place 50 Colony Buildings to earn the Colonist 3 badge.
	Colonist 4	Place 100 Colony Buildings to earn the Colonist 4 badge.
	Colonist 5	Place 200 Colony Buildings to earn the Colonist 5 badge.
	Conquerer 1	Conquer 2 Planets to earn the Conquerer 1 badge.
	Conquerer 2	Conquer 5 Planets to earn the Conquerer 2 badge.
	Conquerer 3	Conquer 10 Planets to earn the Conquerer 3 badge.
	Conquerer 4	Conquer 20 Planets to earn the Conquerer 4 badge.
	Conquerer 5	Conquer 50 Planets to earn the Conquerer 5 badge.
	Diplomat 1	Form 1 Alliance to earn the Diplomat 1 badge.
	Diplomat 2	Form 2 Alliances to earn the Diplomat 2 badge.
	Diplomat 3	Form 5 Alliances to earn the Diplomat 3 badge.
	Diplomat 4	Form 10 Alliances to earn the Diplomat 4 badge.
	Diplomat 5	Form 20 Alliances to earn the Diplomat 5 badge.
	Eco Hero 1	Avert 2 Eco Disasters to earn the Eco Hero 1 badge.
	Eco Hero 2	Avert 5 Eco Disasters to earn the Eco Hero 2 badge.
	Eco Hero 3	Avert 10 Eco Disasters to earn the Eco Hero 3 badge.
	Eco Hero 4	Avert 25 Eco Disasters to earn the Eco Hero 4 badge.
	Eco Hero 5	Avert 50 Eco Disasters to earn the Eco Hero 5 badge.
	Economist 1	Purchase 1 Solar Systems to earn the Economist 1 badge.
	Economist 2	Purchase 3 Solar Systems to earn the Economist 2 badge.

primagames.com

Icon	Badge	Requirement	Icon	Badge	Requirement
	Economist 3	Purchase 6 Solar Systems to earn the Economist 3 badge.		Jack Of All Trades 5	Buy 200 Tools to earn the Jack of All Trades 5 badge.
	Economist 4	Purchase 10 Solar Systems to earn the Economist 4 badge.		Joker	You don't want to earn the Joker badge you cheater!
	Economist 5	Purchase 15 Solar Systems to earn the Economist 5 badge.		Merchant 1	Trade for 500,000 Sporebucks to earn the Merchant 1 badge.
	Empire 1	Expand to 3 Solar Systems to earn the Empire 1 badge.		Merchant 2	Trade for 2,000,000 Sporebucks to earn the Merchant 2 badge.
	Empire 2	Expand to 7 Solar Systems to earn the Empire 2 badge.		Merchant 3	Trade for 4,000,000 Sporebucks to earn the Merchant 3 badge.
	Empire 3	Expand to 13 Solar Systems to earn the Empire 3 badge.		Merchant 4	Trade for 7,000,000 Sporebucks to earn the Merchant 4 badge.
	Empire 4	Expand to 22 Solar Systems to earn the Empire 4 badge.		Merchant 5	Trade for 15,000,000 Sporebucks to earn the Merchant 5 badge.
	Empire 5	Expand to 35 Solar Systems to earn the Empire 5 badge.		Missionista 1	Complete 5 Missions to earn the Missionista 1 badge.
	Explorer 1	Explore 15 Solar Systems to earn the Explorer 1 badge.		Missionista 2	Complete 10 Missions to earn the Missionista 2 badge.
	Explorer 2	Explore 50 Solar Systems to earn the Explorer 2 badge.		Missionista 3	Complete 18 Missions to earn the Missionista 3 badge.
	Explorer 3	Explore 100 Solar Systems to earn the Explorer 3 badge.		Missionista 4	Complete 30 Missions to earn the Missionista 4 badge.
	Explorer 4	Explore 250 Solar Systems to earn the Explorer 4 badge.		Missionista 5	Complete 50 Missions to earn the Missionista 5 badge.
	Explorer 5	Explore 500 Solar Systems to earn the Explorer 5 badge.		Planet Artiste 1	Use 5 Planet Sculpting or Coloring Tools to earn the Planet Artiste 1 badge.
	Frequent Flyer 1	Fly between 50 Solar Systems to earn the Frequent Flyer 1 badge.		Planet Artiste 2	Use 25 Planet Sculpting or Coloring Tools to earn the Planet Artiste 2 badge.
	Frequent Flyer 2	Fly between 150 Solar Systems to earn the Frequent Flyer 2 badge.		Planet Artiste 3	Use 75 Planet Sculpting or Coloring Tools to earn the Planet Artiste 3 badge.
	Frequent Flyer 3	Fly between 400 Solar Systems to earn the Frequent Flyer 3 badge.		Planet Artiste 4	Use 150 Planet Sculpting or Coloring Tools to earn the Planet Artiste 4 badge.
	Frequent Flyer 4	Fly between 800 Solar Systems to earn the Frequent Flyer 4 badge.		Planet Artiste 5	Use 250 Planet Sculpting or Coloring Tools to earn the Planet Artiste 5 badge.
	Frequent Flyer 5	Fly between 1,500 Solar Systems to earn the Frequent Flyer 5 badge.		Sightseer 1	Make 2 Cosmic Discoveries to earn the Sightseer 1 badge.
	Golden Touch 1	Accumulate 500,000 Sporebucks to earn the Golden Touch 1 badge.		Sightseer 2	Make 10 Cosmic Discoveries to earn the Sightseer 2 badge.
	Golden Touch 2	Accumulate 1,000,000 Sporebucks to earn the Golden Touch 2 badge.		Sightseer 3	Make 20 Cosmic Discoveries to earn the Sightseer 3 badge.
	Golden Touch 3	Accumulate 2,500,000 Sporebucks to earn the Golden Touch 3 badge.		Sightseer 4	Make 40 Cosmic Discoveries to earn the Sightseer 4 badge.
	Golden Touch 4	Accumulate 5,000,000 Sporebucks to earn the Golden Touch 4 badge.		Sightseer 5	Make 70 Cosmic Discoveries to earn the Sightseer 5 badge.
	Golden Touch 5	Accumulate 10,000,000 Sporebucks to earn the Golden Touch 5 badge.		Terra-Wrangler 1	Improve the Terraforming Score on planets 2 times to earn the Terra-Wrangler 1 badge.
	Gopher 1	Complete 5 Delivery Missions to earn the Gopher 1 badge.		Terra-Wrangler 2	Improve the Terraforming Score on planets 5 times to earn the Terra-Wrangler 2 badge.
	Gopher 2	Complete 10 Delivery Missions to earn the Gopher 2 badge.		Terra-Wrangler 3	Improve the Terraforming Score on planets 10 times to earn the Terra-Wrangler 3 badge.
	Gopher 3	Complete 20 Delivery Missions to earn the Gopher 3 badge.		Terra-Wrangler 4	Improve the Terraforming Score on planets 20 times to earn the Terra-Wrangler 4 badge.
	Gopher 4	Complete 40 Delivery Missions to earn the Gopher 4 badge.		Terra-Wrangler 5	Improve the Terraforming Score on planets 40 times to earn the Terra-Wrangler 5 badge.
	Gopher 5	Complete 70 Delivery Missions to earn the Gopher 5 badge.		Trader 1	Establish 2 Trade Routes to earn the Trader 1 badge.
	Dance with the Devil	Ally with the Grox.		Trader 2	Establish 5 Trade Routes to earn the Trader 2 badge.
	Badge outta Heck	Beat the Grox.		Trader 3	Establish 10 Trade Routes to earn the Trader 3 badge.
	Jack Of All Trades 1	Buy 5 Tools to earn the Jack of All Trades 1 badge.		Trader 4	Establish 20 Trade Routes to earn the Trader 4 badge.
	Jack Of All Trades 2	Buy 20 Tools to earn the Jack of All Trades 2 badge.		Trader 5	Establish 40 Trade Routes to earn the Trader 5 badge.
	Jack Of All Trades 3	Buy 50 Tools to earn the Jack of All Trades 3 badge.		Traveler 1	Contact 3 Empires to earn the Traveler 1 badge.
	Jack Of All Trades 4	Buy 100 Tools to earn the Jack of All Trades 4 badge.		Traveler 2	Contact 10 Empires to earn the Traveler 2 badge.

Icon	Badge	Requirement
	Traveler 3	Contact 20 Empires to earn the Traveler 3 badge.
	Traveler 4	Contact 50 Empires to earn the Traveler 4 badge.
	Traveler 5	Contact 100 Empires to earn the Traveler 5 badge.
	Warmonger 1	Start 1 War to earn the Warmonger 1 badge.
	Warmonger 2	Start 3 Wars to earn the Warmonger 2 badge.
	Warmonger 3	Start 6 Wars to earn the Warmonger 3 badge.
	Warmonger 4	Start 10 Wars to earn the Warmonger 4 badge.
	Warmonger 5	Start 15 Wars to earn the Warmonger 5 badge.
	Wonderland Wanderer 1	Discover 1 Storybook Planet to earn the Wonderland Wanderer 1 badge.

Icon	Badge	Requirement
	Wonderland Wanderer 2	Discover 2 Storybook Planets to earn the Wonderland Wanderer 2 badge.
	Wonderland Wanderer 3	Discover 4 Storybook Planets to earn the Wonderland Wanderer 3 badge.
	Wonderland Wanderer 4	Discover 7 Storybook Planets to earn the Wonderland Wanderer 4 badge.
	Wonderland Wanderer 5	Discover 12 Storybook Planets to earn the Wonderland Wanderer 5 badge.
	Zoologist 1	Fill out 3 Ecosystems to earn the Zoologist 1 badge.
	Zoologist 2	Fill out 10 Ecosystems to earn the Zoologist 2 badge.
	Zoologist 3	Fill out 20 Ecosystems to earn the Zoologist 3 badge.
	Zoologist 4	Fill out 40 Ecosystems to earn the Zoologist 4 badge.
	Zoologist 5	Fill out 70 Ecosystems to earn the Zoologist 5 badge.

Tools

There are dozens of tools available in the Space Stage. Some of them, like the **Planet Sculpting and Planet Coloring tools,** can be found randomly on unexplored planetary surfaces. Others require you to earn specific badges before you can trade for them with your homeworld, colonies, or friendly empires.

Socialization

Icon	Name	Description	Badges Required
	Mini Happy Ray	Increases relationship with the alien race inhabiting the planet.	Economist 2 or Diplomat 2
	Medium Happy Ray	Increases relationship with the alien race inhabiting the planet.	Economist 3 or Diplomat 3
	Super Happy Ray	Increases relationship with the alien race inhabiting the planet.	Economist 4 or Diplomat 4
	Fireworks	Use near colonies to make them happier.	Missionista 2 or Traveler 2
	Mind Erase	Use on panicked citizens to subdue them and forestall attack.	Brain Surgeon 1 or Cleaner 1
	Global Mind Erase	Subdues all the inhabitants of a planet, they will not attack.	Brain Surgeon 3 or Cleaner 3
	Embassy	Places an embassy on another alien race's planet. Increases your relationship with this empire over time.	Diplomat 5 or Traveler 5
	Crop Circles	Draw crop circles near cities and tribes to interact with them.	Zoologist 1 or Traveller 1
	Monolith	Place on a tribal or civilized planet to uplift the species on this planet.	Zoologist 2 or Traveller 2
	Species Eradicate	Eradicate an entire species of creature to make way for something new.	Missionista 4 or Cleaner 3
	Supersizer	Enlarges a creature to epic proportions. Requires an open foodweb slot to use.	Zoologist 4 or Eco Hero 4
	Creature Tweeker	Select this tool and click a creature on a planet to modify it.	Traveler 2 or Cleaner 3
	Create Creature	Make a creature and get 5 specimens of it in your cargo hold.	Traveler 4 or Cleaner 5

Icon	Name	Description	Badges Required
	Wildlife Sanctuary	Use on a planet to designate it as a wildlife sanctuary, allowing you to place a variety of abducted creatures to live in safety.	Zoologist 3 or Eco Hero 3
	Cash Infusion	Instantly take over systems where you have trade routes established.	Trader Super-weapon
	Fanatical Frenzy	Use on a planet to convert its inhabitants religiously.	Zealot Super-weapon
	Soothing Song	Has a calming effect on the other empires.	Bard Super-weapon

Weapons

Icon	Name	Description	Badges Required
	Mini Laser	Use on ground targets. A precise, but weak weapon.	none
	Laser	Use on ground targets. A medium strength, precision weapon.	Conqueror 2 or Eco Hero 1
	Mega Laser	Use on ground targets. A strong, precision weapon.	Conqueror 3 or Eco Hero 2
	Mini Auto Blaster	A defensive weapon that will automatically fire on enemy turrets and spaceships when attacked. Can be toggled on and off.	Conqueror 1 or Colonist 1
	Auto Blaster	A defensive weapon that will automatically fire on enemy turrets and spaceships when attacked. Can be toggled on and off.	Conqueror 2 or Colonist 2
	Mega Auto Blaster	A defensive weapon that will automatically fire on enemy turrets and spaceships when attacked. Can be toggled on and off.	Conqueror 3 or Colonist 3

Icon	Name	Description	Badges Required
	Mini Pulse	Fires a weak burst in a straight line. Good against ground targets.	Conqueror 1 or Colonist 1
	Pulse	Fires a medium-powered burst in a straight line. Good against ground targets.	Conqueror 2 or Colonist 2
	Mega Pulse	Fires a powerful burst in a straight line. Good against ground targets.	Conqueror 3 or Colonist 3
	Minor Proton Missile	Fires a small homing Proton Missile at its target. Effective against enemy spaceships.	None
	Proton Missile	Fires a homing Proton Missile at its target. Great against other spaceships.	Conqueror 2 or Body Guard 1
	Mega Proton Missile	Fires a powerful homing Proton Missile at its target. Effective against enemy spaceships.	Conqueror 3 or Body Guard 2
	Mini Bomb	A weak bomb, capable of damaging vehicles and buildings.	Warmonger 1 or Colonist 2
	Justa Bomb	A medium-powered bomb, capable of destroying vehicles and buildings.	Warmonger 2 or Colonist 3
	Mega Bomb	A powerful bomb, capable of destroying many vehicles and buildings.	Warmonger 3 or Colonist 4
	Anti-Matter Bomb	A very powerful weapon, capable of destroying entire cities.	Conqueror 3 or Colonist 3
	Anti-Matter Missile	Fires a very powerful homing missile at its target, capable of destroying multiple aircrafts.	Conqueror 4 or Colonist 4
	Planet Buster	Destroys an entire planet. Feared by all. BIG BADDA BOOM.	Conqueror 5 or Colonist 5
	Cloaking Device	Cloak your spaceship, making you invisible to others.	Missionista 5 or Trader 5
	AOE Repair	Repairs all friendly units near you.	Diplomat 2 or Body Guard 3
	Rally Call	Rally's your ally spaceships, momentarily increases the damage they inflict	Warmonger 3 or Diplomat 3
	Shield	Protects your ship from damage for a short period.	Warmonger 4 or Colonist 3
	Repair Pack	Restores some of the health to your spaceship.	Missionista 2 or Trader 2
	Repair Mega Pack	Instantly repairs your spaceship to pristine condition.	Missionista 4 or Trader 4
	Energy Pack	Recharge a portion of your spaceship's energy.	Missionista 1 or Trader 1
	Energy Mega Pack	Recharges your spaceship's energy to full.	Missionista 3 or Trader 3
	Summon Mini-U	Summon a miniature clone of your spaceship to help you in your travels.	Knight Super-weapon
	Gravitation Wave	Destroys all structures on the planet.	Scientist Super-weapon
	Raider Rally	Entices pirates to attack the planet.	Warrior Super-weapon
	Static Cling	Stuns all other ships and turrets on the planet.	Diplomat Super-weapon

Main Tools

Icon	Name	Description	Badges Required
	Scan	Click on plants or animals to get more information about them.	None
	Radar	Signals when you are near important planetside targets. Toggles on and off.	None
	Hologram Scout	Send a hologram to the planet for an up close examination.	Missionista 5 or Trader 5
	Planet Scan	Use on a planet to scan all the plants and animals.	Zoologist 5 or Eco Hero 5
	Return Ticket	Returns you to your home system in a single jump.	Shaman Super-weapon
	Safari Vacuum	Use on a planet to instantly abduct several of each species on the planet.	Ecologist Super-weapon

Colonization

Icon	Name	Description	Badges Required
	Colony Incredi-Pak	Places a colony on a planet.	Interplanetary Drive
	Bio Protector	Place on a planet to slow down the rate of biological disasters.	Zoologist 2 or Eco Hero 3
	Bio Stabilizer	Place on a planet to reduce the liklihood of biological disaster.	Zoologist 3 or Eco Hero 4
	Loyalty Booster	Place on a planet to maintain maximum loyalty.	Warmonger 2 or Body Guard 3
	Happiness Booster	Place on a planet to keep the planet's inhabitants happy.	Golden Touch 3 or Merchant 3
	Spice Storage	Place on a planet to increase the amount of spice that can be stored.	Trader 2 or Colonist 3
	Uber Turret	Place on a planet to provide the ultimate defense for its colonies.	Warmonger 3 or Colonist 4

Planet Atmospheric Tools

Icon	Name	Description	Badges Required
	Cloud Accumulator	Use on a planet to raise its atmosphere level.	Terra-Wrangler 2 or Empire 2
	Cloud Vacuum	Use on a planet to lower its atmosphere level.	Terra-Wrangler 2 or Empire 2
	Refrigeration Ray	Use on a planet to lower the temperature.	Terra-Wrangler 3 or Empire 3
	Heat Ray	Use on a planet to raise the temperature.	Terra-Wrangler 3 or Empire 3
	Staff of Life	Use on planet to totally terraform it instantly.	Center of Galaxy Reward
	Air Conditioning	Use on a planet to lower its temperature and raise its atmosphere level.	Terra-Wrangler 5 or Empire 5
	Hot Cloud Seeder	Use on a planet to raise both temperature and atmosphere level.	Terra-Wrangler 5 or Empire 5
	Hot Cloud Vacuum	Use on a planet to raise temerature and lower atmosphere level.	Terra-Wrangler 4 or Empire 4
	Cold Cloud Vacuum	Use on a planet to lower both its temperature and atmosphere level.	Terra-Wrangler 4 or Empire 4
	Atmosphere Generator	Place on a planet to raise its atmosphere level...give the joint a little 'atmosphere' you know.	Missionista 1 or Empire 1
	Drought Generator	Place on the planet to lower the atmosphere level.	Missionista 1 or Empire 1

Icon	Name	Description	Badges Required
	Ice Storm	Place on the planet to lower the temperature.	Missionista 2 or Empire 2
	Meteor Shower	Use to hurl meteors at a planet to raise the temperature.	Missionista 2 or Empire 2
	Ice Comet	Use on a planet to hurl an ice comet at it. Lowers temperature and raises atmosphere level.	Missionista 4 or Empire 4
	Volcano	Place on the planet to raise both the temperature & atmosphere level.	Missionista 4 or Empire 4
	Asteroid Call Button	Use on a planet to summon an asteroid, raising the temperature and lowering atmosphere.	Missionista 3 or Empire 3
	Atmosphere Freezer	Place on the planet to lower both temperature & atmosphere level.	Missionista 3 or Empire 3

Planet Sculpting Tools

Icon	Name	Description	Badges Required
	Raise Terrain (Small)	Use on a planet to raise the planet's surface.	Terra-Wrangler 1 or Explorer 1
	Lower Terrain (Small)	Use on a planet to lower the planet's surface.	Terra-Wrangler 1 or Explorer 1
	Level Terrain (Small)	Use on planet terrain to level the planet's surface.	Terra-Wrangler 1 or Explorer 1
	Raise Terrain (Medium)	Use on a planet to raise the planet's surface.	Terra-Wrangler 2 or Explorer 2
	Lower Terrain (Medium)	Use on a planet to lower the planet's surface.	Terra-Wrangler 2 or Explorer 2
	Level Terrain (Medium)	Use on planet terrain to level the planet's surface.	Terra-Wrangler 2 or Explorer 2
	Raise Terrain (Large)	Use on a planet to raise the planet's surface.	Terra-Wrangler 3 or Explorer 3
	Lower Terrain (Large)	Use on planet terrain to lower the planet's surface.	Terra-Wrangler 3 or Explorer 3
	Level Terrain (Large)	Use on planet terrain to level the planet's surface.	Terra-Wrangler 3 or Explorer 3
	Terra Hills	Use on a planet to terrasculpt terra hills.	Planet Artiste 1 or Explorer 3
	Terra Plateaus	Use on a planet to terrasculpt terra plateaus.	Planet Artiste 3 or Explorer 4
	Terra Craters	Use on a planet to terrasculpt terra craters.	Planet Artiste 1 or Explorer 3
	Terra Mesas	Use on a planet to terrasculpt terra mesas.	Planet Artiste 3 or Explorer 4
	Terra Seas	Use on a planet to terrasculpt terra seas.	Planet Artiste 5 or Explorer 5
	Terra River	Click and drag on planet to set the start point and direction of a terra river.	Planet Artiste 2 or Explorer 3
	Terra Mountain	Click and drag on planet to set the start point and direction of a terra mountain.	Planet Artiste 3 or Explorer 5
	Terra Canyon	Click and drag on planet to set the start point and direction of a terra canyon.	Planet Artiste 2 or Explorer 4
	Terra Lava Flows	Use on a planet to terrasculpt terra lava flows.	Planet Artiste 4 or Explorer 5
	Chocolate Strand	Click and drag on planet to set the start point and direction of a chocolate strand.	Pick up on Planet
	Chocolate Truffle	Use on a planet to terrasculpt a chocolate truffle.	Pick up on Planet
	Chocolate Swirl Pond	Use on a planet to terrasculpt a chocolate swirl pond.	Pick up on Planet

Icon	Name	Description	Badges Required
	Chocolate Swirl River	Click and drag on planet to set the start point and direction of a chocolate swirl river	Pick up on Planet
	Chocolate Swirl Seas	Use on a planet to terrasculpt chocolate swirl seas.	Pick up on Planet
	Chocolate Swirl Spirals	Click and drag on planet to set the start point and direction of chocolate swirl spirals.	Pick up on Planet
	Chocolate Squares	Use on a planet to terrasculpt chocolate squares.	Pick up on Planet
	Chocolate Truffle	Use on a planet to terrasculpt a chocolate truffle formation	Pick up on Planet
	Swirly Valley	Click and drag on planet to set the start point and direction of a chocolate box.	Pick up on Planet
	Crystal Canyon	Click and drag on planet to set the start point and direction of a crystal canyon.	Pick up on Planet
	Crystal Chasm	Click and drag on planet to set the start point and direction of a crystal chasm.	Pick up on Planet
	Crystal Hills	Use on a planet to terrasculpt crystal hills.	Pick up on Planet
	Crystal Holes	Use on a planet to terrasculpt crystal holes.	Pick up on Planet
	Crystal Mesas	Use on a planet to terrasculpt crystal mesas.	Pick up on Planet
	Crystal Mountains	Click and drag on planet to set the start point and direction of a crystal mountain.	Pick up on Planet
	Crystal Plateau	Use on a planet to terrasculpt crystal plateau	Pick up on Planet
	Crystal River	Click and drag on planet to set the start point and direction of a crystal river.	Pick up on Planet
	Crystal Seas	Use on a planet to terrasculpt crystal seas.	Pick up on Planet
	Cute Canyon	Click and drag on planet to set the start point and direction of a cute canyon.	Pick up on Planet
	Cute Hills	Use on a planet to terrasculpt cute hills.	Pick up on Planet
	Cute Stamps	Use on a planet to terrasculpt cute stamps.	Pick up on Planet
	Cute Mesas	Use on a planet to terrasculpt cute mesas	Pick up on Planet
	Cute Mountains	Click and drag on planet to set the start point and direction of a cute mountain.	Pick up on Planet
	Cute Plateaus	Use on a planet to terrasculpt cute plateaus.	Pick up on Planet
	Cute Rivers	Click and drag on planet to set the start point and direction of a cute river.	Pick up on Planet
	Cute Seas	Use on a planet to terrasculpt cute seas.	Pick up on Planet
	Cute Walls	Click and drag on planet to set the start point and direction of a cute wall.	Pick up on Planet
	Create Gear	Use on a planet to terrasculpt a gear.	Pick up on Planet
	Gear Canyons	Click and drag on planet to set the start point and direction of a gear canyon.	Pick up on Planet
	Gear Craters	Use on a planet to terrasculpt gear craters.	Pick up on Planet

Icon	Name	Description	Badges Required
	Gear Fissure	Click and drag on planet to set the start point and direction of a gear fissure.	Pick up on Planet
	Gear Hills	Use on a planet to terrasculpt gear hills.	Pick up on Planet
	Gear Mesas	Use on a planet to terrasculpt gear mesas.	Pick up on Planet
	Gear Mountains	Click and drag on planet to set the start point and direction of gear mountains.	Pick up on Planet
	Gear Plateaus	Use on a planet to terrasculpt gear plateaus.	Pick up on Planet
	Gear Rivers	Click and drag on planet to set the start point and direction of a gear river.	Pick up on Planet
	Gear Seas	Use on a planet to terrasculpt gear seas.	Pick up on Planet
	Gear Walls	Click and drag on planet to set the start point and direction of a gear wall.	Pick up on Planet
	Tentacle Arm	Click and drag on planet to set the start point and direction of a Tentacle Arm.	Pick up on Planet
	Tentacle Canyon	Click and drag on planet to set the start point and direction of a Tentacle Canyon.	Pick up on Planet
	Tentacle Hills	Use on a planet to terrasculpt tentacle hills.	Pick up on Planet
	Tentacle Mountains	Click and drag on planet to set the start point and direction of tentacle mountains.	Pick up on Planet
	Tentacle Mouth Hole	Use on a planet to terrasculpt a tentacle mouth hole.	Pick up on Planet
	Create Tentacle Plateau	Use on a planet to terrasculpt a tentacle plateau	Pick up on Planet
	Tentacle River	Click and drag on planet to set the start point and direction of a tentacle river.	Pick up on Planet
	Tentacle Seas	Use on a planet to terrasculpt tentacle seas.	Pick up on Planet
	Tentacle Suckers	Use on a planet to terrasculpt tentacle suckers.	Pick up on Planet

Planet Coloring Tools

Icon	Name	Description	Badges Required
	Sky Blueinator	Changes the atmosphere color of the planet to blue.	Pick up on Planet
	Sky Cyaninator	Changes the atmosphere color of the planet to cyan.	Pick up on Planet
	Sky Greeninator	Changes the atmosphere color of the planet to green.	Pick up on Planet
	Sky Orangizer	Changes the atmosphere color of the planet to orange.	Pick up on Planet
	Sky Pinkinator	Changes the atmosphere color of the planet to pink.	Pick up on Planet
	Grape Flavored Sky	Changes the atmosphere color of the planet to purple.	Pick up on Planet
	Skies of Red	Changes the atmosphere color of the planet to red.	Pick up on Planet
	Sky Lemonizer	Changes the atmosphere color of the planet to yellow.	Pick up on Planet
	Planet Color Reset	Restores the planet to it's original colors.	Pick up on Planet
	Blue Terra-Coloring	Changes the terrain color of the planet to blue.	Pick up on Planet

Icon	Name	Description	Badges Required
	Cyan Terra-Coloring	Changes the terrain color of the planet to cyan.	Pick up on Planet
	Green Terra-Coloring	Changes the terrain color of the planet to green.	Pick up on Planet
	Orange Terra-Coloring	Changes the terrain color of the planet to orange.	Pick up on Planet
	Pink Terra-Coloring	Changes the terrain color of the planet to pink.	Pick up on Planet
	Purple Terra-Coloring	Changes the terrain color of the planet to purple.	Pick up on Planet
	Red Terra-Coloring	Changes the terrain color of the planet to red.	Pick up on Planet
	Yellow Terra-Coloring	Changes the terrain color of the planet to yellow.	Pick up on Planet
	Deep Blue Sea	Changes the water color of the planet to blue.	Pick up on Planet
	Cyan Sea	Changes the water color of the planet to cyan.	Pick up on Planet
	Sea of Green	Changes the water color of the planet to green.	Pick up on Planet
	Orange Flavor Crystals	Changes the water color of the planet to orange.	Pick up on Planet
	Sweetheart Sea	Changes the water color of the planet to pink.	Pick up on Planet
	Grape Juice Ocean	Changes the water color of the planet to purple.	Pick up on Planet
	Crimson Sea	Changes the water color of the planet to red.	Pick up on Planet
	Leomonade Sea	Changes the water color of the planet to yellow.	Pick up on Planet

Spaceship Abilities

Icon	Name	Description	Badges Required
	SETI	Automatically detects intelligent life in other star systems. Look for the radio lines in the galactic view.	None
	Abduction Beam	Use to Abduct plants, animals or rares and add them to your cargo bay.	None
	Drop Cargo	Eject items from your cargo bay onto a planet. Hold to drop creatures gently.	None
	Basic Cargo Hold	Increase your spaceship's cargo capacity, so you can fit more loot in your boot.	Collector 1 or Merchant 2
	Medium Cargo Hold	Increase your spaceship's cargo capacity so you can put more junk in your trunk.	Collector 2 or Merchant 3
	Large Cargo Hold	Increase your spaceship's cargo capacity to maximum so you can haul the most of all.	Collector 3 or Merchant 4
	Interplanetary Drive	Your basic interplanetary drive, allows you to leave your planet's orbit.	None
	Interstellar Drive 1	Your basic interstellar drive, allows you to leave your solar system.	None
	Interstellar Drive 2	Increases your spaceship's travel range.	Frequent Flyer 2 or Gopher 1
	Interstellar Drive 3	Increases your spaceship's travel range.	Frequent Flyer 3 or Gopher 2
	Interstellar Drive 4	Increases your spaceship's travel range.	Frequent Flyer 4 or Gopher 3
	Interstellar Drive 5	Increases your spaceship's travel range to maximum.	Frequent Flyer 5 or Gopher 4

Icon	Name	Description	Badges Required	Icon	Name	Description	Badges Required
	Wormhole Key	Allows you to fly through a black hole.	Frequent Flyer 3 or Gopher 3		Basic Health	Increase your spaceship's health capacity.	None
	Basic Energy Storage	Increase your spaceship's energy capacity.	Missionista 1 or Colonist 1		Small Health	Increase your spaceship's health capacity.	Conqueror 1 or Colonist 1
	Small Energy Storage	Increase your spaceship's energy capacity.	Missionista 2 or Colonist 2		Medium Health	Increase your spaceship's health capacity.	Conqueror 2 or Colonist 2
	Medium Energy Storage	Increase your spaceship's energy capacity.	Missionista 3 or Colonist 3		Large Health	Increase your spaceship's health capacity.	Conqueror 3 or Colonist 3
	Large Energy Storage	Increase your spaceship's energy capacity.	Missionista 4 or Colonist 4		Extreme Health	Increase your spaceship's health to maximum capacity.	Conqueror 4 or Colonist 4
	Extreme Energy Storage	Increase your spaceship's energy to maximum capacity.	Missionista 5 or Colonist 5				

Rare Items

Thoroughly explore each planet in every star system to find and collect rare items. Each rare item is extremely valuable in its own right, but if you collect every rare item in a set, the set of items can be traded for 10 times the sum of their individual values!

Icon	Artifact Name	Trading Value	Icon	Artifact Name	Trading Value	Icon	Artifact Name	Trading Value
	Block of Chance Vol. 1	45,000		Stone of Life 1	45,000		A Yellow Geode	45,000
	Block of Chance Vol. 2	45,000		Stone of Life 2	45,000		A Shiny Geode	67,000
	Block of Chance Vol. 3	45,000		Stone of Life 3	45,000		A Green Geode	22,500
	Block of Chance Vol. 4	45,000		Stone of Life 4	45,000		A Pink Geode	67,000
	Block of Chance Vol. 5	45,000		Stone of Life 5	45,000		A Blue Geode	22,500
	Block of Chance Vol. 6	45,000		Stone of Life 6	45,000		A Fuchsia Geode	45,000
	Block of Chance Vol. 7	45,000		Stone of Life 7	45,000		An Orange Geode	67,000
	Block of Chance Vol. 8	45,000		Stone of Life 8	45,000		A Golden Geode	45,000
	Block of Chance Vol. 9	45,000		Stone of Life 9	45,000		An Aqua Geode	90,000
	Block of Chance Vol. 10	45,000		Stone of Life 10	45,000		A Reddish Geode	67,000
Blocks of Chance		**4,500,000**	**Stones of Life**		**4,500,000**	**Rare Geodes**		**6,075,000**
	Scroll of Order I	45,000		Ancient Flyswatter	45,000		Purple-ish Gems of Rabban Ankott	67,000
	Scroll of Order II	45,000		Fossilized Remains of a Big Scary Thing	45,000		Turquoise	22,500
	Scroll of Order III	45,000		The Fossil That Everybody Finds	45,000		Tangeriamonds	67,000
	Scroll of Order IV	45,000		Fossilized Domesticated Animal Treat	45,000		Amethysts	45,000
	Scroll of Order V	45,000		Fossilized Tribal Sheriff's Badge	45,000		Emeralds	22,500
	Scroll of Order VI	45,000		Ancient Epic Boot Scraper	45,000		Jade	67,000
	Scroll of Order VII	45,000		Petrified Sun Dried Nautilus	45,000		Lapis Lazuli	22,500
	Scroll of Order VIII	45,000		Big Dead Fish on a Little Non Living Rock	45,000		Opals	45,000
	Scroll of Order IX	45,000		Fossilized Candy Corn	45,000		Rubies	67,000
	Scroll of Order X	45,000		Mr. Fluffers	45,000		Sapphires	22,500
Scrolls of Order		**4,500,000**	**Rare Fossils**		**4,500,000**	**Rare Jewels**		**4,500,000**

Icon	Artifact Name	Trading Value
	Ancient Urn of the Spurg	225,000
	The Lost Chest of Moozilla	67,000
	Super Old Clay Pot	45,000
	Will's Old Sword	22,500
	Scrolls of the Ancients	67,000
	The History of Spore	22,500
	Tablet of the Tribes	22,500
	Screeble's Column	67,000
	Sporehenge	45,000
	The Mask of Todd	45,000
Rare Relics		**6,700,000**
	Book of Science Pt. 1	45,000
	Book of Science Pt. 2	45,000
	Book of Science Pt. 3	45,000
	Book of Science Pt. 4	45,000
	Book of Science Pt. 5	45,000
	Book of Science Pt. 6	45,000
	Book of Science Pt. 7	45,000
	Book of Science Pt. 8	45,000
	Book of Science Pt. 9	45,000
	Book of Science Pt. 10	45,000
Books of Science		**4,500,000**
	Scroll of Harmony Vol. 1	45,000
	Scroll of Harmony Vol. 2	45,000
	Scroll of Harmony Vol. 3	45,000
	Scroll of Harmony Vol. 4	45,000
	Scroll of Harmony Vol. 5	45,000
	Scroll of Harmony Vol. 6	45,000
	Scroll of Harmony Vol. 7	45,000
	Scroll of Harmony Vol. 8	45,000
	Scroll of Harmony Vol. 9	45,000
	Scroll of Harmony Vol. 10	45,000
Scrolls of Harmony		**4,500,000**

Icon	Artifact Name	Trading Value
	The Hand of Quimby	67,000
	The Statue of The Three Crickets	22,500
	The Bust of Yaman	67,000
	The Bust of Bradford	45,000
	The Wayward Leg of Lamstein	22,500
	The Stone of Pierre	67,000
	The Statue of One-Eyed Kippy	45,000
	The Torch of Chalmers	67,000
	The Upper Torso of Little Lee	22,500
	The Foot of Povey	225,000
Rare Statues		**4,500,000**
	Tablet of Prosperity No. 1	45,000
	Tablet of Prosperity No. 2	45,000
	Tablet of Prosperity No. 3	45,000
	Tablet of Prosperity No. 4	45,000
	Tablet of Prosperity No. 5	45,000
	Tablet of Prosperity No. 6	45,000
	Tablet of Prosperity No. 7	45,000
	Tablet of Prosperity No. 8	45,000
	Tablet of Prosperity No. 9	45,000
	Tablet of Prosperity No. 10	45,000
Tablets of Prosperity		**4,500,000**
	Stone of Force Vol. 1	45,000
	Stone of Force Vol. 2	45,000
	Stone of Force Vol. 3	45,000
	Stone of Force Vol. 4	45,000
	Stone of Force Vol. 5	45,000
	Stone of Force Vol. 6	45,000
	Stone of Force Vol. 7	45,000
	Stone of Force Vol. 8	45,000
	Stone of Force Vol. 9	45,000
	Stone of Force Vol. 10	45,000
Stones of Force		**4,500,000**

Icon	Artifact Name	Trading Value
	Scrolls of Faith Book 1	45,000
	Scrolls of Faith Book 2	45,000
	Scrolls of Faith Book 3	45,000
	Scrolls of Faith Book 4	45,000
	Scrolls of Faith Book 5	45,000
	Scrolls of Faith Book 6	45,000
	Scrolls of Faith Book 7	45,000
	Scrolls of Faith Book 8	45,000
	Scrolls of Faith Book 9	45,000
	Scrolls of Faith Book 10	45,000
Scrolls of Faith		**4,500,000**
	Galactic Core	N/A
	Talked to Steve	N/A
	Black Hole	N/A
	Proto-Planetary Disk	N/A
	BinaryOO	N/A
	BinaryOG	N/A
	BinaryOM	N/A
	BinaryGG	N/A
	BinaryGM	N/A
	BinaryMM	N/A
Galactic Objects		
	Crab Legs	N/A
	Rock Stack	N/A
	Craters	N/A
	Dill Pickles	N/A
	Gears n Cogs	N/A
	Marshmallows	N/A
	Pastry	N/A
	Pineapple	N/A
	Tentacles	N/A
	Rattlesnake	N/A
Story Book Planets		

Spice Harvesting

There are six different colors of spice. Each planet produces one color of spice. The color of spice that it produces is determined by the color of its star and the temperature of its surface (indicated by the color of its orbit trail).

Spice	Red Stars		Yellow Stars		Blue Stars	
	Green Orbit Trail	Red/Blue Orbit Trail	Green Orbit Trail	Red/Blue Orbit Trail	Green Orbit Trail	Red/Blue Orbit Trail
Red	96%	50%	—	—	—	—
Blue	—	—	—	—	100%	20%
Yellow	—	44%	94%	74%	—	—
Green	2%	2%	2%	22%	—	30%
Pink	2%	2%	2%	2%	—	35%
Purple	—	2%	2%	2%	—	15%

Of the five spice colors that each colonized planet does not produce, it randomly chooses three that it wants to buy and two that it will not buy. The price that a planet pays for spice is determined by multiplying the base value of the spice color by a random "premium curve" that is determined by the difficulty setting.

Spice Base Cost

Spice Color	Red	Blue	Yellow	Green	Pink	Purple
Base Cost (Per Unit)	3,375	4,500	6,750	10,125	14,625	22,500

Units Sold	Easy	Medium	Hard
1	0.8	0.6	0.4
2	1	0.75	0.5
3	1.13	0.85	0.56
4	1.33	1	0.66
5	1.6	1.2	0.8
6	1.86	1.4	0.93
7	2.2	1.65	1.1
8	2.66	2	1.33
9	3.33	2.5	1.66
10	4	3	2

Personality

The choices that you make in the Cell, Creature, Tribal, and Civilization Stages determine your personality type at the start of the Space Stage.

Cell	Creature	Tribe	Civilization	Personality
Carnivore	Aggressive	Aggressive	Economic	Warrior
Carnivore	Aggressive	Aggressive	Military	Warrior
Carnivore	Aggressive	Aggressive	Religious	Warrior
Carnivore	Aggressive	Aggressive	unplayed	Warrior
Carnivore	Aggressive	Friendly	Economic	Knight
Carnivore	Aggressive	Friendly	Military	Warrior
Carnivore	Aggressive	Friendly	Religious	Zealot
Carnivore	Aggressive	Friendly	unplayed	Zealot
Carnivore	Aggressive	Industrious	Economic	Scientist
Carnivore	Aggressive	Industrious	Military	Warrior
Carnivore	Aggressive	Industrious	Religious	Knight
Carnivore	Aggressive	Industrious	unplayed	Scientist
Carnivore	Aggressive	unplayed	Economic	Scientist
Carnivore	Aggressive	unplayed	Military	Warrior
Carnivore	Aggressive	unplayed	Religious	Zealot
Carnivore	Aggressive	unplayed	unplayed	Warrior
Carnivore	Friendly	Aggressive	Economic	Knight
Carnivore	Friendly	Aggressive	Military	Warrior
Carnivore	Friendly	Aggressive	Religious	Zealot
Carnivore	Friendly	Aggressive	unplayed	Zealot

Cell	Creature	Tribe	Civilization	Personality
Carnivore	Friendly	Friendly	Economic	Ecologist
Carnivore	Friendly	Friendly	Military	Zealot
Carnivore	Friendly	Friendly	Religious	Shaman
Carnivore	Friendly	Friendly	unplayed	Zealot
Carnivore	Friendly	Industrious	Economic	Bard
Carnivore	Friendly	Industrious	Military	Knight
Carnivore	Friendly	Industrious	Religious	Ecologist
Carnivore	Friendly	Industrious	unplayed	Trader
Carnivore	Friendly	unplayed	Economic	Trader
Carnivore	Friendly	unplayed	Military	Zealot
Carnivore	Friendly	unplayed	Religious	Zealot
Carnivore	Friendly	unplayed	unplayed	Zealot
Carnivore	Neutral	Aggressive	Economic	Scientist
Carnivore	Neutral	Aggressive	Military	Warrior
Carnivore	Neutral	Aggressive	Religious	Knight
Carnivore	Neutral	Aggressive	unplayed	Scientist
Carnivore	Neutral	Friendly	Economic	Bard
Carnivore	Neutral	Friendly	Military	Knight
Carnivore	Neutral	Friendly	Religious	Ecologist
Carnivore	Neutral	Friendly	unplayed	Shaman

Cell	Creature	Tribe	Civilization	Personality
Carnivore	Neutral	Industrious	Economic	Trader
Carnivore	Neutral	Industrious	Military	Scientist
Carnivore	Neutral	Industrious	Religious	Bard
Carnivore	Neutral	Industrious	unplayed	Scientist
Carnivore	Neutral	unplayed	Economic	Scientist
Carnivore	Neutral	unplayed	Military	Scientist
Carnivore	Neutral	unplayed	Religious	Shaman
Carnivore	Neutral	unplayed	unplayed	Scientist
Carnivore	unplayed	Aggressive	Economic	Scientist
Carnivore	unplayed	Aggressive	Military	Warrior
Carnivore	unplayed	Aggressive	Religious	Zealot
Carnivore	unplayed	Aggressive	unplayed	Warrior
Carnivore	unplayed	Friendly	Economic	Trader
Carnivore	unplayed	Friendly	Military	Zealot
Carnivore	unplayed	Friendly	Religious	Zealot
Carnivore	unplayed	Friendly	unplayed	Zealot
Carnivore	unplayed	Industrious	Economic	Scientist
Carnivore	unplayed	Industrious	Military	Scientist
Carnivore	unplayed	Industrious	Religious	Shaman
Carnivore	unplayed	Industrious	unplayed	Scientist
Carnivore	unplayed	unplayed	Economic	Scientist
Carnivore	unplayed	unplayed	Military	Warrior
Carnivore	unplayed	unplayed	Religious	Zealot
Carnivore	unplayed	unplayed	unplayed	Warrior
Herbivore	Aggressive	Aggressive	Economic	Knight
Herbivore	Aggressive	Aggressive	Military	Warrior
Herbivore	Aggressive	Aggressive	Religious	Zealot
Herbivore	Aggressive	Aggressive	unplayed	Zealot
Herbivore	Aggressive	Friendly	Economic	Ecologist
Herbivore	Aggressive	Friendly	Military	Zealot
Herbivore	Aggressive	Friendly	Religious	Shaman
Herbivore	Aggressive	Friendly	unplayed	Zealot
Herbivore	Aggressive	Industrious	Economic	Bard
Herbivore	Aggressive	Industrious	Military	Knight
Herbivore	Aggressive	Industrious	Religious	Ecologist
Herbivore	Aggressive	Industrious	unplayed	Trader
Herbivore	Aggressive	unplayed	Economic	Trader
Herbivore	Aggressive	unplayed	Military	Zealot
Herbivore	Aggressive	unplayed	Religious	Zealot
Herbivore	Aggressive	unplayed	unplayed	Zealot
Herbivore	Friendly	Aggressive	Economic	Ecologist
Herbivore	Friendly	Aggressive	Military	Zealot
Herbivore	Friendly	Aggressive	Religious	Shaman
Herbivore	Friendly	Aggressive	unplayed	Zealot
Herbivore	Friendly	Friendly	Economic	Shaman
Herbivore	Friendly	Friendly	Military	Shaman
Herbivore	Friendly	Friendly	Religious	Shaman
Herbivore	Friendly	Friendly	unplayed	Shaman
Herbivore	Friendly	Industrious	Economic	Diplomat
Herbivore	Friendly	Industrious	Military	Ecologist
Herbivore	Friendly	Industrious	Religious	Shaman
Herbivore	Friendly	Industrious	unplayed	Diplomat
Herbivore	Friendly	unplayed	Economic	Diplomat
Herbivore	Friendly	unplayed	Military	Zealot

Cell	Creature	Tribe	Civilization	Personality
Herbivore	Friendly	unplayed	Religious	Shaman
Herbivore	Friendly	unplayed	unplayed	Shaman
Herbivore	Neutral	Aggressive	Economic	Bard
Herbivore	Neutral	Aggressive	Military	Knight
Herbivore	Neutral	Aggressive	Religious	Ecologist
Herbivore	Neutral	Aggressive	unplayed	Warrior
Herbivore	Neutral	Friendly	Economic	Diplomat
Herbivore	Neutral	Friendly	Military	Ecologist
Herbivore	Neutral	Friendly	Religious	Shaman
Herbivore	Neutral	Friendly	unplayed	Diplomat
Herbivore	Neutral	Industrious	Economic	Trader
Herbivore	Neutral	Industrious	Military	Bard
Herbivore	Neutral	Industrious	Religious	Diplomat
Herbivore	Neutral	Industrious	unplayed	Diplomat
Herbivore	Neutral	unplayed	Economic	Diplomat
Herbivore	Neutral	unplayed	Military	Warrior
Herbivore	Neutral	unplayed	Religious	Diplomat
Herbivore	Neutral	unplayed	unplayed	Diplomat
Herbivore	unplayed	Aggressive	Economic	Trader
Herbivore	unplayed	Aggressive	Military	Zealot
Herbivore	unplayed	Aggressive	Religious	Zealot
Herbivore	unplayed	Aggressive	unplayed	Zealot
Herbivore	unplayed	Friendly	Economic	Diplomat
Herbivore	unplayed	Friendly	Military	Zealot
Herbivore	unplayed	Friendly	Religious	Shaman
Herbivore	unplayed	Friendly	unplayed	Shaman
Herbivore	unplayed	Industrious	Economic	Diplomat
Herbivore	unplayed	Industrious	Military	Warrior
Herbivore	unplayed	Industrious	Religious	Diplomat
Herbivore	unplayed	Industrious	unplayed	Diplomat
Herbivore	unplayed	unplayed	Economic	Diplomat
Herbivore	unplayed	unplayed	Military	Zealot
Herbivore	unplayed	unplayed	Religious	Shaman
Herbivore	unplayed	unplayed	unplayed	Shaman
Omnivore	Aggressive	Aggressive	Economic	Scientist
Omnivore	Aggressive	Aggressive	Military	Warrior
Omnivore	Aggressive	Aggressive	Religious	Knight
Omnivore	Aggressive	Aggressive	unplayed	Scientist
Omnivore	Aggressive	Friendly	Economic	Bard
Omnivore	Aggressive	Friendly	Military	Knight
Omnivore	Aggressive	Friendly	Religious	Ecologist
Omnivore	Aggressive	Friendly	unplayed	Shaman
Omnivore	Aggressive	Industrious	Economic	Trader
Omnivore	Aggressive	Industrious	Military	Scientist
Omnivore	Aggressive	Industrious	Religious	Bard
Omnivore	Aggressive	Industrious	unplayed	Scientist
Omnivore	Aggressive	unplayed	Economic	Scientist
Omnivore	Aggressive	unplayed	Military	Scientist
Omnivore	Aggressive	unplayed	Religious	Shaman
Omnivore	Aggressive	unplayed	unplayed	Scientist
Omnivore	Friendly	Aggressive	Economic	Bard
Omnivore	Friendly	Aggressive	Military	Knight
Omnivore	Friendly	Aggressive	Religious	Ecologist
Omnivore	Friendly	Aggressive	unplayed	Warrior

Cell	Creature	Tribe	Civilization	Personality
Omnivore	Friendly	Friendly	Economic	Diplomat
Omnivore	Friendly	Friendly	Military	Ecologist
Omnivore	Friendly	Friendly	Religious	Shaman
Omnivore	Friendly	Friendly	unplayed	Diplomat
Omnivore	Friendly	Industrious	Economic	Trader
Omnivore	Friendly	Industrious	Military	Bard
Omnivore	Friendly	Industrious	Religious	Diplomat
Omnivore	Friendly	Industrious	unplayed	Diplomat
Omnivore	Friendly	unplayed	Economic	Diplomat
Omnivore	Friendly	unplayed	Military	Warrior
Omnivore	Friendly	unplayed	Religious	Diplomat
Omnivore	Friendly	unplayed	unplayed	Diplomat
Omnivore	Neutral	Aggressive	Economic	Trader
Omnivore	Neutral	Aggressive	Military	Scientist
Omnivore	Neutral	Aggressive	Religious	Bard
Omnivore	Neutral	Aggressive	unplayed	Scientist
Omnivore	Neutral	Friendly	Economic	Trader
Omnivore	Neutral	Friendly	Military	Bard
Omnivore	Neutral	Friendly	Religious	Diplomat
Omnivore	Neutral	Friendly	unplayed	Diplomat
Omnivore	Neutral	Industrious	Economic	Trader
Omnivore	Neutral	Industrious	Military	Trader
Omnivore	Neutral	Industrious	Religious	Trader
Omnivore	Neutral	Industrious	unplayed	Trader
Omnivore	Neutral	unplayed	Economic	Trader
Omnivore	Neutral	unplayed	Military	Scientist
Omnivore	Neutral	unplayed	Religious	Diplomat
Omnivore	Neutral	unplayed	unplayed	Trader
Omnivore	unplayed	Aggressive	Economic	Scientist
Omnivore	unplayed	Aggressive	Military	Scientist
Omnivore	unplayed	Aggressive	Religious	Shaman
Omnivore	unplayed	Aggressive	unplayed	Scientist
Omnivore	unplayed	Friendly	Economic	Diplomat
Omnivore	unplayed	Friendly	Military	Warrior
Omnivore	unplayed	Friendly	Religious	Diplomat
Omnivore	unplayed	Friendly	unplayed	Diplomat
Omnivore	unplayed	Industrious	Economic	Trader
Omnivore	unplayed	Industrious	Military	Scientist
Omnivore	unplayed	Industrious	Religious	Diplomat
Omnivore	unplayed	Industrious	unplayed	Trader
Omnivore	unplayed	unplayed	Economic	Trader
Omnivore	unplayed	unplayed	Military	Scientist
Omnivore	unplayed	unplayed	Religious	Diplomat
Omnivore	unplayed	unplayed	unplayed	Trader
unplayed	Aggressive	Aggressive	Economic	Scientist
unplayed	Aggressive	Aggressive	Military	Warrior
unplayed	Aggressive	Aggressive	Religious	Zealot
unplayed	Aggressive	Aggressive	unplayed	Warrior
unplayed	Aggressive	Friendly	Economic	Trader
unplayed	Aggressive	Friendly	Military	Zealot
unplayed	Aggressive	Friendly	Religious	Zealot
unplayed	Aggressive	Friendly	unplayed	Zealot
unplayed	Aggressive	Industrious	Economic	Scientist
unplayed	Aggressive	Industrious	Military	Scientist
unplayed	Aggressive	Industrious	Religious	Shaman
unplayed	Aggressive	Industrious	unplayed	Scientist
unplayed	Aggressive	unplayed	Economic	Scientist
unplayed	Aggressive	unplayed	Military	Warrior
unplayed	Aggressive	unplayed	Religious	Zealot
unplayed	Aggressive	unplayed	unplayed	Warrior
unplayed	Friendly	Aggressive	Economic	Trader
unplayed	Friendly	Aggressive	Military	Zealot
unplayed	Friendly	Aggressive	Religious	Zealot
unplayed	Friendly	Aggressive	unplayed	Zealot
unplayed	Friendly	Friendly	Economic	Diplomat
unplayed	Friendly	Friendly	Military	Zealot
unplayed	Friendly	Friendly	Religious	Shaman
unplayed	Friendly	Friendly	unplayed	Shaman
unplayed	Friendly	Industrious	Economic	Diplomat
unplayed	Friendly	Industrious	Military	Warrior
unplayed	Friendly	Industrious	Religious	Diplomat
unplayed	Friendly	Industrious	unplayed	Diplomat
unplayed	Friendly	unplayed	Economic	Diplomat
unplayed	Friendly	unplayed	Military	Zealot
unplayed	Friendly	unplayed	Religious	Shaman
unplayed	Friendly	unplayed	unplayed	Shaman
unplayed	Neutral	Aggressive	Economic	Scientist
unplayed	Neutral	Aggressive	Military	Scientist
unplayed	Neutral	Aggressive	Religious	Shaman
unplayed	Neutral	Aggressive	unplayed	Scientist
unplayed	Neutral	Friendly	Economic	Diplomat
unplayed	Neutral	Friendly	Military	Warrior
unplayed	Neutral	Friendly	Religious	Diplomat
unplayed	Neutral	Friendly	unplayed	Diplomat
unplayed	Neutral	Industrious	Economic	Trader
unplayed	Neutral	Industrious	Military	Scientist
unplayed	Neutral	Industrious	Religious	Diplomat
unplayed	Neutral	Industrious	unplayed	Trader
unplayed	Neutral	unplayed	Economic	Trader
unplayed	Neutral	unplayed	Military	Scientist
unplayed	Neutral	unplayed	Religious	Diplomat
unplayed	Neutral	unplayed	unplayed	Trader
unplayed	unplayed	Aggressive	Economic	Scientist
unplayed	unplayed	Aggressive	Military	Warrior
unplayed	unplayed	Aggressive	Religious	Zealot
unplayed	unplayed	Aggressive	unplayed	Warrior
unplayed	unplayed	Friendly	Economic	Diplomat
unplayed	unplayed	Friendly	Military	Zealot
unplayed	unplayed	Friendly	Religious	Shaman
unplayed	unplayed	Friendly	unplayed	Shaman
unplayed	unplayed	Industrious	Economic	Trader
unplayed	unplayed	Industrious	Military	Scientist
unplayed	unplayed	Industrious	Religious	Diplomat
unplayed	unplayed	Industrious	unplayed	Trader
unplayed	unplayed	unplayed	Economic	Trader
unplayed	unplayed	unplayed	Military	Warrior
unplayed	unplayed	unplayed	Religious	Shaman
unplayed	unplayed	unplayed	unplayed	Wanderer

Changing Personality Type

You can change the personality type that you start the Space Stage with by performing certain types of missions. The following chart explains how the different personalities relate to each other:

The decisions that you make during the course of the Space Stage can generally be sorted into one of three categories:

Warrior: Pretty self-explanatory. Any time that you kill, destroy, or blow something up, you're taking a Warrior action.

Trader: Whenever you buy something, sell something, collect rare items, or open a trading route, you're behaving like a Trader.

Shaman: Actions that involve creating or changing a plant, creature, or planetary surface fit into the Shaman category.

Focusing on actions and missions of a certain category move your personality toward that category. For example, if you start out Space Stage as a Wanderer (meaning you began the game at the Space Stage), your personality type is in the dead center of the personality matrix triangle. Focusing exclusively on battle and conquest will eventually make you a Knight, because you're moving toward the Warrior point of the triangle. Continuing along this path will eventually change your personality to Warrior.

To change your personality to one represented on the sides of the triangle, pursue actions that fit into the categories of both points of that side of the triangle. For instance, if you want to become a Diplomat, engage in a lot of wheeling and dealing (Trader actions) and terraform and create as much as possible (Shaman actions).

Mission Types

Your personality type is important, because it determines the percentage chance of alien cultures offering you a certain type of mission or declaring war on you.

		Personality Type								
		Bard	Diplomat	Ecologist	Grox	Scientist	Shaman	Trader	Warrior	Zealot
Mission Type	Fetch an Artifact	100	50	40	30	100	70	70	70	100
	Eradicate Animals	50	40	100	30	70	40	40	40	40
	Eradicate Citizens	40	50	40	80	40	40	40	100	70
	War	40	40	40	100	40	40	40	100	50
	Sample Collection	50	40	90	30	100	70	70	40	40
	Terraform	40	40	100	0	70	70	40	40	40
	Multi Delivery	50	70	40	30	50	50	100	50	40
	Fetch a Commodity	40	40	40	30	100	50	40	70	40
	Destroy All Turrets	50	70	40	100	40	40	40	100	50
	Fetch a Plant	40	40	70	30	100	50	40	40	40
	Fetch an Animal	40	40	70	30	100	50	40	40	40
	Balance Ecosystem	40	40	100	0	50	70	40	40	40
	Fetch a Tribe Member	100	50	40	30	50	50	40	40	100
	Fetch a Civilization's Citizen	100	70	40	60	40	50	40	50	40
	Fetch an Empire's Citizen	70	70	40	100	40	40	40	90	40
	Scan and Abduct	40	50	50	30	70	50	40	40	40

Fetch an Artifact

Recover a single item from a planet's surface with your Abduction Beam and return it to the mission giver.

Eradicate Animals

Sick animals on a planet threaten to infect the rest of the species. Destroy the infected animals within a time limit to save the planet's ecosystem.

Eradicate Citizens

A colony's citizens are sick or insane and threaten the rest of the populace. Euthanize them to preserve the colony.

War

The empire declares war upon your empire.

Sample Collection

Use your Abduction Beam to collect samples of a planet's flora and fauna and bring them back to the mission giver.

Terraform

Terraform a planet with Planetary Atmospheric tools and make it habitable for plants and animals.

Multi Delivery

Deliver a number of objects to several different planets using your Abduction Beam to safely retrieve and drop them off.

Fetch a Commodity

The mission giver is in need of a specific commodity. Find it and bring it back.

Destroy All Turrets

Eradicate all Turrets on all colonies on a specific planet with any Weapons tools you have.

Fetch a Plant

Pick up a specific species of plant from a planet with your Abduction Beam and bring it back to the mission giver.

Fetch an Animal

Use your Abduction Beam to pick up a specific animal type from a planet and bring it back to the mission giver.

Balance Ecosystem

Fill out a planet's Food Web with plants and animals to balance its ecosystem.

Fetch a Tribe Member

Go to a tribal planet, pick up a member of a tribe with your Abduction Beam, and bring it back to the mission giver.

Fetch a Civilization's Citizen

Use your Abduction Beam to transfer a citizen from a civilization into your cargo hold, and then return and drop it off in one of the mission giver's cities.

Fetch an Empire's Citizen

Abduct a citizen of another empire with your Abduction Beam and bring him to the mission giver's city. This may worsen your relationship with the abductee's empire and could lead to war.

Scan and Abduct

Use your Scan tool to examine the plants and animals of a planet and use your Abduction Beam to bring samples of them back to the mission giver.

Spore Achievements

Icon	Achievement	Conditions
	Galactic God	Evolve a creature from cell to intergalactic space traveler in one continuous game
	Photographer	Send a photo or video to a friend from Test Drive mode
	Architect	Create and share 50 buildings
	Automotive Engineer	Make and publish 50 vehicles
	Biologist	Create and publish 100 different creatures
	Spore Fan	Spend 50 hours in your Spore galaxy
	Spore Addict	Spend 100 hours in your Spore galaxy
	Creator	Spend more than 50 hours in the Creators
	Universe in a Box	Play every game level and use every Creator at least once
	Deja Vu	Stumble across one of your own creations when exploring the universe
	Social Engineer	Make 5 Sporecasts of 50 assets or more
	Rising Star	Have 5 different Sporecasts subscribed to by at least 10 people
	Front Page News	Have one of your creations or Sporecasts featured on the Spore website
	Creature Stage Unlocked	Play enough of the Cell stage to unlock the Creature stage
	Tribe Stage Unlocked	Play enough of the Creature stage to unlock the Tribe stage
	Civilization Stage Unlocked	Play enough of the Tribe stage to unlock the Civilization stage
	Space Stage Unlocked	Play enough of the Civilization stage to unlock the Space stage

Cell Stage Achievements

Icon	Achievement	Conditions
	Aluminium Cell	Finish the Cell stage on Hard difficulty
	Landfall	Finish the Cell stage and clamber onto the planet's surface!
	Pacifist	Finish the Cell stage without killing another creature
	Completist	Unlock all the parts in Cell stage
	Speed Freak	Finish the Cell stage in under 8 minutes
	Cell Addict	Finish the Cell stage 25 times

Creature Stage Achievements

Icon	Achievement	Conditions
	Iron Creature	Finish the Creature stage on Hard difficulty
	Evolver	Finish Creature stage
	Everyone's BFF	Finish the Creature stage by befriending at least 20 other species
	Foe	Extinct at least 20 other species in Creature stage
	Max Power	Build a creature with max stats in at least four abilities while playing the Creature stage
	Survivor	Complete the Creature stage without dying
	Socialite	Meet 200 creatures made by other players
	Flight of the Bumblebee	Fly for over 200 meters without touching the ground
	Devourer	Eat 50 different species across any number of games
	Village Folks	Have three posse members from different species
	Speed Demon	Complete the Creature stage in less than an hour
	Bestial	Complete the Creature stage 10 times
	Cerberus	Evolve a creature with three heads
	General Custer	Lead 30 posse members to their death
	Epic Killer	Kill an epic in Creature stage
	Slugger	Finish Creature stage without legs

Tribal Stage Achievements

Icon	Achievement	Conditions
	Steel Tribe	Finish the Tribal stage on Hard difficulty
	Founder	Complete the Tribal stage and build a city
	Tribal Socialite	Convert all 5 other tribes to your belief system
	Vicious	Kill all members of all 5 other tribes and raze their villages
	Domestic Bliss	Domesticate and farm three different species
	Watchful Parent	Complete the Tribal stage without the death of a single tribe member
	Tribal	Complete the Tribal stage 10 times
	Ergonomically Terrific	Complete the Tribal stage in less than an hour